UNDERSTANDING
CONTEMPORARY
CHICANA LITERATURE

Understanding Contemporary American Literature
Matthew J. Bruccoli, Series Editor

Volumes on

Edward Albee • Nicholson Baker • John Barth • Donald Barthelme
The Beats • The Black Mountain Poets • Robert Bly
Raymond Carver • Fred Chappell • Chicano Literature
Contemporary American Drama
Contemporary American Horror Fiction
Contemporary American Literary Theory
Contemporary American Science Fiction
Contemporary Chicana Literature • James Dickey
E. L. Doctorow • John Gardner • George Garrett • John Hawkes
Joseph Heller • Lillian Hellman • John Irving • Randall Jarrell
William Kennedy • Jack Kerouac • Ursula K. Le Guin
Denise Levertov • Bernard Malamud • Bobbie Ann Mason
Jill McCorkle • Carson McCullers • W. S. Merwin • Arthur Miller
Toni Morrison's Fiction • Vladimir Nabokov • Gloria Naylor
Joyce Carol Oates • Tim O'Brien • Flannery O'Connor
Cynthia Ozick • Walker Percy • Katherine Anne Porter
Reynolds Price • Thomas Pynchon • Theodore Roethke • Philip Roth
Hubert Selby, Jr. • Mary Lee Settle • Isaac Bashevis Singer
Jane Smiley • Gary Snyder • William Stafford • Anne Tyler
Kurt Vonnegut • Robert Penn Warren • James Welch • Eudora Welty
Tennessee Williams • August Wilson

UNDERSTANDING
CONTEMPORARY
CHICANA
LITERATURE

Deborah L. Madsen

University of South Carolina Press

Published in Columbia, South Carolina, by the
University of South Carolina Press

Manufactured in the United States of America

04   03   02   5   4   3

Library of Congress Cataloging-in-Publication Data

Madsen, Deborah L.
    Understanding contemporary Chicana literature / Deborah L.
Madsen.
       p. cm. — (Understanding contemporary American
literature)
    Includes bibliographical references (p.) and index.
    ISBN 1-57003-379-X (alk. paper)
    1. American literature—Mexican American authors—History
and criticism. 2. Women and literature—United States—
History—20th century. 3. American literature—Women
authors—History and criticism. 4. American literature—20th
century—History and criticism. 5. Mexican American women—
Intellectual life. 6. Mexican American women in literature.
7. Mexican Americans in literature. I. Title. II. Series.
PS153.M4 M33   2000
810.9'9287'0896872—dc21   00-011471

Grateful acknowledgment is made to the authors and publishers represented in this volume, for permission to reprint their copyrighted material. Source and credit information appears at the end of the book.

CONTENTS

EDITOR'S PREFACE

The volumes of *Understanding Contemporary American Literature* have been planned as guides or companions for students as well as good nonacademic readers. The editor and publisher perceive a need for these volumes because much of the influential contemporary literature makes special demands. Uninitiated readers encounter difficulty in approaching works that depart from the traditional forms and techniques of prose and poetry. Literature relies on conventions, but the conventions keep evolving; new writers form their own conventions—which in time may become familiar. Put simply, *UCAL* provides instruction in how to read certain contemporary writers—identifying and explicating their material, themes, use of language, point of view, structures, symbolism, and responses to experience.

The word *understanding* in the titles was deliberately chosen. Many willing readers lack an adequate understanding of how contemporary literature works; that is, what the author is attempting to express and the means by which it is conveyed. Although the criticism and analysis in the series have been aimed at a level of general accessibility, these introductory volumes are meant to be applied in conjunction with the works they cover. They do not provide a substitute for the works and authors they introduce, but rather prepare the reader for more profitable literary experiences.

M. J. B.

UNDERSTANDING

CONTEMPORARY
CHICANA LITERATURE

CHAPTER ONE

The Contemporary Chicana Renaissance
An Introduction

The growing body of literature produced by Chicanas, or Mexican American women, is part of a contemporary renaissance of ethnic women's writing that has emerged in the period since the civil rights activism of the 1960s. In literary terms this has meant the development of a distinctive feminine ethnic/racial voice through literary themes, imagery, and style—all reworked so that elements of a racial cultural tradition become expressive of a feminist voice instead of expressing traditional patriarchal Mexican values. This literary movement has been theorized in various ways. Most relevant to the understanding of contemporary Chicana literature is the incisive critique of mainstream feminism, on the part of feminists of color, that is based upon a reappraisal of the historical relationship between white feminism and racism. Theorists such as bell hooks argue that Anglo-American feminism has historically struggled to create a place for (white) women within the existing social and political system.[1] Thus, representation of women in positions of power and access for women to positions from which they can become oppressors has taken priority over the transformation of society toward a more equitable distribution of power in which no one is oppressed. In support of this view bell hooks, as does Angela Davis in *Women, Race and Class,* points to the opposition of such white suffragettes as Elizabeth Cady Stanton to the abolition of slavery if black men are to be enfranchised before white women.[2] The exclusion of colored women from male-dominated civil rights organizations and the white-dominated women's movement is seen as a continuation of this same tradition in which access to power takes priority over the redefinition of power relationships within American society.

The liberal or "bourgeois" feminist struggle for equality with men raises the troubling issue that not all men are equal in society. Again it is bell hooks who draws attention to the fact that although various ethnic groups have benefited from equal opportunity and affirmative action programs, still the institutionalized racism, classism, and male supremacy that have always underpinned oppression in America remain unchallenged by liberal feminism. Many colored women were working in exploitative and dehumanizing jobs even as Betty Friedan was claiming that freedom for women must mean paid work outside the home. As bell hooks argues, low-paid work is not liberating for the poor, be they men or women.[3] An associated issue is the feminist "careerism" that has come at a significant cultural price. The emphasis on getting women into positions of power and prestige has meant preserving the existing socioeconomic system, and the result has been increased poverty for the majority of women.[4] By addressing the problem of sexism in isolation from the network of oppressive relationships that include racism and classism as well, feminists have alienated working-class and colored women from the liberation struggle. By focusing upon the relationship between class and race as they crucially affect the experience of gender and sexualized power relationships, literary theory and the literary work produced by women of color exist in a close symbiotic relationship, each supporting, nurturing, and motivating the other.

This racialized theory addresses the problematic status of women of color as "the Other": that which defines by opposition the powerful, the mainstream, the establishment. The concept of women of color as occupying a distinct place on the margins of society has given rise to the development of distinct feminist discourses: black feminism, Chicana/Hispanic feminism, native feminism, Asian feminism. Each forms a distinct theoretical perspective upon the oppression of women by virtue of racialized sexuality. Racism is experienced differently by each group; each group has a distinct historical experience as a racialized community within the United States: blacks in relation to slavery, natives in relation to conquest and dispossession, Asians in relation to immigration, and Mexican Americans in relation to the experience of annexation and the Treaty of Guadalupe Hidalgo, discussed in some detail below, which formalized their entry into the United States. For women, the experience of feminine sexuality is different according to ethnic or racial religious identity: Hispanic Catholicism, Oriental Confucianism, native religions, and black evangelical Christianity. Masculinity is constructed differently according to racial or ethnic groups: Chicanos invented the term "machismo," and femininity is defined in opposition to these dominant images of masculine gender identity. Women in each racial group express the ways in which their individual experience of their sexuality is mediated by their racial identity.

This attention to the marginalizing of women of color

involves the analysis of what W. E. B. Du Bois, in *The Souls of Black Folk,* called "double consciousness": the consciousness of what one is in oneself (self-consciousness) versus the cultural image or stereotype imposed by the racism of others.[5] This analysis and identification of personal authenticity, both racial and sexual, is expressed by the imperative on the part of Chicana writers to construct a feminist "voice" for Mexican American women. "Double consciousness" or double stigma describes the Chicana experience of oppression both as woman and as a member of an ethnic minority. Historically this has described the experience of those who are placed in a position of powerlessness by the racist white culture in which they live. However, women of color describe the same mechanism in operation when they deal with white feminists. The construction of a feminist "voice" for women of color can then be expressed as a series of problems: how to speak in such a way as to be listened to seriously by white women and by men within one's own racial group; how to speak from a discredited cultural position; how to write when established literary forms have been devised to express the lives and thoughts of men (colored and white) and white women. Chicana writers have responded to these problems by seeking to construct or reconstruct ethnic women's literary traditions through the rediscovery of earlier modes of speaking and by challenging conventional distinctions among forms of expression. These writers subvert conventional forms of literary expression to make them express colored women's experiences. Strategies by which this work is done include use of the epistolary form; the use of the *Kunstlerroman;* variations of the memoir form; and repeated challenges to the distinctions among poetry, prose, and fiction. Chicana writers insist that the reader work hard to understand the specialized racial or ethnic references included in the text, such as references to Mexican mythology and cross-cultural references. In important ways the subject of Chicana writing *is* the Chicana subject: feminine subjectivity in a Mexican American context is the primary subject matter of Chicana literature. This is a literature that embodies the quest for self-definition, and so voice is a matter if both form and content.

In a lecture titled "Ghosts and Voices: Writing from Obsession" (1987), Sandra Cisneros describes her own ambivalence about the issue of literary "voice": "As a young writer in college I was aware I had to find my own voice, but how was I to know it would be the voice I used at home . . . ? It's ironic I had to leave home to discover the voice I had all along, but isn't that how it always goes? As a poor person growing up in a society where the class norm was superimposed on a TV screen, I couldn't understand why our home wasn't all green lawn and white wood like the ones in 'Leave it to Beaver' and 'Father Knows Best.' Poverty then became the ghost and in an attempt to escape the ghost, I rejected what was at hand and emulated the voices of the poets I admired in books: big, male voices."[6] She goes on to describe how later, at the Iowa Writers Workshop, she felt different, "other," for the first time and then realized that imitating mainstream voices or even the voices of her classmates would not do; in seeking to identify the knowledge she had and they did not—"third-floor flats and fear of rats, and drunk husbands sending rocks through windows"—she discovered the suppressed voice that is her poetic voice.[7]

Characteristic concerns of Chicana writing that are outlined here and that will be discussed in the chapters that follow include:

- hybrid cultural identity/fragmentary subjectivity
- control of feminine sexuality
- memory and role models: La Virgen and La Malinche, La Llorona
- connection of gender oppression with racial and class oppression
- use of hybrid literary forms

The rest of this introduction sets out contextual issues such as key definitions for words such as "Chicano" and "Chicana," explores in more detail the Chicana feminist theory that informs much contemporary Chicana writing, and explores also the characteristic themes, images, and stylistic devices that make contemporary Chicana writing so vibrant and innovative.

Background and Definitions

The most persuasive explanation of the term "Chicano" claims that the word derives from "Mexicano" (pronounced "me-chicano") and describes someone of mixed Spanish, Indian, and Anglo descent. Generally the term "Chicano" describes someone of this ethnic mix who lives in the United States. Richard A. García describes how the term "Chicano" was used in Mexico to describe lower-class Mexicans but underwent a shift in meaning when the term was taken up by "hyphenated" Mexican-Americans to describe their hybrid character.[8] Thus the term is used by

Mexicans living in the United States; as García points out, when Chicanos travel to Mexico they are considered to be too Anglicized to be authentic Mexicans. It is not "Mexicanness" that the term "Chicano" describes but precisely the mix of Mexican, native (Aztec, Mayan), and European cultural heritage that comprises the Chicano as mestizo, as a person of mixed cultural ancestry. Gloria Anzaldúa gives a full account of the genealogy of the Chicano in *Borderlands/La Frontera: The New Mestiza* (1987).

Early in the sixteenth century the Spanish led by Hernán Cortés invaded Mexico. Tribes that had been subjugated by the Aztecs supported the invaders against their old enemy, and so Mexico was conquered for Spain. Among those associated with Cortés, his Indian courtesan La Malinche has entered into Chicano/a mythology. Some doubt attaches to her willingness to assist the conquistadors—whether she was raped or seduced or gave herself willingly—and her motives are also ambiguous—whether she acted to preserve her people by forging an alliance with the invaders or acted more purely from self-interest. Her status as the mother of the Chicano is unquestioned; from her there issued the mestizo, the people of mixed Indian and Spanish blood whose descendants in the United States call themselves Chicano.

The single most controversial interpretation of the significance of the Malinche figure for modern Mexico is Octavio Paz's discussion in *Labyrinth of Solitude* (1959). "The Sons of La Malinche" describes Mexicans, mestizos, as the offspring of the rape victim (*la chingada*). The cry "¡Viva México, hijos de la chingada!" affirms the positions of Mexicans in relation to the raped indigenous woman but also inscribes specific gender positions. Paz says that the verb *chingar* is "masculine, active, cruel: it stings, wounds, gashes, stains. And it provokes a bitter, resentful satisfaction. The person who suffers this action is passive, inert and open, in contrast to the active, aggressive and closed person who inflicts it. The *chingón* is the *macho,* the male; he rips open the *chingada,* the female, who is pure passivity, defenseless against the exterior world."[9] La Malinche in this interpretation is seen as the origin of macho violence and Chicana passivity; her original betrayal of her people and her abandonment by Cortés have left them fatherless and motherless. The consequence of this national trauma is succinctly described by Debra Castillo: Mexicans "find themselves victims of the evil betrayer, and so have no recourse but to commit violence, including sexual violence, against women and against their fellow man so as to shore up a sagging and threatened identity as the possessor of a powerful and inviolable male body."[10] This accounts for the prominence of sexual violence and domestic violence as themes in contemporary Chicana writing. Writers such as Ana Castillo, Sandra Cisneros, and Alma Luz Villanueva use the figure of La Malinche to represent a feminist revision of inherited Chicano/a gender roles.

Chicanas, however, claim three mothers: "*La gente Chicana tiene tres madres,*" Gloria Anzaldúa writes. "All three are mediators: *Guadalupe,* the virgin mother who has not abandoned us, *la Chingada (Malinche),* the raped mother whom we have abandoned, and *la Llorona,* the mother who seeks her lost children and is a combination of the two."[11] These figures appear repeatedly in Chicana writing and contribute importantly to key definitions of Chicana femininity, and it is important to note the cultural interplay that lends these figures their power. For instance, Anzaldúa shows how the figure of Guadalupe is related to the Aztec serpent goddess Coatlicue, in her more benign aspect as Tonantsi, the good mother. "*Guadalupe* appeared on December 9, 1531, on the spot where the Aztec goddess, *Tonantsi* ('Our Lady Mother'), had been worshipped by the Nahuas and where a temple to her had stood."[12] Where Coatlicue demanded human sacrifice, Tonantsi required the sacrifice of small animals and birds and in return not only protected crops but also gave the life-giving cactus, source of food and milk, to Mexico. Thus Tonantsi easily translated in Christian terms as Guadalupe, maternal protector of the people. And as Guadalupe was imagined a chaste virgin, so Coatlicue and La Chingada (Malinche) were imagined as a whore, la puta, the prostitute, and bad mother. These images then draw upon the ancient cultural roots of the Chicano but also exert great prescriptive force in the present, in the world of which contemporary Chicanas write. Cherríe Moraga, in *Loving in the War Years* (1983), concludes her discussion of La Malinche and the guilt for her transgression that is still borne by Chicanas by confessing: "As a Chicana and a feminist, I must, like other Chicanas before me, examine the effects this myth has on my/our racial/sexual identity and my relationship with other Chicanas. There is hardly a Chicana growing up today who does not suffer under her name even if she never hears directly of the one-time Indian princess."[13] This kind of analysis is precisely what Moraga sees as the urgent work of Chicana feminism: liberating feminine consciousness from the invisible shackles of inherited definitions and stereotypes.

Chicana feminism does draw in part upon the gains made by the Chicano movement, which was part of the civil rights movement of the 1960s and 1970s. The efforts of the Chicano movement were focused especially on the plight of itinerant Mexican farm laborers, especially men, working under exploitative conditions in California and the Southwest. Thus, the particular issues affecting women who live under the same conditions of exploitation went unacknowledged. The term "Chicana" describes the same mixed ethnic heritage as "Chicano" but applies to women. However, the term "Chicana" has a powerful association with a feminist commitment or consciousness of the condition of Hispanic women who live in a highly patriarchal Chicano culture, subject to the constraints of the Catholic Church and the Mexican family, who feel that mainstream feminism excludes them from the gender analysis it offers because of a strong Anglo bias. Chicana feminism, then, has arisen as a distinct feminist theory concerned to address the issues that urgently face Chicanas—among them birth control, domestic violence and abuse, poor working conditions, poverty, family dysfunction, and illness. Among the most prominent theorists are Cherríe Moraga and Gloria Anzaldúa, who write from a Chicana lesbian perspective.

The "Chicana Literary Renaissance" is part of a burgeoning of Latina creativity. This movement derives its impetus and force from the earlier Chicano and women's movements and from contemporary concern with interrogating the literary canon, questioning the exclusion from it of ethnic American voices. Native American, Asian American, African American, and Hispanic women are writing about their lives and analyzing their experiences within the terms of their own feminist consciousness. The ideas articulated by Chicana feminists both in creative and theoretical form are important components of the literary work of most contemporary Chicanas. Contemporary Chicana writers are able to enjoy advantages that have been made possible by the Chicano movement: earlier Chicano literary works have become available, including revised histories of relations between Mexico and the United States and the history of Mexican America; a vocabulary of images and concepts was created; and literary forms appropriate to Chicano experience were forged. The first decade of renewed Chicano literary activity was very much male-dominated; this accounts for the antimachismo tone and feminist voice of later Chicana writing.

The current surge of interest in ethnic writing and the experience of ethnic women in particular has various motives. The questioning of the inherited American literary canon is one important motive. The effort to "deconstruct" and to diversify the literary canon has been made possible by the historical effect of feminist activism. Even more, for ethnic women the questioning of racial bias within the mainstream women's movement has produced a new awareness of the unique experience of women in different ethnic communities, and this in turn has expanded the possibilities for feminine literary expression within the context of the canon. Moraga and Anzaldúa are among the best known of Chicana feminist theorists, but the ideas they articulate both in creative and theoretical form inform the literary work of most contemporary Chicanas. The list of these Chicana writers grows apace: Ana Castillo, Sandra Cisneros, Lorna Dee Cervantes, Denise Chávez, Pat Mora, Mary Helen Ponce, Alma Luz Villanueva, Helena María Viramontes, and Bernice Zamora are among the most prominent, but new names appear every year on the lists of such specialist Hispanic/minority publishers as Third Woman Press (Berkeley), Bilingual Review Press/Editorial Bilingüe (Tempe, Arizona), Aunt Lute (San Francisco), and Arte Público (Houston). To the list of Chicana writers must be added those Latinas whose cultural hybridity derives not from Mexico but from the postcolonial nations of Central and South America. It is within the context of this vast and vibrant canon of literature that Chicana literary achievement must be understood, at least initially; but like all significant artistic production, the work of these women will not be constrained, not even by the conditions of its own production.

Aztlán and Chicano/Chicana Consciousness

In the mid-twentieth century, Chicano resistance to the injustices of the past and the ongoing discrimination against Hispanic peoples was organized initially under the auspices of the United Farm Workers led by César Chávez. The manifesto of Chicano civil rights, "El Plan Espiritual de Aztlán," was written at the First Chicano National Conference in Denver, Colorado, in 1969 and provides the ideological and political framework for the Chicano movement. It begins: "In the spirit of a new people that is conscious not only of its proud historical heritage but also of the brutal gringo invasion of our territories, we, the Chicano inhabitants and civilizers of the northern land of Aztlán from whence came our forefathers, reclaiming the land of their birth and consecrating the determination of our people of the sun, declare that the call of our blood is our power, our responsibility, and our inevitable destiny."[14] Aztlán, of course, signifies those territories annexed by the United States, the homeland claimed by Mexican Americans, the Chicanos/as who trace their cultural roots in the New World to the Aztec, Inca, and Toltec peoples who occupied the land prior to the European invasion of 1492 and who describe themselves as of mixed Indian, Spanish, and, later, Anglo bloodlines. For these people, the post-Columbian past is experienced as a legacy of genocide, dispossession, and deracination. Rudolfo Anaya and Francisco Lomelí explain: "During the decade from 1965–1975, Chicanos not only demonstrated in the streets to increase their opportunities and status, they also struggled to define a sense of a mythic past and history in order to recapture what official history had omitted. Aztlán became a collective symbol by which to recover the past that had been wrestled away from the inhabitants of Aztlán through the multiple conquests of the area."[15] Gloria Anzaldúa, who describes herself as "a Chicana *tejana* lesbian-feminist poet and fiction writer," gives powerful expression to the experience of the mestiza, the mixed-blood, who occupies a cultural, historical, and psychological border territory.[16] In the essay "The Homeland, Aztlán/*El otro México*" she describes the violence of annexation and the redrawn border between Mexico and the United States as a "1,950 mile-long wound / dividing a *pueblo,* a culture, / running down the length of my body, / staking fence rods in my flesh."[17]

The image of the border as an artificial division imposed upon and doing violence to a seamless earth is found throughout Chicana/o writing. Bernice Zamora's poem "On Living in Aztlán" expresses this sense of a people divided:

We come and we go
But within limits
Fixed by a law
Which is not ours;

We have in common
The experience of love.[18]

The division is artificial, imposed, and unrelated to the common
feeling of the people who retain a culture despite the imposition
of Anglo barriers and borders. Anzaldúa concludes her poem:
"This land was Mexican once, / was Indian always / and is. / And
will be again."[19] But this hope, founded on nostalgia, is balanced
by Anzaldúa's account of what life is like now for the descendants of the Mexicans annexed along with the land in 1848. She
describes them as the citizens of a borderland: "a borderland is a
vague and undetermined place created by the emotional residue
of an unnatural boundary."[20] But this border separates and also
brings together the First World and the Third World; it defines
the powerful and the powerless, the legitimate inhabitants and
the trespassers, the "normal" and the alien. The essay concludes
with a diagnosis of the current malaise affecting the people of the
southwestern borderland: the brutal choice "to stay in Mexico
and starve or move north and live." She notes that "North Americans call this return to the homeland the silent invasion," but she
begins with the pseudocolonization of Mexico by the United
States: "*Los gringos* had not stopped at the border. . . . The Mexican government and wealthy growers are in partnership with
such American conglomerates as American Motors, IT & T and

Du Pont which own factories called *maquiladoras.* One fourth of all Mexicans work at *maquiladoras.*"[21]

One of the foremost Chicana voices of the *movimiento* is Angela de Hoyos, who, in collections such as *Arise, Chicano, and Other Poems* (1975) and *Chicano Poems: For the Barrio* (1975), gave expression to the cultural nationalism that accompanied the growing political awareness that the desperate social status of Mexican Americans was not the product of any inherent racial inferiority but had clear historical and economic motives. The ability to express both the reasons for Chicano oppression and the equality of Chicano culture with all world cultures has become a common theme in Chicano/a writing. In the poem "Arise, Chicano!" Angela de Hoyos writes of exactly this problem of discovering a language that is adequate to express Chicano consciousness. For the impoverished farmworker, living in inhuman conditions, the infant's lullaby turns to a dirge: in the fields "the mocking whip of slavehood / confiscates your reverie"; "rude songs of rebellion" and the "hymn of hope" can be imagined only in the safety of dreams. The poem concludes:

> . . . wherever you turn for solace
> there is an embargo.
> How to express your anguish
> when not even your burning words
> are yours, they are borrowed
> from the festering barrios of poverty.[22]

In the introduction to the reissue of her collection of poetry, *My*

Father Was a Toltec, Ana Castillo addresses the anxiety of the mestiza, who is neither Anglo nor Spanish, that she has no legitimate claim to the language of either culture. Experiencing an absence or sense of loss in relation to her Chicana culture, the mestiza must blaze her own trail through a cultural wilderness. Castillo confesses: "As for the *writing* of poetry, having no models that spoke to my experience and in my languages, I decided that I would never ever take—and never have taken—a workshop or a writing class at any time anywhere. I was afraid that I would be told that I had no right to poetry . . . and that I didn't write English or Spanish well enough to write. So, while I was intent on being a good poet, I had to carve out for myself the definition of 'good.'" [23] The necessity for creating a national identity that will redefine values such as "good" in a dominant culture that makes "Mexican" synonymous with "bad," even while resisting the tendency to create a monolithic and hence inauthentic national solidarity, is reflected in Castillo's writing, in her poetry that expresses the consciousness of a Mexican American who is also a woman, a Chicana. "A white woman inherits / her father's library, / her brother's friends. Privilege / gives language that escapes me," she writes in the poem "A Christmas Gift for the President of the United States, Chicano poets, and a Marxist or Two I've known in My Time."[24] The urgency of this work, the imperative under which writers such as Castillo work to reclaim the dignity, the pride, and the minds and souls of their people, is emphasized by the need to argue back, to contradict the persistent ideological pressure of manifest destiny and to proclaim:

We are left
with one final resolution
in our own predestined way,
we are going forward.
There is no going back.[25]

Chicana Writing and the Chicano Canon

In the proceedings of the First International Symposium on Chicano Culture, published in 1984 as *Missions in Conflict: Essays
on U.S.-Mexican Relations and Chicano Culture,* a strong
impression is created of Mexican American writing as over-
whelmingly masculine. Represented here are Rudolfo Anaya,
Rolando Hinojosa, Sabine Ulibarri, Alejandro Morales, Oscar
Acosta, Tomás Rivera, and Ron Arias, with John Nichols (author
of *The Milagro Beanfield War*) as the outsider-insider. There is
a paper discussing images of mothers and grandmothers in Chicano poetry but little mention of Chicana mothers and grandmothers as writers themselves. This deafening silence does have
a historical explanation. It was the struggle for Chicano civil
rights, in the period since the mid-1960s that provided a context
and an occasion for the rapid emergence of Chicano cultural
expression, especially literature. The emergent voices of the so-
called Chicano Renaissance were those listed above: Anaya,
Hinojosa, Ulibarri, Morales, Acosta, Rivera, Arias. The gendered voice of the Chicana was marginalized as issues of racial
discrimination took precedence over those of gender. Only in the
past twenty years has the patriarchal character of the Chicano

movement been challenged by a generation of Chicana writers, including Ana Castillo, Sandra Cisneros, Alma Villanueva, Helena María Viramontes, Cherríe Moraga, and Gloria Anzaldúa, who attempt to discover in language a voice to express Hispanic femininity.

It is no accident, then, that the upsurge in Chicana writing should follow in the wake of both the women's movement and the Chicano movement: caught between the twin pillars of racism and sexism, the connection of gender oppression with racial and class oppression is a common theme in Hispanic women's writing. In the poem "Notes from a Chicana Coed" Bernice Zamora describes the condition of women who are trapped between conflicting allegiances to their race and to their gender:

> To cry that the *gabacho*
> is our oppressor is to shout
> in abstraction, *carnal.*
> He no more oppresses us
> than you do now as you tell me
> 'It's the gringo who oppresses you, Babe.'
> You cry, 'The gringo is our oppressor!'
> to the tune of $20,000 to 30,000
> a year, brother, and I wake up
> alone each morning and ask,
> "Can I feed my children today?"[26]

The patriarchal values of the Chicano movement, and the literary canon that subsequently gave it expression, no more answered

the needs and aspirations of Hispanic women than did the predominantly Anglo-American women's movement of the same
period. White feminists and macho Chicanos provide poor alternatives for women laboring under a triple burden of sexism,
racism, and economic deprivation.

Gloria Anzaldúa writes powerfully of this dilemma in her
essay *"La Conciencia de la Mestiza / Towards a New Consciousness."* Rather than lament the manifold oppressions of
Latinas, Anzaldúa presents a vision of the mestiza, the mixed-
blood woman, as the direction of the future. Mestiza consciousness is described as a capacity to tolerate ambiguity, an ability to
move across the divide between racial and gender identities, to
replicate hybridity across cultures: "[*La mestiza*] puts history
through a sieve, winnows out the lies, looks at the forces that we
as a race, as women, have been a part of. . . . This step is a conscious rupture with all oppressive traditions of all cultures and
religions. She communicates that rupture, documents the struggle. She reinterprets history and, using new symbols, she shapes
new myths. She adopts new perspectives toward the dark-
skinned, women and queers. She strengthens her tolerance (and
intolerance) for ambiguity. She is willing to share, to make herself vulnerable to new ways of seeing and thinking. She surrenders all notions of safety, of the familiar. Deconstruct,
construct."[27]

One of the most dramatic ways in which contemporary
Latina writers struggle against inherited discourses is represented by Chicanas who are writing against the Chicano canon
and the values of Mexican masculinity, *la raza* (the race) and the
barrio, it highlights. Classics of the Chicano Renaissance such as

Rudolfo Anaya's *Bless Me, Ultima* and Tomás Rivera's . . . *y no se lo tragó la tierra* (. . . *The Earth Did Not Devour Him*) represent the dawning awareness of cruel social injustice through the coming of age of a Chicano adolescent. In contrast Helena Viramontes's recent novel *Under the Feet of Jesus,* which reads at first like a Chicana *Grapes of Wrath,* describes the coming of age of an adolescent itinerant farmworker who, significantly, is a girl. Estrella's growing sense of personal maturity is defined by a single act of resistance against racism, economic exploitation, and her own marginal status. Much of the narrative concerns her attempts to heal a young man who has been poisoned by the pesticides sprayed upon crops. Estrella prevails upon her stepfather to drive Alejo to the nearest clinic where a nurse tells them that he requires hospital treatment. However, the money that might have bought gas to get them to the hospital, twenty miles away, has just been given to the clinic nurse for this information that they already knew. Estrella takes up a crowbar and violently demands the return of their money: "Estrella counted nine dollars and seven cents. She lowered the crowbar, unable to catch a breath and showed the nurse what she had taken. She did not feel like herself holding the money. She felt like two Estrellas. One was a silent phantom who obediently marked a circle with a stick around the bungalow as the mother had requested [to keep out evil], while the other held the crowbar and the money. The money felt wet and ugly and sweaty like the swamp between her legs. . . . But it was then that Estrella realized the nurse was sobbing into her hands, her lipstick smeared as if she tried wiping her mouth away."[28] The new sense of empowerment Estrella experiences through violence is in contradiction to her earlier sense of herself as passive, marginal, someone to whom events happen; her experiences are disjointed and recalled as images (like that of her real, absent, father peeling an orange) that lack logical connection. The value of community is represented as real and precious, though tenuous and fragile in this narrative. The importance of women, not only as the source of support and nurture but also as agents in their own histories and the unfolding history of la raza, is emphasized by Viramontes.

Chicana Feminism

This section explores some of the issues that define the distinctive nature of Chicana feminism in opposition to other "feminisms." In particular the control of feminine sexuality, the promotion of Chicana role models, and the relation between Chicana feminism and United States imperialism are discussed below. Through the developing discussion of these various issues it becomes apparent that cultural imperialism is a basic feminist issue for Chicana feminists. In her essay "Chicana Literature from a Chicana Feminist Perspective" Yvonne Yarbro-Bejarano comments that "perhaps the most important principle of Chicana feminist criticism is the realization that the Chicana's experience as a woman is inextricable from her experience as a member of an oppressed working-class racial minority and a culture which is not the dominant culture."[29] To this I would add the reminder that the dominant culture within which Chicana subjectivity is formed is comprised of a matrix of the dominant cultural forms of both the United States and Mexico—not just the cultural imperialism of the United States, expressed in a history of military aggression, conquest, annexation, and ongoing cultural and economic humiliation, but also the cultural imperialism of Mexico and Latin America from the perspective of which Chicanos/as are defined as mestizo, mongrel, Anglicized, and bastardized. Gloria Anzaldúa describes the reluctance experienced by Chicanas to speak in Spanish to Latinas who may criticize their "illegitimate" Chicano Spanish.[30] This fear is as debilitating as the memories of punishments at school for speaking Spanish at all. Both reinforce the perception that the Chicano language is somehow "wrong," and this rejection of the native tongue translates easily into a rejection of the community body, the people, la raza. Anzaldúa writes, "Ethnic identity is twin skin to linguistic identity—I am my language."[31]

A technique used in Chicano/a writing to express this dual linguistic inheritance and this double linguistic consciousness is commonly called "code-switching."[32] Writers choose to use either English or Spanish or a combination of both by selecting English or Spanish phraseology within individual texts. "Interlingualism" is another term to describe the use of two languages in one poem; this term is distinct from "bilingualism," which describes the work of a poet who uses both English and Spanish but in different poems rather than in the same poem. As Marta Sánchez explains, both techniques require that the reader move from one language to another: "The difference lies in how the movement takes place. In a bilingual experience the reader must mentally juxtapose poems in English with poems in Spanish; in an interlingual experience, the tensions in syntax, the connotations, the ironies, and the reverberations of words and images interlock, pulling in two directions at once. Poems written interlingually engage rival sets of reader expectations and desires. They graphically enact on the surface of the page the conflicts and tensions between the two main audiences of Chicana-Chicano poetry, the English-speaking audience and the Spanish-speaking audience."[33]

In the poetry collection *Emplumada,* for example, Lorna Dee Cervantes uses both techniques. She juxtaposes the poem, written entirely in Spanish, titled "Barco de Refugiados," with its English counterpart "Refugee Ship" (it would not be accurate to use the term "translation" because that suggests some kind of prioritizing between the poems, where one is the origin of the other). In the poem "Freeway 39" Cervantes uses interlingualism, placing Spanish words and phrases strategically within the predominantly English-language poem, in lines such as:

Albaricoqueros, cerezos, nogales . . .
Viejitas come here with paper bags to gather greens.
Espinaca, verdolagas, yerbabuena . . .
                    (2.10–12, Cervantes's ellipses)[34]

The word "viejitas," for example, creates a quite different meaning in this context as compared to the phrase "the old women." With great economy and power Cervantes is able to suggest the destruction of the barrio by the building of the freeway and the continuity of Chicano/a life in that place simply by her use of the word "viejitas." The opening line of the same poem works in the same way: "Las casitas near the gray cannery" juxtaposes the Chicano/a residential and cultural world with the world of factories and presents the Anglo perception of this neighborhood as poor and working-class. To use the language of the barrio, to represent life in the barrio, is a subversive gesture on the part of writers such as Cervantes. The deliberate use of Spanish, and an "illegitimate" Chicano form of Spanish (as Anzaldúa describes), violates traditional poetic or literary decorum. But the use of Spanish and English to represent not only Chicano experience but the details of women's lives within this world of the barrio is a particularly subversive act for Chicana writers.

The denial of language and the enforcement of silence upon the women of the Chicano community are urgent issues for Chicana feminism. More than the cultural imperialism of the United States or Mexico or Latin America, it is the imperialism of the male-dominated, patriarchal, misogynistic Chicano culture that Chicana feminists such as Gloria Anzaldúa seek to break down. Silence is described by Anzaldúa as a basic component of Chicana femininity: "good" girls do not answer back, do not gossip, do not tell lies, do not talk too much, do not question what they are told. The language that is available expresses a masculine sensibility: "Chicanas use *nosotros* whether we're male or female. We are robbed of our female being by the masculine plural."[35] Even the term "Chicana," then, is a statement of resistance, of liberation into a feminine Chicano sensibility. To overcome the misogynistic demand for female silence is thus a difficult achievement; first a language must be forged. Just as Chicano Spanish expresses the mestizo consciousness of Chicanos, so a Chicana language must express and represent authentically the consciousness of Chicanas. Anzaldúa proclaims, "I will have my voice: Indian, Spanish, white. I will have my serpent's tongue—

my woman's voice, my sexual voice, my poet's voice. I will overcome the tradition of silence."[36]

Anzaldúa links the enforced silence of Chicanas within traditional Chicano culture with the expression of feminine sexuality. The reason why women must be silent is part of a broader cultural imperative that women seek invisibility and a denial of their being. In this resides the fundamental misogyny of traditional Mexican society. The Church, the family, the culture require that women be subservient to men, that women renounce themselves in favor of men. Selflessness and humility define the "good" women; "bad" women, in contrast, are selfish and value their own selves, to which they give expression. But still there is confusion between the cultural imperative to be strong yet also submissive, to be rebellious yet also conformist; the culture sends mixed messages.[37] The Church emphasizes the spirit and preaches denial of the body, of the carnal flesh, yet the family emphasizes motherhood and the importance of the maternal body. It is because of the identification of femininity with the carnal that in patriarchal Chicano culture women must be protected from their own sexuality, protected from themselves. Invisibility, silence, incorporeality—the strategy of denying the body is pursued in patriarchal society. And so sexuality becomes the most potent means of expressing rebellion against the strictures of Chicano patriarchy: "For the lesbian of color, the ultimate rebellion she can make against her native culture is through her sexual behavior. She goes against two moral prohibitions: sexuality and homosexuality."[38] It is no accident, then, that a number of prominent Chicana feminists are lesbians, that they choose to express through their sexuality their rejection of traditional Chicano culture, patriarchy, machismo. But Chicana lesbianism is not simply a means of rebellion. In *Waiting in the Wings: Portrait of a Queer Motherhood* Cherríe Moraga describes one of her students, victim of a dysfunctional family, with a "white rapist father [and] silent latina mother."[39] Moraga goes on to describe how "I want something more than 12-step for Rosie and her Latina lesbian kind. She deserves more than Christianity or goddess worship, more than politically correct lines that take away our edges, our outrage, our pasión. She deserves familia resurrected and repaired by us."[40] This is the transformative power of Chicana lesbian feminism, the desire to construct out of the destruction of patriarchy a better society, a better culture, a better world.

In the essay "Art in America con Acento" Cherríe Moraga discusses the Chicana feminist implications of United States imperialism in Latin America for the Latinas/os living within the belly of the beast: "*las entrañas del monstruo.*" Her essay was written one week after what she calls "the death of the Nicaraguan Revolution" by cause of the U.S.-financed Contra War and economic embargo. She goes on:

Once again an emerging sovereign nation is brought to its knees. A nation on the brink of declaring to the entire world that revolution is the people's choice betrays its own dead. Imperialism makes traitors of us all, makes us weak and tired and hungry.

I don't blame the people of Nicaragua. I blame the U.S. government. I blame my complicity as a citizen in a coun-

try that, short of an invasion, stole the Nicaraguan revolution that *el pueblo* forged with their own blood and bones.
After hearing the outcome of the elections, I wanted to flee
the United States in shame and despair.[41]

Moraga questions not only the impact of North American imperialism upon the nations of Latin America but, more important,
the ways in which imperialism promotes complicity, making
imperialists of all citizens. She describes the rapturous reception
of President George Bush by Latinos who celebrated the defeat
of the revolution in Nicaragua and wonders how monolithic is
the vision of the United States and the global relevance of U.S.
interests. Daughter of an Anglo father and Mexican mother, and
"a testimony to the failure of the United States to wholly angli-
cize its *mestizo* citizens,"[42] she is consumed by the fact of U.S.
domination and control in the Americas coupled with the consciousness of a very different kind of America, an America that
resists the artificial divisions imposed by imperialistic ideologies: "We stand on land that was once the country of México.
And before any conquistadors staked out political boundaries,
this was Indian land and in the deepest sense remains just that: a
land *sin fronteras*. . . . Chicanos are a multiracial, multilingual
people, who since 1848, have been displaced from our ancestral
lands or remain upon them as indentured servants to Anglo-
American invaders."[43] In Moraga's view it is this consciousness,
this historical condition—coupled with the fact that Chicanos are
not a monolithic group, and nor are the other dispossessed
groups victimized by North American imperialism—that poses a
threat to the coherence, the power, of the ideologies and cultural

mythologies like manifest destiny that fuel America's imperialistic ambitions. "Ironically, the United States' gradual consumption of Latin America and the Caribbean is bringing the people of the Americas together. What was once largely a Chicano/ Mexican population in California is now *guatemalteco, salvadoreño, nicaragüense.* . . . Every place the United States has been involved militarily has brought its offspring, its orphans, its homeless, and its casualties to this country: Vietnam, Guatemala, Cambodia, the Philippines."[44] Thus, the Third World comes to the First World—but this is only a vision, a hope for the future that American exceptionalism may, by its own contradiction, fracture and disintegrate. Right now, Moraga writes, "we witness a fractured and disintegrating América, where the Northern half functions as the absented landlord of the Southern half and the economic disparity between the First and Third Worlds drives a bitter wedge between a people."[45] The transformation of consciousness from the "Americas" to "Our America" envisioned by Moraga requires the transformation of a resilient and powerful cultural ideology. Not only the transformation of the patriarchal structure of Mexican social and gender relations but the imperialistic assumptions of United States self-definitions—challenged by the Chicano movement—are targeted by the transformative politics of Chicana feminism.

Control of Feminine Sexuality

The definition of Chicana femininity by patriarchal Mexican institutions, specifically the control of Hispanic women through the Catholic Church and the traditional structure of the Mexican family, forms the basis of Chicana criticism of the Chicano movement. This is Helena María Viramontes's concern in the short narratives collected as *The Moths and Other Stories.* For example, in the story "Growing" (which is also reprinted in Roberta Fernández's anthology *In Other Words*) Viramontes describes the momentous significance of feminine maturity, of becoming a woman, as the denial or confiscation of the freedoms of childhood. Naomi has yet to appreciate the huge difference between being a child and being a woman; she cannot understand why her femininity is viewed negatively, and so she resents her young sister's role as chaperone at her father's insistence: "It was Apa who refused to trust her and she could not understand what she had done to make him so distrustful. TU ERES MUJER, he thundered like a great voice above the heavens, and that was the end of any argument, any question, because he said those words not as truth, but as a verdict, and she could almost see the clouds parting, the thunderbolts breaking the tranquillity of her sex. Naomi tightened her grasp with the thought, shaking her head in disbelief. 'So what's wrong with being a mujer,' she asked herself out loud."[46] The story simply describes an interrupted walk with her younger sister, as they stop to watch and become involved in a game of stickball played in the street. At the end of the story Naomi experiences a new sense of tenderness toward her sister and her childhood that now seems so temporary and will soon give way to the restrictions and denials that are womanhood: "When she was Lucia's age, she hunted for lizards and played stickball with her cousins. When her body began to bleed at twelve . . . she began to act differently because everyone began treating her differently and wasn't it crazy? She could no longer be herself and her father could no longer trust her, because she was a woman. . . . She felt Lucia's warm deep breath on her neck and it tickled her."[47] Despite a sense of shared feminine experience, a bond of sisterhood, it is the father who defines the significance of Chicana femininity with a definition that depends crucially upon the presumed duplicity and shamefulness of feminine sexuality. In this view women need to be controlled, and the primary agents of control are the Church and the family.

A drama by Edit Villareal, *My Visits with MGM,* one of the plays collected by Linda Feyder in the volume titled *Shattering the Myth* (1992), explores the control that can be exerted by the Church over vulnerable and dependent Hispanic women. This is a memory play; memories are recalled in the ashes of the family home by Marta Feliz, who has returned to the ruins of the house in which she was raised by her grandmother Marta Grande and her great-aunt Florinda. As the play progresses, it becomes clear that Florinda has never managed to adjust to life across the border, and she takes refuge in an increasingly hysterical Catholicism. As Marta Feliz observes to the audience, "Poor Florinda. For her, crisis became a religion. When I think of her now, I always see her far away. And alone." At this moment in the action Florinda unveils a large statue of the Virgin Mary and cries, "She is your mother. She is a virgin. Her son died. And we must suffer. You hear me? Suffer! We are born to suffer! We live to suffer! It is our one true joy."[48] Marta Grande, however, who married and raised children, manages to carve out of her life small freedoms and areas of independence for herself—accordingly she advises her granddaughter always to keep her financial independence, using the homely example of chickens. But Florinda immerses herself in her own dependence upon the Church, identifying with the tenets of her religion to the point where she believes herself to be repeating the sufferings of Christ. She identifies with an imaginary community of the chosen against Marta Feliz, who comes to represent all that Florinda fears. The two women struggle against each other for possession of the family home. Finally Florinda takes possession to create a hospice for the poor (ignoring Marta Feliz's pleas that she *is* the poor). Thus, Florinda dispossesses her American-born, "gringa" niece who "immigrates" to Los Angeles: "My tia Florinda had turned into somebody I didn't know. And worse, somebody I didn't even like. And the house had changed, too. The foundation was the same, but the rooms were furnished with ghosts, dead memories, shadows and the rotting remains of a dying Church. My grandmother was right. Poverty is not a god and starvation has no virtue, no matter what anybody says."[49] So, as Marta Grande had to flee Mexico, persuading her sister Florinda to accompany her, so Marta Feliz has to flee Texas for a new life in the West. Marta Feliz leaves behind the same corruption, dispossession, and lack of choice that her grandmother left, and particularly she leaves behind the Church.

Josefina López's play *Simply María* is a much angrier and more passionate representation of the pressures placed upon women by the traditional Hispanic family (rather than pressures exerted by the Church). María is brought as a child to the United States by parents who want a better life for her, and she rewards them by studying hard and progressing well. The crisis comes when she wants to go to college instead of marrying young, and then the conflicts and contradictions of a cross-cultural existence come fully into play. Her mother, Carmen, tries to explain the conventional expectations of a Mexican woman: "María, don't cry. Don't be angry at us either, and try to understand us. M'ija! We are doing this for you. We don't want you to get hurt. You want too much; that's not realistic. You are a Mexican woman, and that's that. You can't change that. You are different from other women. Try to accept that. Women need to get married, they are no good without men."[50] To this María responds, "Mother, we are in America. Don't you realize you expect me to live in two worlds? How is it done? Can't things be different?"[51] The posing of this question is followed by an allegorical sequence, starting with a dream-vision: the character representing Myth introduces a fairy-tale image of marriage to Prince Charming; she is chased off the stage by Mary, who promises liberation and self-determination: "Self independence, economic independence, sexual independence. We are free! María, in America, you can be anything you want to be. A lawyer. A doctor. An astronaut. An actress!! The Mayor. Maybe even the President . . . of a company. You don't have to be obedient, submissive, gracious. You don't have to like dolls, dishes, cooking, children and laundry. Enjoy life! Enjoy liberation! Enjoy sex! Be Free!"[52] She is banished by the figure of María 2, who undergoes a mock marriage ceremony, promising her husband to "love, cherish, serve, cook for, clean for, sacrifice for, have his children, keep his house, love him even if he beats you, commits adultery, gets drunk, rapes you lawfully, denies you your identity, money, love his family, serve his family, and in return ask for nothing."[53] This is followed by a Kafkaesque mock trial in which María stands accused of rebellion against her wifely duties. In the following, final scene María leaves home observing, "Mexico is in my blood. . . . And America is in my heart."[54] The extreme difficulty of reconciling or even living with the conflicting demands of contemporary American culture and the traditional values of the Mexican community places unbearable pressures upon the Hispanic family structure.

The problematic nature of feminine sexuality is frequently depicted within the dual context of family and Church. Sexuality, that which defines femininity, is perceived as an obstacle, a burden, and a constraint. In the story "Cimarron" (signifying an escaped slave) Alicia Gaspar de Alba describes an exchange between the main character, the mestiza Concepcion, and her Spanish grandmother, who is also the Mother Superior of the convent in which Concepcion lives: "Destiny is the cage that each of us is born with, and we can't ever leave that cage, Concepcion. We are all slaves to our destinies."[55] In response to the girl's suggestion that she will never be free because she is a mestiza, the older woman tells her, "Because you're a woman. That's the cage you're born with, Concepcion. It doesn't matter that you're a mestiza or a criolla or a servant or a nun. If your destiny is to be a woman, you will never know what it means to fly."[56] Concepcion's grandmother concludes that if destiny does originate with God, God made the men who impose destiny upon all women. As the story reaches its inevitable conclusion, Concep-

cion resists the position of slave into which she has been forced
and chooses instead death.

Chicana Role Models

In the attempt to represent the restrictions that are placed upon
Hispanic feminine identity, Latina writers often draw on a traditional cultural iconography of woman as the virgin or the whore.
I have discussed in some detail above the three primary images
of Chicana femininity (La Virgen de Guadalupe, La Malinche,
and La Llorona), but here I want to draw attention particularly to
the latter, the figure of La Llorona, who is favored by contemporary writers for the ambiguity of her symbolic significance. La
Llorona is the weeping woman, who is said to have drowned her
young children in order to punish her husband for his infidelity;
but she hid the little bodies so well that when she went to bury
them she could not find them, and now she haunts rivers and
streams, any body of water, calling and weeping for her lost children. Destroyer and creator; mother and murderer, the wronged
woman who searches eternally for her dead children—La
Llorona offers a powerful image that speaks to all the dispossessed people of the Americas as well as the Chicanas who find
that the lives they lead cost them their children. The multiple
meanings embraced by the figure of La Llorona are the subject
of Naomi Quiñónez's poem "La Llorona." Here, La Llorona is
the woman of irresolvable contradictions, the phantom murder-
ess, the rejected mother, the all-forgiving part of being, the
defiled woman, "La india amorosa / La mujer dolorosa." La

Llorona encapsulates the contradictions of the Chicana condition:

> La madre who grieves
> at bringing children into a world
> that may destroy them
> and will kill them.[57]

The woman who is the giver of life is also the woman who condemns her children to death. The mortality that is her gift is also the burden her children must bear, and the knowledge that life is death is her particular lament.

Alma Luz Villanueva's story "La Llorona," from the collection of that name, describes La Llorona's mythological significance as a woman who has killed her children to save them from a worse destiny.[58] Villanueva uses La Llorona in a complex symbolic motif to represent the transformation of her character Carmen, who uses her sexuality in order to survive but at the expense of her spirit and her humanity. The loss of the children is represented by a broader loss of family relationships in Carmen's rejection of her own mother and her refusal to comfort her abused daughter Luna, who has been sexually assaulted while playing in the park. Her grandmother and Luna take refuge in a rare bus journey to the seaside, where for the first time Luna has a vision of La Llorona seeking her lost children—all the lost children—and finds a profound comfort in the vision. In this way La Llorona becomes symbolic of the violence that arises from oppression, sexism, and racism and destroys the most fundamental of kinship ties. Interestingly, in Rudolfo Anaya's Chicano classic, *Bless Me, Ultima,* La Llorona is referred to as the destroyer of men; in Villanueva's use the figure represents the sacrificial destruction of the family as the price of survival.

Hybrid Literary Forms

The specific conditions of Hispanic femininity have produced an imperative that new literary forms, forms that accurately portray rather than distort Hispanic subjectivity, be developed to supersede the literary forms of a masculine-defined or Anglo-America. Gloria Anzaldúa describes the linguistic mix characteristic of her writing in these terms. In the preface to *Borderlands/La Frontera: The New Mestiza* (1987) she explains that her language switches from English to Castillian Spanish to North Mexican Spanish to Tex-Mex to Nahuatl because her language is a new language and a necessary expression of a new consciousness, that of the Borderlands. Anzaldúa refuses to translate for us, to simplify this new language and make easy our access to the new consciousness. She will not apologize for her difference and requires instead that we meet her halfway on this linguistic territory. This kind of hybridity not only is found in relation to the linguistic usage of contemporary Chicana writers but marks the use of narrative form as well. Upon opening Ana Castillo's *The Mixquiahuala Letters* we are encouraged to resist the linear narrative by Castillo's preface, which reads:

Dear Reader:
    It is the author's duty to alert the reader that this is not

a book to be read in the usual sequence. All letters are numbered to aid in following any one of the author's proposed options.[59]

These are then specified as The Conformist, The Cynic, and The Quixotic, with a final reminder: "For the reader committed to nothing but short fiction, all letters read as separate entities. Good luck with whichever journey you choose! A.C." Castillo thus prescribes the act of reading as an act of self-definition on the part of the reader rather than the discovery of the definitive nature of the characters created in the text.

Contemporary Hispanic women's writing is highly innovative, producing literary styles that are hybrid and provisional, using an associative logic in place of coherent linear narrative, and that use linguistic code-switching to express cross-cultural identities: in short, this is a literature that locates itself in the cultural borderland of the mestiza. For many of the characters created by Chicana writers, life is experienced in fragments, in unrelated images or vignettes; these women are denied the authority to create a unified vision of their lives. Chicanas express a sense of powerlessness that arises from life lived on the margins and captured in moments, scenes, and images rather than developed narratives. Here are the women imprisoned in upper-floor flats because their husbands/fathers/sons forbid that they should venture out; women who are afraid to leave the barrio because they do not speak English; women who are afraid to speak for themselves because of the pervasive violence, sexual and otherwise, that begins at the home and does not end. Fear, intimidation, self-doubt, and imposed constraints are the daily realities of Chicana lives, and these are the realities that contemporary Chicana writers are seeking to represent in new and authentic ways. How to give voice to subjectivity experienced as marginal and fragmentary is the challenge and the great achievement of much Hispanic women's writing.

Helena María Viramontes presents a series of vignettes in the story "The Broken Web" that are more like interior monologues spoken by the characters woven into a complex web of relationships. Tomás, his lover Olivia, his daughter Martha and her aunt, and the woman who remains unnamed and is referred to only as "Tomás's wife" gradually reveal a situation that is unknown to any one of them but becomes known to the reader. Tomás's wife has sought to break out of the constraints imposed upon her by her family and traditions through a sexual liaison with another man. The rage this fuels in Tomás is released only when his wife accuses him of infidelity and in the violent clash that ensues she shoots and kills him. Only when he is dead does he begin to appear to his wife as an equal: dead as she has felt dead throughout the years of her marriage. "How could she explain to him that she was so tired and wrinkled and torn by him, his God, his word? She had tried to defy the rules by sleeping with another man, but that only left her worse off. And now she could not leave him because she no longer owned herself. He owned her, her children owned her, and she needed them to live. And she was tired of needing."[60] But this act of rebellion brings physical incarceration in place of the spiritual bondage she has suffered. She has only killed a man, when the real enemy is the patriarchal law of the fathers that generates the oppression, suffering, and feminine servitude she has sought to destroy. The discontinuous, hybrid form of the narrative allows a story to develop without falsely imposing a unity or coherence that does not exist for the characters.

Sandra Cisneros uses provisional, discontinuous, loosely associative forms of narrative logic in *The House on Mango Street* to represent the fragmentary sense of self possessed by characters whose lives have no completion, no closure, none of the assurance that is conveyed by an omniscient narrator telling the story of lives that have clearly defined beginnings, middles, and ends. The violence and abuse experienced by Esperanza and her friend Sally are disguised by the stories they are told of romance and happy endings, stories that correspond in no way to the actual lives led by these characters. The sequence of narrative vignettes that tell the story of Esperanza's friend Sally explore the dangers of sexuality, of female power, of body image, of the life story Sally has expected to live, the fantasy of escape.[61] Denise Chávez's *The Last of the Menu Girls* uses a similar discontinuous form to explore the developing consciousness of the protagonist Rocío Esquibel as an artist and writer. Both texts can be named generically as Chicana feminist Kunstlerromans, narratives that describe the coming to consciousness of the artist as a poor Latina woman, and as such the authority to speak and the discovery of a subject about which to speak is the central motive of the narrative. The advice given to Rocío at the end is taken not only by Denise Chávez but by Sandra Cisneros in her writing as well: "I'll tell her, Roque, just write one *Gone With the Wind.* That's all. Just one. You don't have to go anywhere. Not down the street. Not even out of this house. There's stories, plenty of them around."[62] Both Chávez and Cisneros, like so many Chicana writers, find their subjects in the immediate world in which they live, a world that so often lacks the logic of justice and the closure of self-fulfillment.

The Chicana voice is not always black and pessimistic and depressing; the subject of this writing is not always deprivation and suffering. These negative issues are explored in a context that looks forward, in the directions indicated by Chicana feminist theory, and in a style that is required formally to innovate in order to represent without distorting the very subject and subjectivity it seeks to express. A frequent theme is the joyful transgression or defiance of inherited misogynistic definitions of Mexican American femininity. The corresponding theme is the celebration of the potential for liberation offered through the expression of feminine sexuality. Cisneros's poetry in titles such as "Loose Woman" and "My Wicked, Wicked Ways" represents precisely this celebration of a liberated Chicana sexuality, as does the narrator of Denise Chávez's *Face of an Angel* who questions her mother about the significance of the phrase "sanitary napkin," commenting that "they aren't a bandage to swab up something dirty. The blood that comes out of me is beautiful."[63] Her mother is, of course, scandalized, exclaiming that such things are dirty, not to be spoken of or even thought about. Chávez and Cisneros represent the new mestiza/Chicana consciousness of daughters who resist and refuse to accept the constraints against which their mothers and grandmothers have chafed and which limited their lives. Contemporary Chicana literature celebrates this breaking of constraints and liberation of possibilities.

CHAPTER TWO

Bernice Zamora

It is appropriate to begin the analysis of key Chicana writers with the poet Bernice Zamora, for Zamora's poetic career spans the entire period of the Chicana Renaissance, from the 1970s to the present. Her poems published in 1976 in *Restless Serpents* represent her writing from 1966 to 1976. Her second collection, *Releasing Serpents* (1994), represents her work from that time in a kind of revisiting of her earlier work from the vantage point of the 1990s.[1] This is because the poems of *Restless Serpents* are reprinted in the second volume, in front of the new poems that reread the old. Juan Bruce-Novoa has written of her that "most notable of the first flurry of Chicana texts was Bernice Zamora's half of *Restless Serpents* (1976), a feminist manifesto written in thoughtfully crafted poems that proved instantly that Chicanas could write as well as, if not better than, Chicanos."[2] Zamora's work continues to reinforce her reputation as a skillful and complex poet not only of the Chicana experience but also of the human condition.

Bernice Zamora was born on 28 January 1938 in Aguilar, a small village in Southern Colorado, to a well-established but poor farming family of mixed Spanish and Taos Pueblo Indian descent. Her ancestors had farmed the land for six generations, but poor conditions forced her father to seek work in the coal mines of Valdez, Colorado, and the family lived in the company section of the town of Segundo until Zamora was six years old. From there the family moved to live with her mother's family in

Denver, but when Zamora was twelve years old they moved again to Pueblo, which is located in between Denver and Aguilar. Zamora lived in Pueblo with her own family after her parents returned to Denver and remained there until her divorce when she was thirty-six, at which time she moved to California, where she lives today. After marrying and raising two daughters, Zamora was twenty-eight when she returned to her studies. She received her B.A. in English and French from Southern Colorado University, her M.A. from Colorado State University in Fort Collins, and her Ph.D. in English and American Studies from Stanford University in 1986.

Zamora describes the importance of education for her and the sacrifices she has had to make in her life in order to become the well-educated woman she is. She tells how her father forbade reading in the house and placed pressure upon her to leave school as soon as the law allowed, though her mother struggled to keep her in school. She attributes several reasons for her father's attitude: first, the family needed the money that she could earn by working, and so the compromise she struck was that she would work at a full-time night job while attending high school during the day. Second, she recognizes that in Latino culture an educated woman is perceived to be a danger; she possesses a thinking, questioning consciousness rather than the submissive attitude prescribed for Latina femininity.[3] Gloria Anzaldúa in *Borderlands/La Frontera* describes education as the recently available fourth alternative for Chicana lives, an alternative to the Church (as a nun), the street (as a prostitute), and the family (as a mother).[4] Zamora's education has allowed her a kind of liberation from the conservatism of the region in which she grew up and spent so much of her adult life. This conservatism affected Zamora's sense of herself, and while she was reluctant to rebel openly, she sought instead an internal accommodation with the constraints placed upon her. She has taught at various times, though she describes teaching as a way to pay the rent while she focuses on her real work, which is writing. Most recently she has taught ethnic and world literatures at the University of Santa Clara, and she has acted as guest editor of the Chicano movement journal *El Fuego de Aztlán*.[5] Her work has been widely anthologized and reprinted in such journals as *El Fuego de Aztlán, De Colores, Atisbos, Mango,* and *Coracol.*

There is a relatively close relationship between Zamora's life and her work, from the physical landscapes, to the people of her family and community, to her particular experiences of prejudice and oppression. Each of these aspects of her work will be discussed in turn. The landscapes of Colorado are important as scenery and background to Zamora's writing. She describes her childhood memories of the place in which she lived: "The landscape, especially the mountains, instructed us in the way the day would evolve. We looked at the mountains to see if it was going to rain. We related to the mountains on a daily basis."[6] Zamora attributes the importance of religion in her life and her poetry to the close proximity with the mountains of her childhood. Rather than the rituals of religion, it is the knowledge of God that comes from a close relationship with nature and the natural world that represents the centrality of religion or spirituality in Zamora's work. She describes this consciousness of the spirituality inherent in nature as arising from her Native American inheritance. It is in connection with the practice and conception of religion that

Native Americans appear in Zamora's poetry. For example, the poem "Trinkets" describes the contrast between native versus European conceptions of god and transcendent powers (*Restless Serpents,* 66). In this poem a Navajo Indian sells bright ethnic baubles to Anglo tourists; it is said that he "knows our god" (1.2). But the Navajo lives in a close relationship with the spirit of the land so that after each heavy rainfall he moves his home to a different location by the river. Zamora uses a clever reversal of the notion that natives are seduced by bright glittering worthless things and that they will abandon their tribal religious practices if tempted with such baubles. In Zamora's poem it is the Anglos who have no real idea of spiritual values or of the true worth of things.

The corruption of the Indians of the Americas, the ancestors of the Chicanos, is lamented in poems such as "Moctezuma's Treasure" (*Restless Serpents,* 35). In this poem Zamora asks, "How did it happen?"—"it" being the dissolution and debasement of native society, culture, and spirituality. In the first stanza she draws attention to the superiority of native spirituality over that of Western Christianity. In contrast to the Christian observation of a set of commandments, traditional native life conceived of every day as holy, the family as divine and covetousness was unknown. The second stanza deals with the terms of native destruction by identifying all those things natives would not have participated in before European contact, such as entering and desecrating crypts, learning and using strange languages, or trading "lands for candles / and a coffin" (2.15–16), where the candles signify Western Catholicism and the coffin the fatal diseases spread by the conquistadors. The final stanza describes ironically how Europeans, who cannot know that the treasure was the life lived by these people before contact with Europe, question the natives about Moctezuma's treasure. The neglect of the native spiritual inheritance is lamented in the poem "Unattended," which closely follows "Moctezuma's Treasure." In this poem Zamora describes how it is easy to observe a European religion but impossible even to gain access to the temples of Native America. The doors are guarded so that access is denied "even to janitors / who wish only to clean / the fouled tombs of / ancestors so that inscriptions / of Tlaloc may be seen (2.9–13). No sign or indication of the spiritual significance of these tombs is permitted. The dominance of Western modes of religion allows no competitors. But Zamora warns us that this willful neglect of the lessons that are to be learned from these ancestors comes at a terrible price. In a series of violent images she describes torrential "rains from unknown skies" (1.16) that will wash the tombs clean and bodily "spit us, one after another" (1.18) onto those inscribed slabs until we are forced to read, to understand, and to venerate.

In some later poems this apocalyptic response of nature and the neglected old gods is linked to an ecological concern that temporarily takes precedence over issues of race and gender, though the violence done to the planet is linked to the exploitative and repressive assumptions that underpin racism and sexism. In "Summer's Rage" Zamora begins with images of unnatural climatic conditions such as snow in July, the Mississippi uncontrollably flooding, heat waves in Houston to describe a planet in crisis, a crisis like a Medieval plague.[7] The perspective she adopts in relation to this ecological crisis is the contrasting perspective of adults and children. "We adults race fatigued / From reality to betrayal" ("Summer's Rage," 2.6–7), she writes, while the refrain throughout the short poem repeats the paralysis of children who know "our confusion" but are powerless to act. "Piles of Sublime" similarly contrasts adults' with children's perspectives (*In Other Words,* 261). The imagery of ice is used to represent a world in which the lessons of the past are neglected; past history goes unexamined, and the consequence for children is that they are unable to imagine a future that will release them from this icy existence. Within this context Zamora redefines the notion of "endangerment," suggesting that it is not so much species that are endangered as it is "beauty / unfrozen" ("Piles of Sublime," 2.7–8) that is threatened with extinction in this world of ignorance and denial. The extinction of beauty in a culture dominated by images of death is the theme of the poem "Shade" (*In Other Words,* 259). The artifice of the plastic shades alienates us from the world and confines us to a realm of life-lessness or death; this is far from a life lived in close physical and spiritual proximity to the natural world, which is how Zamora describes her own childhood and the lives of her native ancestors.

As remarked on above, the image of Native Americans appears in important but incidental ways in Zamora's work. Her poetry is characterized by the vivid representation of the people she knows in terms of their race, gender, history, religion, language, and regional identity as well as the places she has experienced. In the poem "Luciano" she describes her attempt to observe a lunar eclipse that is frustrated by a vision of Uncle Luciano. The interruption proves to be more valuable than the eclipse she had hoped to see because what she is privileged to see and hear is a breaking of the silence that a life of back-breaking labor, suffering, and oppression has forced upon Luciano. The man she knew when he was alive was "a man of extraordinary traits: / unhappiness / integrity / silence / devotion" (2.8–12), but the ghostly vision she records in this poem reveals something of what was buried beneath that silent exterior (*Releasing Serpents,* 90).

Humor is a device sometimes used to express the poet's fondness for landscapes and people, as in "El Burrito Café" and "Martha." In "El Burrito Café" the use of words lends the poem its gentle humor. The poet describes the work in the café kitchen of the woman Augustina Godínez, to whom the title "chef" seems inappropriate. The humor arises from the conflict of perspectives between the Chicana whose work of nurturing and care far transcends that of a mere chef—she is described as preparing *menudo,* a remedy for hangovers, for the drunks who will visit the café—and the class-bound European definition of a chef as far superior to a mere cook. Zamora describes how many of her poems are written for or about specific people: such as the aunt of her former husband whose voice is heard in the poem "¿A que hora venderemos todo?" This is the second of the sequence of poems that make up *Restless Serpents,* and it is in this poem that Zamora uses the figure of the woman to establish her specific concern with the condition of women in the Chicano community, a concern that will be explored throughout the poem sequence. In the opening poem of *Restless Serpents,* "Penitents," Zamora establishes the poetic identity that is to control the entire sequence of poems. Here identity is characterized through childhood memories of the sacred chanting of the *alabados,* the penitents, echoing through the Rocky Mountains at Easter, and this image establishes the connection between nature and spirituality that is so important in Zamora's aesthetic and throughout this poem sequence.

Central to her work are the Chicano cultural traditions of her community and the experiences she has witnessed of women within those traditions, though her poetry expresses anger against oppression in all forms. Zamora's racial memories are deeply felt and vividly recollected; these memories take the form of scars from the wounds she suffered in adolescence when her childhood innocence was destroyed by the growing awareness of the racially prejudiced nature of the world.[8] She describes having a vague awareness of racial prejudice as something that existed outside the world of her family and community. But she recognizes that the Catholic Church and the Catholic school she attended insulated her from knowledge of racism. The common experience and shared rituals of the church members obscured the racial differences between them. It was when she had to leave the Catholic schooling system, because her family could not afford to send her to Catholic high school, and entered the public school system that the full force of racial discrimination hit her. She describes an incident in which her mother instructed her to tell a boy who has shown her some favor that these favors are inappropriate because he is not Catholic; before Zamora can deliver this message, however, the boy tells her that his mother has instructed him to keep away from Mexicans. Painful and humiliating experiences such as this have left emotional scars on Zamora's poetic sensibility, and they are compounded by her recollection of the poverty of her childhood.

This struggle for the opportunity to be creative informs in a fundamental way Zamora's artistic views: her poetics and her sense of the role of the writer. Basically she writes poetry out of a need to write poetry, to express herself, her subjectivity, and the pain of her past. She describes her "brutal childhood" and unhappy marriage as powerful motivators of her poetry. She writes, and has written, as a means of controlling the pain and surviving the psychological and emotional suffering she has experienced. For this reason she is a prolific writer, measuring her average creative output at a poem per day, although her published work is relatively modest. One of the points of development throughout her career as a poet is the increasingly internal motivation or inspiration for her work. Poems are inspired less in reaction to an event or image and more as part of an ongoing internal dialogue. The creation of poetry in this way is a healing process; Zamora describes how when she is ill, rereading her own poetry makes her well again: "It's about the closest I can get to a spiritual experience, maybe a mystical experience, and then it's on paper and I can re-read it."[9]

Bernice Zamora's view of the world is shaped by her consciousness of herself as a Chicana. This means that feminism and the Chicano movement are crucial reference points for her. The movement gave her an audience and a way to describe herself. It provided an answer to the question she poses in the one-line poem "Sin Titulo": "What if we survive?" (*Restless Serpents,* 82). Since she was always aware that she could not be an authentic Mexican, like those who were born in and live their lives in Mexico, she had experienced herself as occupying a kind of cultural limbo. But the concept of the Chicano/a subject both named and gave reality and legitimacy to that limbo state. As a consequence, she no longer had to risk the feeling of being lost or suspended between cultures and instead could see herself as engaging with and addressing both Mexican and Anglo cultures. Zamora is not, however, unaware of the ambivalent position of women within the Chicano movement. As pointed out in the introduction, in the poem "Notes from a Chicana Coed," Bernice Zamora describes the condition of women who are trapped between conflicting demands made by their race and their gender. By giving priority to the struggle of the Chicano community she betrays her Chicana sisters to ongoing patriarchal oppression within the traditional Mexican cultural units of church and family. By giving priority to her gender and the liberation of Chicana femininity from oppressive cultural paradigms she splits the movement and betrays her people to continuing racial oppression. But it is not the trapped woman who is the subject of her poem so much as the hypocritical Chicano who fights white oppression while oppressing women, especially Chicanas. The reality of the movement for so many women was precisely this experience of being oppressed in the name of liberation.

Zamora describes the exhilaration of the early days of the movement, when she took her daughters with her on street marches and demonstrations, but she also describes the emergence to positions of relative prominence of those who want to insist that the civil rights struggle has been won, that the Chicano movement is dead because it has outlived its moment, and that Chicanos do not in any case form a distinct culture but simply form part of the immigrant culture of the United States. It is the Chicano who desires this kind of assimilation that Zamora fears and despises. This is the man who is not committed to his family or his community or his culture but on the contrary wants to deny and obliterate them. Zamora remarks, "When the macho becomes assimilated he's even uglier than the Mexicano macho because he's trying to kill everything that he came from; I think there's so much self-hatred that he will kill anything that reminds him of his culture and that includes women and children."[10]

This desire for access to Anglo structures of power, with the concomitant self-denial and self-hatred this involves, has a counterpart in what Zamora calls "the white-woman feminist movement."[11] Zamora rejects the feminist movement, which she sees as being dominated by an agenda prescribed by the Anglo women who are not seeking genuine liberation for all women and an end to oppression in all its forms but instead want to empower women to adopt masculine values and behaviors. Just as some Chicanos/as want to "pass" for white in Anglo society, so feminists of this kind seek to "pass" for male within the existing power structure. In Zamora's view the woman who has made it to the top of a corporate ladder is still constrained by male structures and a patriarchal bondage to the masculine images she must emulate. Feminine values and patterns of behavior find no space for expression within patriarchal social and economic institutions. Zamora asks, where are the women healers? She sees healing, especially the healing of other women, as a power possessed by women specifically, but it is a power squandered by feminists who seek a place in the white medical profession and once there take up invasive and brutalizing surgical practices. However, the necessary healing of bodies, minds, and spirits by women who know how to heal naturally and by female definitions is not considered a feminist issue. In her poetry

Zamora balances her concerns with racial and gender oppression. Chicano culture, and the position within that culture of Chicanas, is her primary theme.

"On Living in Aztlán" is about the condition of dispossession that afflicts all Mexican Americans. Zamora's poem describes in succinct and powerful form the injustice imposed by this division of the land by the U.S.-Mexico border. The people are divided (Mexicans from Americans) where they were once one; families (such as the Arias family, to whom the poem is dedicated) are divided from each other. Zamora insists that the arbitrary imposition of a national border, a political principle, "a law / Which is not ours" (2.3–4), cannot defeat the love that unites the people, but it imposes restraints upon what they can do, go, become (*Restless Serpents,* 25). Mexicans experience the injustice of this border construction as a form of partitioning, the creation of a border that cuts across family, community, and cultural relations with no regard for the consequences this will have for the Mexican people. Zamora responds to this historical fact of Mexican American history in a number of ways. There is the simple exposure of the Chicano perspective upon this episode in the national history and mythology of the United States, as in poems such as "On Living in Aztlán."

In "Among the Ordained" Zamora addresses the trivializing and negation of Mexican American culture that promotes the interests of the colonization of minds as well as bodies. To express this concern she develops a carefully controlled confusion over the attribution of the term "miscreant" (*Restless Serpents,* 54). The poem begins by moving from the religious association of the title to an image of military ("ordinance") rather than spiritual power. Zamora then affirms the image of natives as miscreants who live in a culture that is being destroyed, natives who have been "miscreated" because there is no longer any world in which they belong. Then she contrasts with the positive religious imagery of "the ordained" the image of "hellish" miscreants who are forced to commit "gothic" acts "by ordinands / Villainous miscreants" (2.12–13). From this point in the poem the term "miscreants" is applied ironically to the colonizers, "who rape the wrongs" (1.14) as well as continuing their colonizing rhetoric but applying it to describe the crimes they have committed "wronging miscreants" (1.16). Juxtaposed between these two lines (14 and 16) is the line that applies equally to the colonizers and the colonized, who are both caught up in "avenging wrongs" (1.15) and, as a result of this cycle of violence, are both transformed into "miscreants."

There is also a sense in which Zamora represents the creation of the Mexican-U.S. border as absurd and that rests upon her recognition that nature is entirely separate from the human world and so is ultimately unknowable except in inauthentic human terms. This is the theme of the poem "'The Extraordinary Patience of Things'" (*Restless Serpents,* 59). In this poem Zamora makes explicit the perception that has informed the developing poetic meaning of *Restless Serpents.* In the first stanza she sets out examples of the humanizing of nonhuman nature: horses aware of "the spoiler"; flowers that are "walled in" and "stooped" by the cliffs that tower above them. The second stanza reminds us of the ephemerality of human works and human perceptions while in the following, final stanza the poet observes: "We humanize the unhuman" (1.11). In our self-consciousness and self-absorption we ignore all but our own projected meanings and assume a false confidence in the semantic edifices that we construct. This idea that we project meaning onto the nonhuman world and then willfully mistake the projection for reality is explored with great subtlety in "Pueblo Winter" with the suggestion that the entire poem is an externalization of the poet's consciousness. Though the subject is exclusively the birds of Pueblo, the poem refers to one of the robins as "the silent other" who "lays witness" to the actions of the other birds. It is the poet who equally shares this status of "silent witness" (*Restless Serpents,* 65). Writing of the birds watching each other as they (the birds) watch each other creates a connection between the birds and the poet who watches and records their behavior. In this way the subject of the poem could be read not as the birds but as the poet's witnessing consciousness.

The shallowness of the human mind is contrasted with the deep mind of nature in the poem "Anton Chico Bridge," but this contrast is softened by the awareness that the poet possesses a privileged insight into this contrast (*Restless Serpents,* 68). So the fact that Zamora can understand the significance of the difference between human consciousness and the natural world suggests that not all humans are superficial and self-absorbed. Like the water flowing beneath the bridge, the poet has "a deeper, wider mind whose water, / even in its clearest moments, / knows itself to be muddy with adobe" (2.18–20). There is in this poem, then, a gently ironic expression of poetic self-awareness that indicates to us the importance of the poet who sees more, and more deeply than us. A much more negative and depressed view of the poet is expressed in "Having Drowned," in which the poet describes herself as one of the "seasoned dead," being dead to the experience of the spirit, unable to confront even the shallowest of water, and hopeless of resurrection (*Restless Serpents,* 28). But even in the depths of despair the poet is able to offer a diagnosis of her condition; she is able to understand the terms of the spiritual alienation that affects her in this way. This despair turns angry in the poem "Supping On . . . ," which expresses contemptuously the distinction between human and transcendent perspectives, in terms of which the human appears minuscule and foolish, "holding up our pebble minds / as gems to be admired" (*Restless Serpents,* 30, 2.6–7). Earthbound, in a drunken stupor, the poet like her companions can see no further than themselves, but the image of the mountain, in poems such as "Andando," represents the privileged perspective of the poet that allows her to see the cultural and spiritual terrain on which human life is lived, even though it might not afford her insight (*Restless Serpents,* 52).

Along with many early Chicana writers, who were approaching the same issues addressed by the Chicano movement but from a predominantly feminist perspective, Zamora and her work were attacked for representing a betrayal of la raza by criticizing the machismo of the men in the Chicano community. Juan Bruce-Novoa observes, "The questions that Zamora and Portillo and other Chicanas raised about the oppression women suffered at the hands of men within traditional Chicano culture brought cries of protest from Chicanos. The women were accused of betraying the political struggle by criticizing the behavior of Chicanos, just as those men who wrote other than political works were accused of selling out."[12] Zamora is quick to point out that while she criticizes the gender discrimination to be found in the Chicano movement and expressed in the ideology of machismo, she respects the unquestioned bravery of those Chicanos who risk everything in order to commit themselves to the struggle for civil rights. In poems such as "When We Are Able" the feminine voice reveals the humiliations and degradations that weaken and disempower the entire Chicano/a community (*Restless Serpents,* 18). In each of the three stanzas this feminine voice reassuringly promises that when some condition of Anglo oppression is lifted, then "we will marry, querido, / we will marry." These two lines form a refrain concluding each stanza. The condition described in each stanza is different: when they move from "this colony / of charred huts" (2.1–2); when the stranger no longer comes in the night "to sleep in / our bed and ravish what is yours" (2.7–8); and when her unnamed lover is whole again, able to walk, to smile, to eat without fear—then a future, a marriage, a family will become possible.

The contrasting images of Chicano masculinity represented in the poems "Morning After" and "The Sovereign" reveal precisely Zamora's attitude. The dissolute, hungover man of "Morning After" (*Restless Serpents,* 32), who prefers to live a fiction rather than confront the ugly facts of his life, is contrasted starkly with the Christlike figure of César Chávez in "The Sovereign" (*Restless Serpents,* 33). Chávez is compared to the figure of Sisyphus but is judged to be less given to impractical abstraction and so is more like Atlas, bearing the weight of the world's injustice on his shoulders and resolutely refusing to acknowledge the power of those who seek to usurp or destroy him. "Luciano," a poem already mentioned, describes the poet's uncle as a victim of the lies told to Chicanos about the possibilities open to them in the United States. The burden of his disillusionment breaks Luciano's spirit: "A look of permanent shock stocked his face, stooped his frame" (*Restless Serpents,* 90, 1.14). The lies he has been told, attributed by the poet ironically to "Life" rather than the U.S. mythology of individual progress and self-realization within American democracy, weigh him down, grind him into the ground, and "silenced him at the end with comprehension and incomprehension" (1.17). The knowledge that he has been duped, every day of his life, is a crushing burden. Zamora questions the metaphor and reality (in the poem of that name) of the American dream by contrasting different Chicano perspectives on the idea of progress, advancement. In the first stanza the reality of working in the canneries or in the fields is represented as a "metaphor of being" to which the corresponding reality is the dream, described in the second stanza as belonging to those who believe the promises made to them, even as they live with those who would destroy them and tell monstrous lies about it: "Grendel and Godzilla / as they pick their teeth / with your children's bones" (*Restless Serpents,* 81, 2.8–10).

Zamora is, then, fully aware of the painful challenge to Chicano masculinity that is part of the racist culture of the United States, but that does not stop her from questioning the male-dominated rituals of her culture. The marginalization of Chicanos in the United States is set within the wider context of oppressive attitudes and behaviors. So Zamora not only seeks to identify the racist oppression of Chicanos but strives also to recognize the marginalization of women within Chicano culture and to reinscribe the role of women in that culture. *Restless Serpents* begins with the poem set at Easter, "Penitents" (16); later in the sequence appears the poem "Good Friday, 1973" (55), and this poem is revisited in the poem "Good Friday, 1984," which appears in *Releasing Serpents* (99). The concept of the death and rebirth of the old god is important in terms of the redefinition to include the role of women in Chicano religious traditions. "Penitents" depicts the exclusion of women from such rituals as the alabados' penitential journey, though the poet confesses that the ceremony beckoned to her. In "Good Friday, 1973" the day is described as lacking balance, and though the hours are described as "pregnant," still there will be no birth. The gender inequalities that are revealed so starkly on this day deny even the possibility of "balance." The later poem, "Good Friday, 1984," depicts a soldier who represents a doubly gendered figure. A soldier, he is unarmed, submissive, and weakened by the love he cannot articulate; he is fearful of "his own resurrection / his love for Mary Magdalene / his own summons to act" (2.12–14). This figure combines the masculine with the feminine; in a comparable way Zamora plays on the sound of the word "God" in a woman's name, "Godínez," in "El Burrito Café": because of the accent her name sounds like the phrase "God in you" (*Releasing Serpents,* 70). Zamora repeatedly depicts the image of a strong woman who is able to destroy when necessary. Included with images such as this is the killing or sacrificing of oppressive gods in the poem "California" (*Releasing Serpents,* 29) and the image of the woman who decides to take upon herself the sacrifice of the goat, an image associated with the scapegoat, in the poem "Propriety, 1972" (*Restless Serpents,* 77). That this woman, Loretta, takes upon herself the role of the enactor of ritual is emphasized by the way in which the poem dwells upon her rosary, suggesting that the killing of the goat will have a spiritual significance.

The concept of resurrection, which becomes important in *Restless Serpents* as the poem sequence reaches its resolution, is explored in poems such as "Progenitor" and "Having Drowned." In "Progenitor" the poet adopts the personae of key Chicano/a roles—the *padre,* the *madre,* the *primo,* the *puta,* all the children—in order to emphasize that the resurrection of one depends upon the resurrection of all. Salvation is to be obtained collectively, by and for the community, or not at all (*Restless Serpents,* 20). But immortality is defined as applying differently to men and to women in the poem that expresses Zamora's response to Hermann Hesse's rejection of the ephemeral yet material world, "Without Bark" (*Restless Serpents,* 42) The title of this poem suggests a skinless condition, trees "without bark," in which racial difference is obliterated; yet this rejection of the material is represented not as favoring some superior commitment to the transcendent but instead as a kind of banishment from the material world "that is forbidden us" (1.5), forbidden to those who curse its imperfections and its beauty.

Bernice Zamora's work reveals a self-reflexive concern with what it might mean for a Chicana to be a poet. Many of her themes—marriage, sex, love, and infidelity—directly address the issue of gender and women's experience. But for a woman within Chicano culture, to "be" a poet, to adopt a public voice in that way, is a difficult identification to make and one that is fraught with difficulty. Above is mentioned the opposition Zamora's father expressed to the idea of his daughter reading books, let alone writing her own, and the issue of a public Chicana voice is discussed at some length in the introduction. These are urgent and difficult issues. Zamora asks herself in her poetry about the significance of her own rejection of the silence and self-denial demanded of women by patriarchal culture: what is it in favor of? In a humorous poem such as "A Willing Abdication," Zamora depicts the Chicana poet as incompetent at performing traditional women's roles—for example, cooking (Fernández, 260).

Another response to the questioning of the significance of her role as a poet is to make the writing itself a subject for poetry, so writing becomes both the activity and the subject of the poetry. "Chaff," the central section of *Restless Serpents,* is concerned with the complexity of the artwork or the living being. In an important respect this is the structural center of the poem sequence. Since woman, and her marginalization, was at the center of the first section, titled "On Living in Aztlán," woman and art are from this central point in the sequence conjoined. This is suggested strongly in the first poem of the final section, "Stone Serpents," where the spiritual and creative paralysis symbolized by the image of stone serpents keeps women silent, submissive, and infertile (*Restless Serpents,* 76). Stone has been associated throughout the sequence with spiritual blindness, in poems such as "Morning After" and "'The Extraordinary Patience of Things.'" As explained above, this association is cleverly used in the following poem, "The Sovereign," dedicated to César Chávez, whose heroic stature is likened to that of Sisyphus, the mythical figure whose punishment was the rolling of stones. The "insane" suggestion that women might be artists is explored in the penultimate poem, "A Litany for Mad Masters," where the image of maternal milk is linked with the power of creative insight. The image of milk is developed in poems such as "Bleating" and "'The Extraordinary Patience of Things.'" The connection among woman, madness, and art is first forged in "'What Sweet Delight a Quiet Life Affords'" (*Restless Serpents,* 48). The figure of the feminine artist is characterized by madness, the insane capacity to move "eternity / with a pulse / we do not know" (2.9–11) and to fill the universe with music. Beauty and art are then the compensation for the imperfect world in which we live, as Zamora suggests in "Without Bark."

At the end of the sequence restless serpents are identified with the woman as writer and her art is what soothes the restlessness; to express this vision, images used throughout the poem sequence are revisited. These images include: resurrection in "Progenitor" and "Having Drowned"; corners such as the "painted corner" in "Bleating"; music such as that of cellos in "'What Sweet Delight a Quiet Life Affords'" and the image of the musician as a wise fool in "Denizens"; the image of "droppings" or feces such as the barrel of dung in which the poet finds herself swimming in "Girding Us," the phrase "shit from Shinola" repeated in "Martha," and the words that are like the "turds of the golden goose" in "Let the Giants Cackle"; and stroking, as the "Bearded Lady" in the poem of that name strokes the beard that is her treasure.

Zamora thus emphasizes the importance and power of the feminine artist. In poems such as "Awaiting Grace," "Luciano," and "After Image" the theme is the process of writing, the act of poetic creation. In "Luciano" the occasion of the poem is a vision, an exterior perception that interrupts the poet's consciousness. In "Awaiting Grace" it is a series of noises that inspire the poetic imagination. The poet is represented in the position of witness in "Sheen," where she watches yellow butterflies and a cyclist dressed in yellow circles around the Mission Cemetery, "marauding death's mission" (*Releasing Serpents,* 86, 1.17), and in the following poem, "Endurance," where she watches a pregnant woman visit the grave of her dead child. In "Original Seeding" it is not a specific scene that the poet witnesses but instead a historical process, a "slow plague" that is passed from man to woman to child, "Like English history, language, lore" (1.6), the effect of which is "Degendering the whole of human life" (1.7) (Fernández, 261). In other poems the poet is represented as the mediator between humanity and God. Zamora writes of this explicitly in "The Warmer Climate," where she confesses, "I argue with God in spite of his name" (1.9) but qualifies this assertiveness with the recognition that her voice is probably a "mediocre mouthing" (1.2) that is meaningless from the perspective of the powerful, the transcendent. She acknowledges both her arrogance and her lack of reverence but allows that the silence of God is to her intolerable (*Releasing Serpents,* 100). That irreverence is needed to break through complacency and silence is the theme of the poem "Letter." Here, Zamora argues that only a letter that is anonymous and "ambiguously rude" (1.5) will be sufficient to rouse "the priests, / popes and poets" (2.7–8) to the fury needed "to set the universe into new / tremors" (*Releasing Serpents,* 94, 2.2–3). In "Awaiting Grace" the poet anticipates "an angel's visit" (1.25), and in "From the Vestibule" the excommunicant poet recognizes her power to understand what years of listening to sermons had failed to communicate to her and acknowledges her own part as mediator or translator of spiritual knowledge into human terms (*Restless Serpents,* 53). In addition to, or complementing, its role as the medium of spiritual understanding, poetry is also represented as a natural, necessary, process in poems such as "Upward." In this poem Zamora vows that as a poet she will "fulfill the law / of the universe"; she uses the image of a falling autumn leaf to emphasize the significance of her title and the direction in which her words will travel (*Releasing Serpents,* 113).

For the Chicana poet, the representation of Chicana femininity is central to her work. In poems such as "Pueblo, 1950" Zamora engages the good girl/bad girl dichotomy that in Chicana terms is related to the complex cultural oppositions of virgin versus whore, and Guadalupe versus Malinche, which were discussed in the introduction (*Restless Serpents,* 21). Her recollection depicted in "Pueblo, 1950" is of her first kiss at the age of twelve and the attribution of guilt afterward: her mother blames her, her teacher blames her, she blames herself, but no one says a word to the boy. This distinction between male and female sexuality Zamora relates to the pervasive controls upon Chicana sexuality within traditional Chicano culture. In her poetry Zamora seeks to identify and to resist this control in all its forms. In the poem "So Not To Be Mottled" she refuses the simple division of feminine sexual identity into "good" and "bad" by proclaiming, "*My* divisions are infinite" (*Restless Serpents,* 61). The figures of La Llorona and La Malinche, both closely associated with death and loss, haunt the poem "Widow's Barter," in which a woman alone addresses the spider that has taken up residence with her and confesses in a moment of almost joyful self-revelation her appreciation of death. Sexual self-revelation, in a carnivalesque atmosphere, characterizes the poem "As Viewed from the Terrace." Zamora sets out the terms of a choice between the repressed sexuality of the sacred and the sexual abandonment of the profane. To choose the latter involves blind leaping and the abandonment of all constraints; the poem takes on a theatrical dimension as Zamora describes stripping off the masks of convention and the performance of a liberated sexual self. In the sequence *Restless Serpents* Zamora articulates those sexual and cultural silences that are imposed by the cultural conventions that control women through their sexuality. Though her poetry seeks to discover a form of cooperation between men and women, she finds that it does not work; her love poems end in self-mocking humor, as in "As Viewed from the Terrace" and "Chaff."

In connection with the control of women and the prescription of feminine sexuality, Zamora's poetry is concerned with the violence that is part of her culture, especially violence against women. In "Ancient Knowledge" she uses the images of the owl and the hawk to symbolize wisdom and force, but both are used against the figure of the praying woman: "The beating of wings / the beating of women / Ancient art" (*Releasing Serpents,* 102). "Peatmoss" also uses imagery to represent the use of violence to oppress and control women through fear. The peatmoss that is created through downward force or repression is juxtaposed with the poet's observation that "A woman's laugh is the envy of Heaven" (Fernández, 261). It is not only patriarchy that demands the violent subjugation of women but also such patriarchal institutions as the Church with its repressive notions of heaven and hell. In many of Zamora's poems men are associated with death and women with life, especially within the context of marriage. In "Situation" the fiancé is described as an undertaker, his affianced a midwife. The association of marriage with death is forged in the preceding poem, "State Street," which describes a crippled couple, an aged Mexican and his young but lame black bride, tottering down the street in the direction of the nearest bar. This symbolic link develops a theme explored earlier in "Mirando aquelos desde los campos," where the marriage bed is associated with death, decay, senility, and ruin.

It is not only the patriarchal institution of marriage, which every Chicana is expected to enter, but the entire ideology of romantic love that serves to control the expression of feminine sexuality. In "Sonnet, Freely Adapted" Zamora retells the story of Shakespeare's Sonnet 116, "Let me not to the marriage of true minds / Admit impediments," but from a feminine perspective that questions the inherited concept of masculinity and redefines the masculine abstractions "Love" and "Time" from the Chicana feminist point of view of "this weary woman" (*Restless Serpents,* 56). The idea of love that motivates Shakespeare's poem is revised, and in the process is revealed the ideology of romantic love that has been so destructive of feminine lives. Such an ideology, inherited through the generations along with the literary canon of literary works by men such as Shakespeare, exerts an influence that is pernicious and highly corrosive to the relationships it informs. Women are left alone, separate from the men with whom they can never realize the fantasy of perfect love, the "marriage of true minds." Expectations of romantic fulfillment are encoded in language like the literary language of the great poets, and Zamora finds herself locked in struggle with both the expectations and the words that represent them.

Romantic love tempts women to adopt a particular sexual vocabulary and emotional register, and in this way to adopt a persona or mask, that of the patriarchally approved "lover." Zamora, however, recommends the removal of the masks that have been adopted by Chicanas in response to racial and gender oppression, and which express the internalization of the values of the dominant culture. This inauthenticity and self-denial represent the death of the self. The image of the mirror, in which the masked self can be seen with the reality of a self-reflection, is used in poems such as "Open Gate," in which Zamora addresses the issue of "passing" or creating the appearance of belonging to the dominant culture. In this poem the unnamed woman surrenders the opportunity to choose her own identity. She walks past the open gate, and adopts the mask of conventional being; she walks "into mirrors" (Fernández, 260). "Angelita's Utility" represents the death of the self that is the consequence of internalizing the negative self-images acquired from Anglo and Chicano cultures: "Prostrate I can taste / The ground I disgrace" (*Restless Serpents,* 79, 1.13–14). A response to this negative self-mirroring is given in the following poem, in which "A greater reflection / of the black mirror" (2.1–2) provides the motivation to seek alternative modes of existence (*Releasing Serpents,* 80). The title of this poem, "Bleating," is resonant of the sacrificial goat, the scapegoat, the subject of "Propriety, 1972." While in Zamora's poetry women are most frequently subjected to the oppressive mirror gaze, it is not reserved for women: the figure of a man confronts his negative "mirrored self" in "Morning After."

Releasing Serpents offers a range of Chicano/a identities formed by family conflict, racial struggle, nostalgia for the loss of the past, or the traumatic break with the Chicano community. Many potential definitions of the self are written into the poems, each in contradiction with the other and resisting the creation of a monolithic Chicano/a identity. In this respect *Releasing Serpents* continues the concern Zamora expressed in *Restless Serpents* with the variety of Chicana subjectivity that goes unrepresented in the stereotypes that oppress and control feminine sexual identity. "Progenitor" represents a variety of Chicana subject positions that are defined by a corresponding masculine subject position. The speaker adopts in turn the personae of padre, madre, primo, puta, and child (*Restless Serpents,* 20). Women are placed by their men in the positions of wife, mother, whore; but men are placed in defined positions by Anglo stereotypes of "the Chicano." Zamora's poetry can be seen within the context of the ongoing Chicano movement as an effort to reconstruct and to retrieve Chicana history, culture, and expression. In "Our Instructions" Zamora describes a dream in which a group of women is engaged in "Tracing spirits of women and female children" (1.8), their images as guides, as the women "train to scale reality" (Fernández, 262, 1.12).

The refusal of Chicana stereotypes, discussed above, is expressed not only in the themes of Zamora's poems but also in the hybridity of her poetic language. She mixes images and definitions, as she describes it, "using the images in very Western technological ways but using the symbolic meanings of Indian culture."[13] For example, the pickup truck is juxtaposed with images of pristine nature in "And All Flows Past" (*Restless Serpents,* 78). The poetry thus demands that the reader be conversant in several different cultural idioms—Spanish, English, and Indian—in order to appreciate the full meaning of the poems. For example, the serpent image that is so often used as a symbol of sexuality in post-Freudian European literature is used by Zamora in its Indian sense as the symbol of wisdom in the poem "Stone Serpents" (*Restless Serpents,* 76). Throughout the sequence of *Restless Serpents* the dominating image of the serpent is used not so much to signify sexuality but in the symbolic idiom of the Nahua Indians as a symbol of wisdom. Zamora observes, "I was born under the year of the serpent and the day of the serpent in the Aztec calendar."[14] In this respect the serpent represents the mythical attempt to recover the full Chicano past.

The "restlessness" of the serpents in the poem "Restless Serpents" is associated with language and language use. At times Zamora expresses impatience with English, a language that expresses the values and experiences of white middle-class males and not those of Chicanas. While Spanish translated into English sounds to Zamora like "romantic sentimentalism," English is seen as a challenge, the challenge to make a fundamentally unemotional language express feeling authentically. But her ability to write poetry in Spanish is limited by Zamora's education, which was in English; her training as a poet was in English, and so she is most comfortable writing in English.[15] The humorous poem "Let the Giants Cackle" expresses some of Zamora's ambivalence about the English language (*Restless Serpents,* 43).

BERNICE ZAMORA

She describes English words as "turds of the golden goose" (1.2) that might be prepared and served "as canapés to the lordly lords" (1.5); in a clever switch of perspective she suggests that in this way they can digest again "their famished thoughts" (1.7), thus making the lords identify with the golden goose and their precious linguistic droppings.

Zamora writes some poems in English and others in Spanish, and she pursues a third strategy that is quite common among Hispanic writers, which is called code-switching. This involves moving from one language to another while preserving the grammatical integrity of the expression. Zamora switches between English and Spanish in a technique that she, echoing Alurista, says "reflects our people's fractured human experience."[16] Zamora does not use native (Nahuatl) phraseology to express her mestiza identity as do some Chicano/a writers, but she does use native symbols. Code-switching is used in such poems as "Anton Chico Bridge," "Mirando aquellos desde los campos," and "Anadando."

Code-switching is a form of juxtaposition, a stylistic device favored by Zamora as a way of expressing her meaning in an economical, compact, and powerful way. For example, the juxtaposition of natural and human worlds in the poem "Plumb" places the two robins warming each other against the cold against the image of two people sharing food and talking, and in this way the two relationships comment upon each other without the poet's consciousness intruding to comment in any bald or clumsy way (*Releasing Serpents,* 46). A similar juxtaposition of symbols—wine, water, blood, the serpent, which are analyzed below—is used for the purposes of comparison and contrast to realize the primary structural principle of the sequence *Restless Serpents*. Zamora has said that she did not deliberately structure the poems with a specific pattern in mind and in fact was assisted by a friend in determining the sequence in which the poems should appear. Nonetheless, a definite thematic pattern based upon the principle of structural juxtaposition is clearly discernible in the poem sequence.

Each of the six sections has as its title that of the poem that closes the section: "On Living in Aztlán," "Girded Us," "Chaff," "So Not to Be Mottled," "Situation," and "Restless Serpents." So the title of the last poem of the sequence echoes that of the concluding section and the entire set of poems, thrice emphasizing its importance. I would like to dwell for a while on the structural importance of these six key poems that determine the form and development of the sequence.

Comments were made above on the significance of "On Living in Aztlán" from the point of view of the Chicano political struggle, but the short poem is also resonant with significance for the definition of Chicana selfhood in terms of arbitrarily imposed limits and prescriptions for Chicana sexuality. The "law / Which is not ours" (2.3–4) could be read as the law of Chicano patriarchy, or of patriarchy in general, which imposes upon women the terms under which they must live their lives: "We come and we go" (1.1). In this way Zamora sets up the twin political poles of her poem sequence: the racial and the sexual terms of liberation for both Chicanos and Chicanas. The poems in the second section dwell on the theme of death: drowning, sacrifice, murder, dissipation, assassination, and genocide. As well as physical death, poems in this section also deal with spiritual death through neglect of the old religions and willful escapism through drunkenness and willed ignorance. The poem "Girded Us," then, encapsulates these themes by focusing on escapism, decay, and aging through images of garbage and dung. The third section of the poem sequence addresses the relationship between men and women, and the final poem, "Chaff," takes the form of a direct address, through questions and exclamations. The poem begins, "Recreate man, you say?" (1.1) and ends, "Bastard, unyielding as before!" (1.13). This is a humorous poem; it considers the possibility that woman might remake man in her image but the result is that he does not smile. This poem summarizes and places in a broadly feminist context the perception presented in each poem in this section that there is a basic hostility underlying all relations between men and women. The next section develops this idea by presenting a diversity of Chicana identities and exploring the forces that keep women from expanding the selves they could experience, and the concluding poem, "So Not to Be Mottled," issues the challenge: "*My* divisions are / infinite" (2.4–5). The section that follows extends Zamora's speculation about the limits imposed upon Chicana subjectivity and asks whether there is a relationship between the repression of Chicana femininity and the repression of Chicano spirituality. The incommensurability of the natural and the human, the feminine and the masculine, is linked with human, masculine violence and aggression that cannot comprehend and exists in absolute opposition to a nature-inspired feminine spirituality. The poem "Situation" represents these gender positions, where man is allied to death and woman to life in a marriage that can beget only conflict. The final section, "Restless Serpents," expresses Zamora's identification of the woman as writer with the wise serpents and her art as the power to soothe the restlessness. The poems in this section present images of strong women who are subjected to repressive forces but who overcome them in various ways. The poem offers no easy resolution of the conflicts Zamora represents in this section and in the sequence as a whole, but the association of femininity with the spiritual power of imagination and images of resurrection does offer hope.

The poems that comprise *Restless Serpents* are related to each other by a complex pattern of repeated symbolic motifs that highlights wine, water, blood, and the image of the serpent. These images, in the absence of the key serpent image, are used in "As Viewed from the Terrace," which sets in the context of gender relations, and specifically sexual relations, the urgent choices to be made between the sacred and the profane, freedom and conformity, life and death. Water is a key image in poems such as "Penitents" and "Having Drowned." The opposite of water as the symbol of spirit is the image of the "prairie sea," the dry desert or spiritual wasteland of the poem "Plainview," within which context the shade offered by a tree becomes valued as a sign of natural benevolence, as in "Re: An Egyptian King." Water in the form of a violent rainstorm represents the neglected spiritual inheritance of the ancestors, which forces the poet to turn to the abandoned temple in "Unattended." The image of drowning in "Girded Us" is juxtaposed with the ironic image of swimming, which rather than indicating some kind of spiritual buoyancy, instead signifies merest survival: the poet is swimming in a barrel of dung. Water offers a haven and breeding ground for insects in "Orangethroats"; it is linked with woman, art, and spirituality in "'What Sweet Delight a Quiet Life Affords'"; and the spiritual nature of water is made explicit in "Anton Chico Bridge," the poem that complements Zamora's representation of Navajo spirituality, expressed by the human relationship with the natural cycle of rain and flooding, in the poem "Trinkets." The image of wine is used significantly in the poems "California," "Supping On . . . ," and "Morning After." The image of blood appears in "Penitents" and "At Hand." The serpent image appears in the key poems, "Stone Serpents" and "Restless Serpents." Significantly, the serpent is associated with the image of chains in the poem "Penitents," and the chain image is used in place of the serpent in "As Viewed from the Terrace": the choice of "Whether to immerse our desires / in grapes and chains" (2.4–5), to repress desire in conformity (chains) and drunken forgetfulness (grapes), would in this way supplant wisdom (the serpent) (*Releasing Serpents*, 57).

Zamora's poetry is characterized by her skillful use of emphasis, especially in the placement of line breaks that lead us into one train of thought only to be abruptly turned around in the next line. For example, in "'What Sweet Delight a Quiet Life Affords'" the line "Madness, madness" (1.4) suggests the common association of woman with the moon, the sea, and insanity, but the following lines, "it is to be less / than a legend" (2.5–6), suggest instead the spiritual power and force of this woman (*Restless Serpents*, 48). In "Girded Us" the image "ubiquitous garbage" (1.5) is qualified by the following line, "collectors chant" (1.6) (*Restless Serpents*, 38). Zamora's linguistic play on the sounds "eye" and "I" to represent the dynamic between blindness and insight in "Phantom Eclipse" depends upon the break between the lines "searching in a world of eyes, / seeing nothing, nothing" (2.8–9), because the first of these lines and the image of a "world of I's" makes as much sense as a "world of eyes" (*Restless Serpents,* 69). In fact Zamora's play on the concepts of spiritual myopia and egotism depends on this double meaning.

If egotism or self-absorption is associated with spiritual blindness and death, in several of the poems of Zamora's later collection, *Releasing Serpents,* it is art that is represented as the transcendence of death. The poet observing the butterflies and the cyclist circling the cemetery is inspired to create the song that "Is marauding death's mission" (1.17) and which becomes the poem "Sheen" (*Releasing Serpents,* 86). In these poems poetry has been obliged to take the place of an ineffectual and oppressive religion: once-sacred images of water and wine are associated with corrupt spirituality in the poem "Gringos," which uses the apocalyptic image of a powerfully destructive wind that Zamora introduced in the poem "After Image." A new dispensation is needed, a new covenant that will infuse the letter with spiritual power. This is the theme of the poem "Letter," in which Zamora offers to address God directly in an attempt to break through the spiritual silence that has descended upon the world. The terror of awaiting such an experience is vividly expressed in the poems "Awaiting Grace" and "Mistral." In these poems, as throughout her work, Bernice Zamora links the oppression of Chicanos by racism, of Chicanas by sexism, and of nature by human civilization to the corruption and weakening of our capacity for spiritual understanding. Her artistry, her poetry, offers the possibility of transcendence and, if we read closely and attentively enough, the hope of resurrection.

CHAPTER THREE

Ana Castillo

Ana Castillo is a prolific writer in a variety of literary genres: poetry, fiction, the short story, essays; and she enjoys a reputation for innovation and experimentation in all the literary forms in which she works. In 1988 Castillo was honored by the Women's Foundation of San Francisco for her "pioneering excellence in literature." Since her early involvement in the Chicano movement she has been a part of Chicano/a political organizing, specifically in terms of Chicano/a literary expression. Her activities as an editor, of the essay collection *Goddess of the Americas/La Diosa de las Americas* (1996) and the literary journal *Third Woman* that she cofounded, have facilitated the promotion of Chicana literature in general and individual writers in particular. Castillo's work expresses the values of a new radical brand of feminism, what she calls Mexic Amerindian feminism or "Xicanisma," which replaces the United States–based orientation of "Chicana feminism" with a broader concern for the oppression of mestizas on both sides of the U.S.-Mexican border. In the introduction to her collection of essays, *Massacre of the Dreamers* (1995), Castillo explains: "Here is the juncture in our story where I believe Xicanisma is formed: in the acknowledgement of the historical crossroad where the creative power of woman became deliberately appropriated by male society. And woman in the flesh, thereafter, was subordinated. It is our task as Xicanistas, to not only reclaim our indigenismo—but also to reinsert the forgotten feminine into our consciousness."[1] In all of her work Castillo devotes her energy toward this kind of feminine empowerment and the destruction of negative, passive stereotypes for women.

Ana Castillo was born 15 June 1953 in Chicago to a family of Mexican migrants. She describes her earliest recollection of writing poetry at the age of about nine, upon the death of her paternal grandmother.[2] In the University of California, Santa Barbara archive is Castillo's first poetry manuscript titled "I Close My Eyes . . . To See," which is dated 1975. She has lived in California, New Mexico, and Gainesville, Florida; she currently lives in her hometown of Chicago with her son, Marcel. She has written the novels *The Mixquiahuala Letters* (1986), *Sapogonia (An Anti-Romance in 3/8 Meter)* (1990), and *So Far from God* (1993); the fiction collection *Loverboys: Stories* (1996); and the collection of essays *Massacre of the Dreamers: Essays on Xicanisma* (1995). The volume of poetry *My Father Was a Toltec and Selected Poems, 1973–1988* (1995) reprints Castillo's selection from her earlier books of poetry: *Otro Canto* (1977), *The Invitation* (1979; 2d edition, 1986), and *Women Are Not Roses* (1984) with the complete text of *My Father Was a Toltec* (1988). Castillo, along with Norma Alarcón and others, cofounded the literary magazine *Third Woman;* she has since been a contributing editor to *Third Woman* and *Humanizarte* magazines. She has also written essays and columns for newspapers and magazines on various topics, such as the murder of Tejano singer Selena and, most recently in the *Los Angeles Times,* gender roles in the farmworkers' movement. She received an American Book Award from the Before Columbus Foundation for her first novel, *The Mixquiahuala Letters.* Her third novel, *So Far from God,* was awarded both the Carl Sandburg Literary Award in Fiction for 1993 and the Mountains and Plains Bookseller Award of 1994. Castillo has been the recipient of fellowships from the National Endowment for the Arts in fiction and poetry. She was featured, along with Sandra Cisneros, Julia Alvarez, and Denise Chávez, in *Vanity Fair* (September 1994). Her work has been widely anthologized in the United States and Europe.

Ana Castillo was educated in Chicago. Following her graduation from Jones's Commercial High School, she attended Chicago City College for two years before entering Northeastern Illinois University, where she received a B.A. in art and secondary education in 1975. During her college years Castillo was active in organizing Latino artists, such as the Association of Latino Brotherhood of Artists. She then relocated to Sonoma County, California, where she taught ethnic studies at Santa Rosa Junior College in 1975–76. Her first major work dating from this time, the chapbook of poetry *Otro Canto,* reflects her involvement in the struggle against the oppression of Third World men and women. In her next published collection of poetry, *The Invitation,* the thematic emphasis in her poetry shifts decisively toward issues of feminist and Latina sexuality. Between 1977 and 1979 she was a writer-in-residence for the Illinois Arts Council. Due to her keen interest in Latin America, she became a graduate fellow in 1979, earning an M.A. degree in Latin American and Caribbean studies in the Social Science Division at the University of Chicago. She was a community activist during the 1970s. Throughout that period Castillo taught English as a second language and Mexican and Mexican American history in community colleges in the Chicago and San Francisco areas. She returned to California in 1986, where from then until 1990 she taught feminist journal writing, women's studies, creative writing, and Chicano literature at various colleges and universities. From 1989 to 1990 Castillo was a dissertation fellow in the Department of Chicano Studies at the University of California, Santa Barbara. There she continued her work on a new collection of poetry, *I Ask the Impossible,* and her collection of essays *Massacre of the Dreamers.* From 1989 to 1994 she taught fiction writing and Latina literature at several colleges, including the University of New Mexico; Mill College in Oakland, California; and Mount Holyoke College in South Hadley, Massachusetts. Supported partly by a fellowship from the National Endowment for the Arts in this period, in 1993 Castillo finished the novel *So Far from God.* Castillo received a Ph.D. in American Studies from the University of Bremen, Germany, in 1991. In 1995 she won a fellowship from the National Endowment for the Arts for creative writing (fiction). The novel *Peel My Love Like an Onion* appeared in 1999.

In addition to her published work, Ana Castillo is involved in an extensive program of speaking engagements both in the United States and abroad. International sponsorship of her public readings has included the Sorbonne University (1985–1986) and the German Association of Americanists (1987). She admitted in a "Platica" at New Mexico State University in March 1998 that she was "devastated by the antagonism of my male counterparts in the movement." She describes the year 1977 as the worst year of her life, when her emotional and intellectual energies were sapped by the conflicting exclusions of a white-dominated women's movement and a Latino movement that saw issues of sexuality as irrelevant to the revolutionary work: "All of the important decisions I made at that time were inextricably tied to being a brown, penniless female. And a poet."[3] She withdrew from political engagement and devoted herself to writing *The Invitation,* in which she hoped "to appropriate our sexuality, our own sense of sensuality, and to invite others to a celebration of self-love."[4] Castillo said she wrote the "naughty" book as her way of shocking her male antagonists and to expose their Latin machismo. In her 1998 "Platica" she declared, "One of my goals is to have the Pope ban all of my works."

The experience of herself as a Chicana informs every aspect of Castillo's work. In the autobiographical statement that heads her website (www.anacastillo.com) she explains how even the claim to be a writer, a poet, with a public voice is a political statement for the Chicana: "I cannot say I am a citizen of the world as Virginia Woolf, speaking as an Anglo woman born to economic means, declared herself; nor can I make the same claim to U.S. citizenship as Adrienne Rich does despite her universal feeling for humanity. As a mestiza born to the lower strata, I am treated at best, as a second class citizen, at worst as a nonentity."[5] As a Chicana writer Castillo acts as a witness to the everyday realities of Chicano/a life in the modern United States. Yet in her recording of the realities of Chicana life, Castillo makes no significant reference to the concept of Aztlán, preferring instead to focus on the fluid nature of Chicano/a cultural geography. As Mary Louise Pratt describes, the opening paragraph of *The Mixquiahuala Letters* "is profoundly Chicano—LA, the San Fernando Valley, family ties, bilingualism, the relatives on both sides of the border, and the differing cultural codes between them." She continues: "Yet it is emphatically not the sovereign homeland of Aztlán where an ancient people lives rooted in the soil. It is a porous space of mobility where people come and go by air and car, entering and leaving. The 'bronze people' are the result, in part, of sunbathing. . . . Instead of a monolithic united brotherhood, it is a nation of men and women, young and old—their relations defined by conflict and difference as well as by love and unity. In this feminocentric description the sole patriarchal figure is an antiheroic individual driven by an antiquated sexual code."[6]

This is precisely the image of Mexico as the homeland represented in the story "My Mother's Mexico."[7] The border has an economic and political reality that does not match the fluidity of the personal and family space Castillo experiences and documents. As a novelist, Castillo also acts as a kind of ethnographer, according to Alvina Quintana's reading of *The Mixquiahuala Letters,* a narrative that compares and contrasts the lives of women in Mexico and the United States in an ethnographic style of discourse that is both interpretive and objective.[8] The ethnographic interest of the feminist novelist, according to Quintana, is female gender identification. She argues: "Unlike both the conventional anthropologist and the classical Chicano writer of fiction, the Chicana feminist is also interested in scrutinizing the assumptions that root her own cultural influences, unpacking so-called tradition and political institutions that shape patriarchal ways of seeing."[9] In these terms Castillo in *The Mixquiahuala Letters* is concerned to address the canonical patriarchal structures that create gender limitations and legitimize oppressive practices in both Anglo and Chicano cultures, and also she opposes the exclusion of the values and experiences of Chicana femininity from the canon of Anglo-American feminist practices. The work of a Chicana novelist such as Castillo, then, involves the work of deconstructing, negotiating and mediating, and asserting a positive Chicana voice, a voice dedicated to Chicana self-definition; in this way Castillo engages as a reader of her own texts as well as their author. *The Mixquiahuala Letters* is "a personal narrative which mediates between objective and subjective narratives," in Quintana's analysis.[10] One specific example of this mediation that Quintana analyzes is letter 4, which concerns the impact of the Catholic Church on feminine subjectivity. This letter begins with Teresa asking her friend rhetorically, "Do you know the *smell* of a church?"[11] She goes on to describe the memories evoked by that complex smell and the emotions stirred by those recollections of the aggressive ways in which the priests pursue the promotion of deep-seated feelings of feminine passivity and sexual guilt. Teresa attributes to the church the power to inhibit the development of a political consciousness.

In some of her work Castillo engages with the terms of colonial representation—the colonizer's symbolic vocabulary—in order to make explicit the condition of Chicanos as a colonized people. In the poem "Our Tongue Was Nahuatl" (1976), for example, the feminine voice tells of an idyllic precontact native world which is shattered by the arrival of the strangers who "made us bow to them. / In our ignorance of the unknown / they made us bow" (2.52–54).[12] The image of bowing then acquires a series of meanings that consolidate the significance of the word and the gesture within the context of colonial conquest—rape, oppression, self-loathing. These colonial meanings then attach to the description of contemporary Chicano/a experiences of racism, such as bodies bowed on buses and hungry eyes averted in factories, and Castillo repeats in an outraged tone, "WE BOW!" (1.72).

In other poems themes of social protest combine with the assertion of positive Chicano images. The poem "We Would Like You To Know" (*Toltec,* 81) catalogs some of the stereotypes that fail to describe Chicanos/as: revolutionaries, armed car thieves, Zootsters, fruit pickers, factory workers, illegal immigrants; the poem then goes on to distinguish varieties in physiognomy and coloring, differences in political affiliation, and the unfortunate historical events the result of which they are "residents of a controversial / power" (2.45–46); and the poem ends with a final explanation: "We are left / with one final resolution / in our own predestined way, / we are going forward. / There is no going back" (2.55–64). The refusal of racial stereotypes is complemented in Castillo's work by her refusal of gender stereotypes, which will be discussed below. In poems that directly address the suffering that is the consequence of racial and gender stereotyping, the documenting of experience takes precedence over speculation about its causes. So the reality of poverty is the theme of the poem "Red Wagons," which contrasts the role of the wagon in the grammar school primer addressed to middle-class white children, "Silly Sally pulled Tim / on the red wagon" (2.9–10), with the reality of the wagon's use out of school in Chicano households: "Father pulled it to the gas / station / when he was home / and if there was money" (2.15–18). When there was not, the poem ends bitterly, these children went to bed dressed in "silly" clothes, already dressed for school in the morning (*Toltec,* 5).

Revolutionary talk or speculation versus revolutionary action is contrasted in the poem "1975," in which each stanza begins with the line "talking proletariat talks" and goes on to describe in specific examples the reality of poverty, racism, Christmas without Santa for the children, unemployment, crime, violence against women, and extortionate slum rents.[13] The poem ends: "talking proletariat talks / talking proletariat talks / talking proletariat talks / until one long / awaited day— / we are tired / of talking" (2.64–70). The emphasis on class at the expense of race and gender requires that "choosing one or the other splits the subject into the domains that heretofore have been symbolically marked feminine or masculine," as Norma Alarcón points out.[14] But Castillo's personae or poetic voices refuse to make these choices. She explores in "In My Country" the possibility of imagining a world without oppression, which is also a world that erases not so much the marks of racial and gender difference but the significance of difference. In this world difference is not pejorative: "I speak all languages. I don't / negate aging, listen to myths / to explain my misery or create them" (*Toltec,* 88, 2.88–90).

Where the poems in Castillo's first published volume, *Otro Canto,* dealt in social protest, as indicated above, those in her next collection, *The Invitation,* explore the diversity of Chicana femininity through the expression of her erotic desires. The title poem, "The Invitation," is a playful, languorous, and erotic exploration of the connection between sexuality and poetry.[15]

ANA CASTILLO

The layout of the words in sinuous pattern across the page enacts in words the movement of a finger tracing slowly the curves of the body even as those words say just that: "I will compose a verse: / Long and Winding / from your mouth / to just below / the thighs" (2.2–5). It is through the exploration of poetic language that Castillo approaches the relationship between her political concerns and erotic themes, and her feminist commitment to the representation of feminine sexuality. Castillo engages with and exposes the limitations of, and constraints imposed by, an inherited vocabulary that is both political and literary, and which forms the material with which she is to describe and represent Chicana femininity. Consequently, Castillo struggles to create an authentic vocabulary of her own. In the poem "Ixtacihuatl Died in Vain" Castillo draws upon Aztec symbolism to express this relationship between two women (*Toltec*, 39–41). In legend Ixtacihuatl and her twin volcano, Popocatepetl, were once a warrior and princess whose love was opposed by their rival tribes. Castillo uses the image of the twin volcanoes but shifts the attribution of gender so that the women can say, "We are Ixtacihuatls / sleeping, snowcapped volcanoes / buried alive in myths / princesses with the name of warrior / on our lips" (2.6–10).

In *The Mixquiahuala Letters* Teresa and Alicia create a language of their own, as Teresa reflects in letter 21 when she adopts an external perspective in the sight of herself and Alicia and asks, "There are words between them, not many, but one will speak and the other nods her head seriously. What do they say to each other? How intimate they are! What language do they speak?" (72). This private code includes, significantly, the word

"Mixquiahuala," which signifies the value and importance of their relationship.[16] Teresa reminds Alicia in letter 3 how "For years afterward you enjoyed telling people that I was from Mixquiahuala" (26). Teresa's plan for the return trip that they will make together to Mexico is conceived as a return to Mixquiahuala (18). The symbolic value of Mixquiahuala is suggested in letter 3 where the place is described as "a Pre-Conquest village of obscurity" (25); the conquest referred to here may be read as not so much the conquest of Mexico by Spain as the conquest of women by patriarchy. The time Teresa and Alicia spend together in Mixquiahuala is characterized by feminine bonding and sharing, apart from men. Teresa says of her friend that "[you] saw yourself isolated, even unwanted by men and their world" (28), and it is only at the end of this idyllic time that Teresa returns to her husband and Alicia falls in love with the Indian caretaker.

In the vignette "Extraordinarily Woman" Castillo's contribution to the essay collection she edited, *Goddess of the Americas/La Diosa de las Americas,* she describes her childhood recollection of the church her family attended. In particular it is the dominating image of the Virgin that stood before the altar that Castillo remembers: "Quite naturally, I believed then that this pious place was Her home; that this beautiful Indian woman with the enigmatic gaze was Mother God. God the Father was absent, though like the men in my family, who were often shadowy and silent, He nevertheless was the ultimate authority. He watched us with a close and critical omnipotent eye and mostly wielded His power by instilling fear. Our Mother, on the other hand, watched over her children without condemning our acts.

Our Mother simply loved us."[17] In *The Mixquiahuala Letters* Teresa recounts overhearing the medical student with whom they are staying talking drunkenly on the telephone. "He made demands, accusations of noncaring, unfaithfulness"; without any other clues than the voice in which he is addressing his respondent, Teresa realizes, *"This jerk's talking to a woman"* (60, Castillo's italics). The attempt to stir feelings of guilt, the violence implicit in his tone, would never be addressed to a man. The poem "The Toltec" (*Toltec,* 3) describes the machismo of traditional Chicano masculinity in the image of the street fighter. But it is in poems such as "Saturdays" and "The Suede Coat" that Castillo relates machismo to the experience of Chicanas. The poem "Saturdays" begins by explaining that her mother did laundry on Saturdays because she worked from "5 to 5" every day of the week; continues by describing how her mother helps her father dress in his finest clothes, "bought on her credit"; and ends with the observation: "That's why he married her, a Mexican / woman, like his mother, not like / they were in Chicago, not like / the one he was going out to meet" (*Toltec,* 6, 2.19–22). The irony of the sharply contrasting images of the wife standing over the ironing board while her husband prepares to meet another woman is bitter. The unrelenting drudgery of Chicana life is expressed in poems such as "Me and Baby" and poems that express Castillo's fear that her life will be just like her mother's: "I am not ready to echo those / trying years," she confesses in "El ser muter. . . ."[18]

It is in response to the fear that her life will not be different than her mother's that in "Wyoming Crossing Thoughts" the poet vows never to marry a Mexican man (*Toltec,* 46). She lays down conditions that exclude the traditional attitudes of feminine submission and subservience to masculine superiority. With her authority as a daughter, sister, and mother she vows that she will never say to a Mexican man "Sí, mi señor" or serve him tortillas; she would rather "drive an obsidian blade / through his heart, / lick up the blood" (2.39–41). The image here of the obsidian blade is significant. In her autobiographical sketch, "Extraordinary Woman," Castillo tells how the Mother Goddess, in her manifestation as Cihuacoatl or the Snake-Woman, was thought to abduct children from their beds and leave in their place an obsidian knife, "as a symbol of their sacrifice to the gods."[19] But the image of a woman choosing under what circumstances she will engage sexually with a Mexican man, in conjunction with the image of stabbing, is powerfully reminiscent of Castillo's novel *Sapogonia (An Anti-Romance in 3/8 Meter)*.

In *Sapogonia* Castillo investigates the relationship between masculine individuation and violence, feminine individuation and the ethic of sharing. In *Sapogonia* the "antihero" of the narrative, Máximo Madrigal, desires unity in the world around him, including the subjective unity of the novel's feminine protagonist Pastora Velásquez Aké, represented by his identification of her with the goddess Coatlicue, the unifier of opposites.[20] However, he must be viewed as an individual; he struggles to maintain his own separateness from the unity and consistency upon which he insists in others. Initially he sees Pastora as sexually voracious or as a lesbian to whom he is sexually irrelevant, and later he sees her as passive, accepting, and undemanding; either way, he cannot see her on her own terms or on terms that are not sexual. Máximo both fears and desires Pastora, needs her, and in the end murders her. This is an obsessive relationship; he thrills at Pastora's refusal to allow herself to be conquered by holding something of herself aloof from him in every encounter they share; she enjoys playing out an aspect of her femininity that is not engaged in her other relationships while she revels in the sexual power game that teases Máximo with the deferred promise of her complete surrender to him.

It is within this framework of male desire that Pastora struggles to define her sense of herself, and it is in terms of this expression of masculine desire that we are invited to view what Norma Alarcón calls Pastora's complicity in her own objectification and ultimately in her own destruction. This same kind of objectification is attributed to Alicia's Indian lover in *The Mixquiahuala Letters.* Teresa describes him playing "lover's games with a complacent wife and a hot, young gringa" and finding the situation "as glamorous as the film he'd seen long ago because this scene would include him as the star" (35). Pastora's is not a passive complicity, a surrender to masculine fantasy, but a choice deliberately to transgress the prohibition against feminine sexual freedom. She chooses to submit to Máximo; she chooses to participate in and thereby subvert his patriarchal fantasy for her own intellectual pleasure. She shares Máximo's powerful attraction to the image of her as a mysterious object of desire, his fantasy of her as Coatlicue, but this undermines her relationship with Eduardo. Yvonne Yarbro-Bejarano describes this marriage as "almost like a parody of the Holy Family (Eduardo is even a carpenter). And there is a snake in this paradise,"[21] who is of course Máximo and Pastora's self-destructive desire for him.

Her subversion of the ideology of feminine submission is

the occasion of her death: Pastora transforms passivity into an aggressive act to which Máximo responds by murdering her. In their final encounter Pastora forces Máximo to acknowledge that his need for her is greater than her need for him; this is an inversion of the power relationship that Máximo, or any machismo, cannot tolerate, and so he is compelled to destroy her. This destructive act reconfirms his separation and individuation. Early in the novel Máximo tells of his compulsion to conquer women who do not want him and to destroy those who reject him: "somehow it occurred to me to choose this [girl] and once I realized that she didn't love me, that she didn't even like me, it was too late. I was committed to having her" (*Sapogonia,* 13–14). Sexual relations are, in his view, power relations, and Máximo's responses are determined by this power struggle. His willful creation and destruction of relationships or patterns of personal connection express the triumph of his ego. Máximo generalizes this behavior as something all men know and understand. Violence against women is then placed in the context of masculine egotism. Sexual rejection is a denial of male selfhood and must be punished; the confirmation of the male self that arises from the act of violence is then in some ways the same confirmation that is obtained through sexual conquest: in either case, sexuality and violence are conjoined in Máximo's experience of masculinity. This conjunction of sex, violence, and the assertion of masculinity is also represented in *The Mixquiahuala Letters.* In the first letter Teresa explains why her tía Filomena refuses to speak to her son Ignacio, who has broken his wife's teeth. The act of violence was Ignacio's response to his wife's confession that she had never loved him and had married him only because she could order him around; but the declaration that earned her two broken teeth was the claim that his lovemaking repelled her: "It feels like a little fish wiggling inside me!" (21). Ignacio's instinctive response to the denial of his sexual power is physical violence.

Castillo's epigram to *The Mixquiahuala Letters* is taken from Anaïs Nin: "I quit loving my father a long time ago. What remained was a slavery to a pattern." This patriarchal pattern of masculine dominance and feminine submission is explored through the changing nature of the relationship between Teresa and Alicia, and the effect of their various romantic relationships upon their friendship. In *The Mixquiahuala Letters* romantic ideals are debunked early on, with Teresa's description of the marriages of her various relatives in letter 1. In letter 2 she refers to the "cesspool" of her years of romantic failure. The poem "An Idyll" offers an image of the idealized romantic man, represented in both artistic and social terms as the embodiment of masculine beauty and as a statue in the form of a satyr. But, the poet reflects in the fractured words that represent the profound disruption of obsessive love, "how silly t/o want to run of/f, and live with / forever, bene/ath its weight."[22] The romantic fantasy serves an enslaving reality. Self-destruction is implicit in the masochistic patriarchal fantasy of the submissive woman and her godlike lover. In letter 16 Teresa describes her attraction to Alvaro Pérez Pérez, which is neither physical nor emotional but is a trained reflex. When Teresa rejects his sexual advances and his confession of need, she is threatened with physical violence. The women find themselves repeatedly threatened with sexual violence: Teresa recalls that Alicia is threatened by a man who whispers in her ear "that he'd slit your vagina" (83); and Teresa recognizes, fearfully, that "there is little in the end I can do. I have a vagina too" (84). The violence is sometimes the implicit assumption that the women without men are sexually available, and so the refusal of sexual advances is a threat to masculine egotism. A situation like this arises when the women accept a lift to Mexico City from the bosses of the engineers with whom they have been staying. It is only by their quick thinking and skill at manipulating the expressions of conservative patriarchy that the women make these elderly men feel guilty at offering insult to these "good girls" and so they are able to escape.

There is at work here a kind of verbal violence that can substitute for the physical violence of male domination and its requirement that women submit. Teresa's account in letter 21 of the destructive effect her relationship with Alexis had upon her is prefaced with a list of violent acts perpetrated against women, including female genital mutilation in Arabia and bride burning in India. She defines love: "In the classic sense, it describes in one syllable all the humiliation that one is born to and pressed upon to surrender to a man" (117). She then tells how the housework was hers to perform, not because she is good at it (Alexis criticizes her constantly) but because Alexis has more important things to do: "He was the artist, I, a useless poet" (117). Recalling and reflecting upon this relationship that so nearly destroyed her, and which she now calls a "deathtrap" (118), Teresa finally confesses to Alicia the truth of her attractiveness to men: "You had been angry that I never had problems attracting men. You pointed out the obvious, the big breasts, full hips and thighs, the kewpie doll mouth. Underlining the superficial attraction men felt for me is what you did not recognize. I was docile" (119). The emotional associations of this relationship with the erasure or death of her self are complicated by the literal association with the death of the child she aborted. The abortion of his child, which she thinks of as getting rid of him "like a cancerous tumour" (116), marks the final end of their relationship, as Alexis leaves her in disgust at her action, and Teresa is left with the self-loathing that is the internalization of Alexis's patriarchal violence.

In her writing Ana Castillo works to question the perceptions, status, and opportunities available to women in patriarchal culture. The notion of destiny in *The Mixquiahuala Letters* is represented by Teresa and Alicia as the power to write one's own script and take charge of one's life independent of patriarchal narratives of romance and true love (as found in the *telenovelas* read by some of the Mexican women they encounter). This impulse to create unitary narratives of romance out of experience is questioned by the alternative readings recommended by Castillo in the opening of the novel (addressed to the reader). Each suggested reading leads to a conventional ending[23] but does not answer the question of which reading Teresa would desire: she is trapped, like the rest of us, among patriarchal meta-narratives that shape our experiences as we attempt to make sense of them. Castillo subverts this invisible and silent process of constructing ideologically determined narratives of our own lives to the extent that she exposes this process and causes us to question it. Teresa shifts voices and personae as she attempts to understand her experiences. In the process she reveals a myriad of selves that are facets of her hybrid self: docile, clever, vampish, fearful, liberated, oppressed—reflections of the cultural images that she has to negotiate as a modern Chicana. Hybridity as the condition of Chicana subjectivity characterizes the relationship between the two major characters, though it is notable that Alicia appears only through the traces of her responses and in Teresa's interpretations of her letters, letters to which the reader never has access. They need to unlearn the patriarchal strategies for self-knowledge that keep them separate from each other and themselves.

Teresa and Alicia do strive to achieve a perfect unity of mind and sharing of experience, but, as Yarbro-Bejarano observes, the image of the mirror "works paradoxically against their identification. . . . In the other each sees the reflection of her own need and dependence from which she must avert her gaze."[24] The significance of these feminine self-reflections is given early in the novel, in letter 3, where Teresa describes their early friendship: "We needled, stabbed, manipulated, cut, and through it all we loved, driven to see the other improved in her own reflection" (29). But ultimately anything that is communicated between them is devalued by the patriarchal reflex to devalue everything feminine; in letter 13 Teresa concedes that her words "were only the words of another woman" (52), lacking the vital legitimization of a man. The women are compromised by their upbringing in the patriarchal society in which they live.

Castillo rejects the patriarchal image of woman as passive and submissive and uses Chicana role models like La Malinche, reinterpreted from Octavio Paz's negative figure of La Chingada as the woman who has been violated, to represent instead the figure of the sexually empowered woman. The sexual woman, rather than being a traitor to her people, her sisters, uses her sexuality to express the full reality of her femininity and in this way realizes the liberation of her gender. It is patriarchy she betrays in the interest of La Chicana. The figure of La Malinche echoes through *Sapogonia,* particularly the episode in which Máximo tells of the circumstances of his mestizo inheritance: his grandfather's rape of an Indian girl who becomes his wife and Máximo's grandmother. This initiates the pattern of sexual use/abuse of women by the men in Máximo's family: Mamá Grande tells the young Máximo that he has an old soul, by which she means that he has inherited precisely this sexual compulsion. The figure of Mamá Grande offers a contrast with Pastora's choice to accept Máximo's fantasy construction of her as the mysterious and sexually passive mestiza. Mamá Grande, the raped indita (indigenous Spanish woman), had no choice to make beyond the passive subject position into which she was forced by sexual violence. Sexual identity is linked with the speaking subject: passivity, erasure except through masculine retrieval, the docility that Teresa recognizes as the secret of her attractiveness to men. Castillo's use of the lower case "I" rather than "I" in *The Mixquiahuala Letters* expresses the identification with the collective subject that is the Chicana, as Castillo explains, to "put to rest the question most frequently asked of my early writing."[25]

Transgression is represented in Castillo's writing as a strategy of liberation, a breaking of patriarchal taboos. For example, Castillo transgresses by addressing the taboo subject of the body, by articulating the reality of the female body and so taking control of it. In *The Mixquiahuala Letters* Castillo offers us sensual descriptions of the female body such as Teresa's "inventory" of Alicia's physical beauty in letter 13 and the description of her friend making love in letter 11. According to Tey Diana Rebolledo, Castillo was one of the first Chicana writers to represent "a tampon experience" in the poem "A Letter to Alicia," where she writes: "I covered for you at the ruins of monte albán / while you changed your tampon / before the eyes of gods and ghosts / and scorpions" (2.10–13).[26] This poem appears, in a revised form, as letter 2 of *The Mixquiahuala Letters.* Even the title of the collection in which this poem first appeared, *Women Are Not Roses,* resists the romanticizing of the bodily reality of women. The transgression of taboos that keep in place the unspoken laws that confine women to traditional roles include: deliberately "making trouble" (being an *escandalosa*); occupying forbidden space; female violence as in the poem "Dirty Mexican"; and sexual transgression, as in poems such as "Cherry Stained Lips and Thick Thighs." Unchaperoned travel or journeying is transgressive, as in *The Mixquiahuala Letters,* which is motivated by "the idea of the journey that would lead from ruin to ruin" (52)—in the sexual as well as archaeological sense of "ruin." Teresa asks in letter 19 "What was our greatest transgression?" and answers "We traveled alone" (65).

Transgressive forms of sexuality such as lesbianism and promiscuity are explored in the stories collected in *Loverboys.* The narrator and protagonist of the opening story is a hard-drinking lesbian who becomes involved in an obsessive sexual relationship with a much younger man: her "loverboy"; the narrator of the story "Who Was Juana Gallo?" describes her as "not the marrying type";[27] the seemingly perfect conventional couple of

"If Not for the Blessing of a Son" live in a house described by their son, with sinister unspoken sexual overtones, as "the house of secrets" (*Loverboys,* 37); Castillo tells of the woman who confronts her aged father, the retired factory foreman who raped her mother, in "Ghost Talk"; in a parody of the masculine objectifying of women, she documents women's careful sexual cataloging of men, "vatos," into "Veteran Vatos" or "Junior Vatos" in the humorous story "Vatolandia."

The transgressive nature of unchaperoned travel or journeying is discovered early by the female protagonists of *The Mixquiahuala Letters:* in Mexico, to be unchaperoned means to be sexually available. Castillo is questioning the modern Chicana's status as a free agent in *The Mixquiahuala Letters* and discovers that a woman's sexuality is always controlled by someone else— husband, father, even her employer in the case of Nene the servant they encounter. Teresa finds herself torn in the several directions of her mestiza inheritance: Anglo, Mexican, and Indian.[28] To the Mexican men she meets she is a gringa; she rejects the church and is married to an African American in the Anglo fashion of the time, in a park, by a Hare Krishna (22); even her attempt to maintain her close friendship with Alicia is a transgression of the Chicano requirement that once a woman is married she surrenders all her close relationships in favor of her husband: "Her needs had to be sustained by him. If not, she was to keep her emptiness to herself" (35).

For a Chicana, the assumption of a public voice through writing is transgressive; the process of writing is the theme in the poems "Everywhere I Go" and "A Christmas Gift for the President of the United States, Chicano Poets, and a Marxist or Two

I've Known in My Time" (62). The latter poem explores the exclusion of women's voices and feminine experiences from the realm of the serious and particularly from the artistic canon (*Toltec,* 62). Castillo has described how she swore never to take a creative writing class for fear that she would repeat the experience of being convinced that her artwork, in this case her drawing and painting, was no good. She tells how "negative social attitudes toward people of humble origins, as well as the institutional racism and sexism of the university, discouraged me, so that by the time I finished my B.A. I was convinced that I had no talent. I couldn't draw and I had no right to paint."[29] This denial of legitimacy to the Chicana writer is attributed both to the masculine domination of philosophy and poetry, and to the white women who at least have access to the English language and to the resources—"her father's library / her brother's friends"— from which to write. Chicana experience is not a legitimate subject for poetry: "Rape is not a poem. Incest is not a rhyme" (2.32–33); these issues contrast with the subjects of canonical masculine poetry and are shown to be "so unlike the embellishment of war / or man's melancholy at being / neither earth nor heaven bound" (2.38–40). The poem is not negative, though; the title suggests that Castillo is going to challenge the race, gender, and class constraints that operate against her as a Chicana poet, and in the concluding stanzas she asserts: "Something inherent resists / the insistence that I don't exist" (2.53–54). The rhyming couplet emphasizes Castillo's determination to fight these racist patriarchal definitions of what constitutes poetry, in part by challenging the assumption that art must be serious: in her poetry she will indulge herself, her pleasures, her fancies.

Transgression is a way of resisting and subverting the power of patriarchy, but Castillo is concerned to expose the mechanics of both gender and ethnic oppression. Her work places emphasis upon traditional Chicana cultural practices as an assertion of cultural identity and resistance to assimilation. These practices include cooking—for example, La Loca's recipes in the novel *So Far from God*—and the traditional healing practices and the figure of Caridad the curandera in the same novel. It is the youngest of the four sisters, La Loca, who at first heals her sisters "from the traumas and injustices they were dealt by society."[30] In her role as healer and mediator she is resonant of the image of the Virgin; the novel opens with the miracle of her resurrection after three days of being thought dead. When the infant regains consciousness, she claims that she was transported back to the living world in order to pray for and intercede on behalf of the people she meets. Her mother, Sofi, then takes her for a full medical examination at the hospital in Albuquerque rather than the county clinic where she had been wrongly declared dead. This becomes the first episode in a sustained contrast between modern medicine and traditional healing that is explored through the novel. La Loca's eventual death is postponed and the symptoms of her illness eased by the efforts of traditional healers who succeed in this limited way when modern medicine is powerless to act.

Caridad heals herself after she is horribly mutilated in a sexual attack and conventional medicine can only give up on "what is left of her," as the narrator repeatedly emphasizes. It is Caridad's capacity for healing through the force of her will in combination with her power of prophecy and her special relationship with animals that marks her as a curandera in the perception of the ancient curandera doña Felicia. In the same way that doña Felicia operates both outside and within the Church, so the practice of *curanderismo* uses a combination of traditional religious symbols and massage, herbs, and folk remedies to restore a patient's spiritual and physical equilibrium. The character of her sister Fe offers a point of contrast with the valuation of Chicano/a tradition represented by Caridad and La Loca.

Fe attempts assimilation, with her respectable clerical job, neat coiffure, and conservative fiancé; she regrets her flat Pueblo buttocks, the sister she thinks of as mentally ill rather than inspired, and her modest life in a small town. Her desire to escape through assimilation into middle-class white America kills her. In a sense her denial of her family, her ancestry, and her Chicana self is always a form of death—the death of her authentic subjectivity. In order to have the trappings of this lifestyle she works at the highest-paid job she can get, in the factory that uses toxic chemicals to manufacture parts for high-tech weapons. She is killed by the cancer caused by what the narrator describes as "her chemical joyride at Acme International, which was eating up her insides like acid" (186). Before she dies, however, she is subjected to the torture of high-tech medical treatment in the form of bungled invasive surgeries and drug therapies that leave her as mutilated as her sister Caridad once was, so that the narrator describes Fe's dead body in terms that echo the description of Caridad after her mutilation: Fe is cremated by special permission of the Church because "there was so little left of her" to bury (186). In turn each of Sofi's daughters comes to be described thus: Caridad is mutilated in an attack; Fe is mutilated by modern medicine; La Loca shrinks as she dies of AIDS; and Esperanza, the journalist sent to report the conflict in the Middle East, is tortured to death by her political captors. In contrast to her sisters, all of whom return from the dead and participate irregularly but fully in the life of the family, Fe just dies and does not ever return. This difference reflects the spiritual death of self-denial and cultural self-hatred experienced by Fe before her body dies.

The integration of the marvelous or miraculous or physically impossible within the realistic textures of mundane daily life reflects the hybrid cultural milieu—Anglo, Chicano, native—with its multiple perspectives and explanations of experience within which the characters move. Castillo's refusal to privilege one perspective over the others represents her allegiance to the hybridity and diversity that characterize the condition of the mestiza. The "doubling" that this commitment to diversity promotes also gives rise to the irony that critics have noted as a feature of Castillo's style. This ironic style has been described by Norma Alarcón: "irony often appears when experience is viewed after-the-fact or in opposition to another's subjectivity."[31] For example, the sexually explicit nature of Teresa's language in *The Mixquiahuala Letters* is a deliberate transgression of the taboo against talking openly about sex: "We licked our wounds with the underside of penises and applied semen to our tender bellies and breasts like Tiger's Balm" (106). But this passage is ironic in that while Teresa's language is transgressive, what she actually says is conditioned by the same patriarchal system she attempts to transgress. The wounds inflicted by patriarchy cannot be soothed with heterosexual promiscuity that serves the desires of the very men who oppress and wound her. More genuinely transgressive, and not in the least ironic, is Teresa's explicit description of her abortion, from "the cold clamp that spread the vulva wide" to the "soft membrane, tissue, undefined nerves, sightless eyes, a minuscule [*sic*], pounding heart, sunless flesh, all sucked out in torn, mutilated pieces" (114).

Castillo's work is characterized by formal experimentation. Her choice of the epistolary style for *The Mixquiahuala Letters* is in itself innovative, but Castillo's refusal to prescribe the order in which the letters are to be read, and the resolution to be obtained, marks a particular innovation in Chicana writing. This technique owes something to Julio Cortázar's 1963 novel *Rayuela* (*Hopscotch*), which also offers two sequences in which the novel can be read. *The Mixquiahuala Letters* is prefaced with an address to the reader in which the author observes her acknowledged duty to "alert the reader that this is not a book to be read in the usual sequence," and so the letters are numbered rather than follow a simple chronological sequence. Castillo proposes three different sequences, one each for "The Conformist," "The Cynic," and "The Quixotic." Thus this technique requires that the reader declare his/her personality type and his/her own role in the reading process; the reader cannot be the passive consumer of the text or take a voyeuristic pleasure in the experiences of the protagonists—Teresa, who writes the letters, and Alicia, her respondent. The reader must become what Cortázar called a "*lector cómplice,*" a reader able to make choices and prepared to share with the author the authority over the meaning of the text.[32] The text refuses to provide a neat conclusion and in so doing to surrender its own dynamic; even if the forty letters are read in the sequence in which they appear, the reader is left with three endings from which to choose.

It was mentioned above that Castillo uses Chicana role models such as La Malinche to contest the patriarchal image of woman as passive and submissive and to represent instead the figure of the empowered woman. La Malinche, in Castillo's revision, subverts patriarchy, and this is the true nature of her betrayal, which is also a sign of her allegiance to her gender. In *So Far from God* the image of La Llorona, the woman who weeps for her lost children, appears in chapter 10. The narrator indicts something of the genesis of this mythical figure, pointing out that she probably owes a great deal to the ancient Aztec goddesses Matlaciuatl, Ciiuapipiltin, and/or Cihuacoatl, all of whom were said to weep and wail in the night. The Christian interpretation of this figure tells that she drowned her children so as to abandon her family and run off with her lover, and ever since she has haunted rivers and bodies of water, weeping and searching for her children. The narrator observes that it is appropriate that Esperanza, the politically motivated of Sofi's daughters, should choose La Llorona to communicate the news of her death to her mother. Esperanza is active in the Chicano movement as well as the regional native community, and she chooses the figure described by the narrator as "a woman who had been given a bad rap by her people since the beginning of time, and yet to Esperanza's spirit mind La Llorona in the beginning (before men got in the way of it all) may have been nothing short of a loving mother goddess" (162–63).

In the novel, then, the figure of La Llorona is given multiple revisionary interpretations; she is also emulated by the spirit of Esperanza, who chooses to haunt the local river. If the primary mother figure, Sofi, somehow represents the figure of La Llorona, this is reflected in the death of all her children before her. But rather than simply weep for them, Sofi mourns her children by seeking to improve the condition of life for all the children of the community. The independent life she has lived since being abandoned by her husband prepares her to take on an even more challenging role as mayor of Tome. Sofi is politicized by her experience in Washington, D.C., while searching for news of Esperanza's fate, and by her experience of the illegal practices of Acme International, the company that uses Fe's ambition and desire for assimilation to get done their dirty work and kills her, and maims many of the women with whom she worked, in the process. She founds the organization called M.O.M.A.S. (Mothers of Martyrs and Saints); her work in the community is devoted to local Chicano/a issues of land use, employment rights, community enterprises, and cooperative ventures. Mostly Sofi wants to resist the danger of becoming what she calls a conformist; she explains to her *comadre:* "That's what my 'jita Esperanza used to call people who just don't give a damn about nothing! And that's why, she said, we all go on living so poor and forgotten!" (139). This could explain the entire project of Ana Castillo's work: the ongoing effort to resist conformity to racial and gender limitations; to resist invisibility and powerlessness by engaging with the most urgent issues that face Chicanas, and doing it with skill and humor.

CHAPTER FOUR

Sandra Cisneros

In a 1990 interview Sandra Cisneros joked that after ten years of writing professionally she had finally earned enough money to buy a secondhand car.[1] Her struggle for recognition as a Chicana writer earned her critical and popular acclaim with the publication of *The House on Mango Street* (1984), the success of which was followed by *Woman Hollering Creek and Other Stories* (1991). Her poetry collection *My Wicked, Wicked Ways* was published by the Berkeley-based Chicana Third Woman Press in 1987, and the outrageous themes of these poems continued in the poems collected in *Loose Woman,* which appeared in 1994. Cisneros's work is characterized by the celebratory breaking of sexual taboos and trespassing across the restrictions that limit the lives and experiences of Chicanas. These themes of trespass, transgression, and joyful abandon feature prominently in her poetry. The narrative techniques of her fiction demonstrate daring technical innovations, especially in her bold experimentation with literary voice and her development of a hybrid form that weaves poetry into prose to create a dense and evocative linguistic texture of symbolism and imagery that is both technically and aesthetically accomplished.

Sandra Cisneros was born in the Puerto Rican district of Chicago on 20 December 1954. Her parents' mixed ethnic background (Spanish-speaking Mexican father and English-speaking Mexican American mother) is reflected in the cultural hybridity that is one of Cisneros's recurring themes. She is the third child and only daughter in a family of seven children, a condition that Cisneros has described as leaving her marginalized as a consequence of her gender.[2] During Cisneros's childhood her father's restless homesickness caused the family to move frequently between Chicago and her paternal grandparents' house in Mexico City, and always she lived in urban neighborhoods. Although her early years were spent in cramped urban apartments, Cisneros recalls her childhood as solitary. Cisneros ascribes to the loneliness of those formative years her impulse to create stories by re-creating in her imagination the dull routine of her life.

She graduated with a B.A. degree from Loyola University in 1976 and completed an M.F.A. in creative writing at the Iowa Writers Workshop in 1978. It was at Iowa that Cisneros discovered, first, a sense of her own ethnic "otherness" and, second, the unique literary voice that characterizes both her poetry and her fiction. She describes her early writing as inferior imitations of the work of mainstream writers; in the discovery of her difference came a rejection of this attempt to join the American literary orthodoxy. The voice she discovered, the voice she had unconsciously suppressed, is the voice of the barrio.

An ongoing commitment to those who grow up in the barrio has led Cisneros to become involved as a teacher in educational projects designed to assist the urban underprivileged, such as the Latino Youth Alternative High School in Chicago. She has worked variously as a teacher, a counselor, a college recruiter, a poet-in-the-schools, and an arts administrator in order to support her writing. Cisneros has taught creative writing at the University of California at Berkeley, the University of California at Irvine, and the University of Michigan in Ann Arbor. She is the recipient of a National Endowment for the Arts Fellowship; the Before Columbus Foundation's American Book Award; a Lannan Foundation Literary Award; the PEN Center West Award for the best fiction of 1991; the Quality paperback Book Club New Voices Award; a MacArthur Foundation Fellowship; and the Frank Dobie Artists Fellowship, Austin, Texas. Sandra Cisneros moved to the Southwest in 1984; she now lives in San Antonio, Texas, and is currently working on a novel, *Caramelo.*

Cisneros describes writing as something she has done all her life from the time when, as a young girl, she began writing in spiral notebooks poems that only her mother read. Her first published book, *Bad Boys,* appeared as the Chicano Chapbook No. 8 (1980). Her novel *The House on Mango Street* was published by a small regional press in 1984 and the following year was awarded the Before Columbus Foundation's American Book Award. The novel draws heavily upon childhood memories and an unadorned childlike style of expression to depict life in the Chicano community. Issues of racial and sexual oppression, poverty, and violence are explored in a sequence of interconnected vignettes that together form a modified autobiographical structure. *Woman Hollering Creek and Other Stories* continues the exploration of ethnic identity within the patriarchal context of Chicano culture. The stories in this volume offer snapshots of Mexican American life: sights and smells recalled in childish memories, stories told by witches who see all of Chicano history from past to future, the hopes and aspirations of grandparents and grandchildren, friends and neighbors, Mexican movies, and "Merican" tourists. Her first volume of poetry, *My Wicked, Wicked Ways,* is described by Cherríe Moraga as "a kind of international graffiti, where the poet—bold and insistent—puts her mark on those travelled places on the map and in the heart."[3] *Loose Woman* similarly invokes the cultural and the emotional in an intoxicating sequence of outrageously confessional moments. Cisneros has also published essays on writing and her role as a writer, most notably the selections titled "From a Writer's Notebook. Ghosts and Voices: Writing from Obsession" and "Notes to a Young(er) Writer," both of which appeared in the *Americas Review* (1987). Her books have been translated into ten languages.

In Cisneros's work the effort to negotiate a cross-cultural identity is complicated by the need to challenge the deeply rooted patriarchal values of both Mexican and American cultures. Cisneros writes, "There's always this balancing act, we've got to define what we think is fine for ourselves instead of what our culture says."[4] Chicana feminism has arisen largely from this need to contest the feminine stereotypes that define machismo, while at the same time identifying and working against the shared class and racial oppression that all Chicanos/as—men, women and children—experience. To adopt models of femininity that are thought of as Anglo is, as Cisneros describes, to be "told you're a traitor to your culture. And it's a horrible life to live. We're always straddling two countries, and we're always living in that kind of schizophrenia that I call, being a Mexican woman living in an American society, but not belonging to either culture. In some sense we're not Mexican and in some sense we're not American."[5]

Patriarchal definitions of feminine subjectivity, some Anglo but mostly Mexican, affect all of Cisneros's characters by creating the medium in which they live. The protagonist of *The House on Mango Street,* the girl Esperanza, compares herself with her great-grandmother with whom she shares her name and the coincidence of being born in the Chinese year of the horse, "which is supposed to be bad luck if you're born female—but I think this is a Chinese lie because the Chinese, like the Mexicans, don't like their women strong."[6] This fiery ancestor, "a wild horse of a woman, so wild she wouldn't marry" (*Mango Street,* 11), is forcibly taken by Esperanza's great-grandfather, and her spirit broken, she lived out her days staring from her window. The narrator remarks, "I have inherited her name, but I don't want to inherit her place by the window" (11). This woman is the first of many Esperanza encounters who are broken in body and spirit by the patriarchal society that defines the terms by which they live.

The primary effect of these prescriptive definitions is the experience of the self as marginal, as failing to belong in the culture in which one lives. Cisneros challenges marginality but in subtle ways and using the weapons at her disposal as an artist: imagery, symbolism, forms of narrative connectivity that are at odds with rational, discursive logic. Like so many Chicana writers, Sandra Cisneros rejects the logic of the patriarchy in favor of more provisional, personal, emotional, and intuitive forms of narrative. She creates stories, not explanations or analyses or arguments. The stories that comprise *The House on Mango Street* are linked according to a loose and associative logic. In this way the fragmented structure of the text embodies a quest for freedom, a genuine liberation that resolves rather than escapes the conflicts faced by the Chicana subject. María Elena de Valdés describes how Cisneros's narrative technique relates to the theme of feminist resistance: "The open-ended reflections are the narrator's search for an answer to the enigma: how can she be free of Mango Street and the house that is not hers and yet belong as she must to that house and that street. The open-ended entries come together only slowly as the tapestry takes shape, for each of the closed figures are also threads of the larger background figure which is the narrator herself."[7] The threads with which the story is then woven are the complex image patterns Cisneros gradually develops and the imagistic connections she builds among the vignettes. The first story, which describes the houses in which Esperanza has lived, ends with her father's promise that their cramped and shabby house is temporary. The next story, "Hairs," begins with a description of her father's hair and goes on to contrast it with her mother's. The contrast between mother and father is continued and generalized in the third story, "Boys and Girls," which ends with Esperanza's hope that she will one day have the best friend for whom she yearns. The fourth story concerns the meaning of Esperanza's name, "Hope." In this way Cisneros creates vignettes that are self-contained, autonomous, yet link together in an emotionally logical fashion and build to create a picture of life in the barrio, seen through the experiences of the young Esperanza and her developing consciousness of herself as an artist.

The stories collected in *Woman Hollering Creek* are organized according to a similar associative logic. The volume is divided into three named sections: "My Lucy Friend Who Smells Like Corn," "One Holy Night," and "There Was a Man, There Was a Woman." Each section shares a loosely defined theme: the experience of Chicano/a children in "My Lucy Friend Who

SANDRA CISNEROS

Smells Like Corn," "Eleven," "Salvador Early or Late," "Mexican Movies," "Barbie-Q," "Mericans," and "Tepeyac"; the betrayal of Chicana girl children in the stories "One Holy Night" and "My Tocaya"; and the limited choice of adult relationships available to women in patriarchal Chicano/a society in "Woman Hollering Creek," "The Marlboro Man," "La Fabulosa: A Texas Operetta," "Remember the Alamo," "Never Marry a Mexican," "Bread," "Eyes of Zapata," "Anguiano Religious Articles Rosaries Statues . . . ," "Little Miracles, Kept Promises," "Los Boxers," "There Was a Man, There Was a Woman," "Tin Tan Tan," and "*Bien* Pretty." Though many of these stories depict the lives of individuals who are comprehensively defeated by the sheer burden of work, worry, and care they are required to bear, in some of them Cisneros creates characters who are able to subvert oppressive definitions of gender identity in favor of marginal, hybrid selves.

The story "Never Marry a Mexican," for example, begins with the disappointment of the narrator's grandparents that their son should have married a United States–born Mexican—a woman who is neither white like an Anglo nor raised properly in the ways of Mexican femininity: "what could be more ridiculous than a Mexican girl who couldn't even speak Spanish, who didn't know enough to set a separate plate for each course at dinner, nor how to fold cloth napkins, nor how to set the silverware."[8] The lesson learned by the narrator is "Never Marry a Mexican," which she generalizes into a determination never to marry. Instead she cultivates a hybrid identity, belonging to several socioeconomic classes and yet to none. She describes herself as "amphibious"—capable of surviving in radically different environments. And although she is United States–born, still the native idiom does not come naturally to her. She exclaims, ironically in the very idiom she denies, "I can't ever get the sayings right even though I was born in this country. We didn't say shit like that in our house" (73). This awareness of cross-cultural marginality extends even to the endearments used by her lover; he calls her Malinche, "my courtesan," the native woman taken by Cortés and mother of the hybrid Chicano race. But this woman, Cisneros's narrator, takes her own peculiar revenge upon her adulterous lover: in his wife's absence she plants around the house a trail of sticky sweets, in places only his wife will look—her makeup bag, her nail polish bottles, her diaphragm case. Then she seduces this faithless lover's son, and the significance of the story becomes clear as a confession to this son and an explanation of the relationship in which he has become involved. This vengeance is more than personal; it is revenge upon an Anglo man who believes he can "Never Marry a Mexican." This is vengeance sought on behalf of La Malinche for all her Chicana daughters who are good enough to seduce but never good enough to marry. This is vengeance on behalf of all the women who are led to believe that marriage is the only mechanism by which their lives may be validated and if they are not married then they themselves are somehow not valid.

The legacy of La Malinche is the fragmentary subjectivity commonly experienced by Chicanas: women who seek approval on both Anglo and Mexican terms, so that the unitary sense of self is inevitably sacrificed. The Chicana writer perhaps experiences this conflict most intensely: "the Chicana has had to be a cultural schizophrenic in trying to please both the Chicano and

Anglo publishers, not to mention pleasing the readers, who may
neutralize her potential to create within her own framework of
ideas."[9] In these words Marcela Christine Lucero-Trujillo
describes the experience of cross-cultural identity and alienation
that is perhaps the single most common theme in ethnic women's
writing. To lose one's sense of self in the effort to satisfy mutu-
ally antagonistic sets of cultural values is the danger negotiated
by Cisneros's characters. The image of living under occupation,
of living in an occupied territory or even of becoming occupied
territory, describes the experience of both a woman under Chicano patriarchy and a Chicana under Anglo dominance. This
accounts for Cisneros's use of the image of the window in several of the stories in *The House on Mango Street.* Women are
depicted sitting by their windows, forbidden or afraid to enter the
world represented by the street, literally and physically trapped
in their imposed domesticity. Esperanza's friend Sally is beaten
by her jealous husband if she so much as speaks to anyone in his
absence; Rafaela's husband locks her in their apartment, so she
communicates with the world solely through the window;
Mamacita refuses to leave her building because she cannot speak
English. Such women experience the world in a series of
vignettes which permit no unifying structure. They live lives
without narrative, without context, but representing a logic of
oppression and cruelty too ugly to confront. In her fiction Cisneros tells of living with a double burden imposed by white
women and by men of all colors. The complexities of gender,
race, and class, which will not remain distinct but instead com-
pound their oppressive effects, form the labyrinth that Cisneros
seeks to map.

Fiction is used to expose the many lies that are told to children, especially girl children, in order to regulate their desires, ambitions, and aspirations. The narrator of the story "One Holy Night" tells her girl cousins who are curious to know "how it is to have a man": "It's a bad joke. When you find out you'll be sorry" (*Woman Hollering Creek,* 35). But these girl children seem to have no choice other than to "find out," eventually. The juxtaposition of the vignettes in *The House on Mango Street* dramatizes the attempts of the adolescent Esperanza to reconcile her childish naïveté with the realities of adult Chicana life. In the story "Papa Who Wakes Up Tired in the Dark" Esperanza makes an important distinction between her own father and other men as she struggles to reconcile her love for her father with the treatment she receives from other men and the patriarchal attitudes that inform their behavior toward her. In the preceding story, "First Job," Esperanza describes her first experience of sexual harassment, by a man old enough to be her father: "he said it was his birthday and would I please give him a birthday kiss. I thought I would because he was so old and just as I was about to put my lips on his cheek, he grabs my face with both hands and kisses me hard on the mouth and doesn't let go" (55).

In one of the pivotal stories of *The House on Mango Street,* "Red Clowns," Esperanza describes her sexual initiation. She is assaulted by a group of Anglo boys while waiting at the fairground for her friend Sally. Esperanza's feelings of helplessness, confusion, and pain are overwhelmed by the sensation of betrayal: betrayal by Sally who was not there when Esperanza needed her but also betrayal by all the women who ever failed to contradict the romantic mythology of love and sex. Esperanza says, "You're a liar. They all lied. Only his dirty fingernails against my skin, only his sour smell again" (100). Esperanza directs her anger and shame not at the perpetrators of this violent act; she does not have the words, the language with which to direct blame at men, and privileged white men at that, and so she internalizes that sense of blame and accuses women instead. As María Herrera-Sobek explains: "The diatribe is directed not only at Sally the silent interlocutor but at the community of women who keep the truth from the younger generation of women in a conspiracy of silence: silence in not *denouncing* the 'real' facts of life about sex and its negative aspects in violent sexual encounters, and *complicity* in embroidering a fairy-tale-like mist around sex and romanticizing and idealizing unrealistic sexual relations."[10]

In the earlier story "Beautiful and Cruel" Esperanza tells of her desire to become like the movie actresses who are beautiful and cruel. The kind of actress Esperanza most wants to be "is the one who drives the men crazy and laughs them all away. Her power is her own. She will not give it away" (*Mango Street,* 89). This image of an empowered woman is quite distinct from the imagery of femininity encountered in popular culture. The character Marin, for example, represents the young victim of patriarchal popular culture. Esperanza recalls that Marin sings popular songs of romantic love, and she tells the younger girls "how Davey the Baby's sister got pregnant and what cream is best for taking off moustache hair and if you count the white flecks on your fingernails you can know how many boys are thinking of you and lots of other things I can't remember now" (*Mango Street,* 27). Marin's ambition is to work in a department store, where she can look beautiful and wear fashionable clothes and meet someone to marry. Romantic love and personal beauty are the ideologies that inform her sense of herself, her worth, and the direction of her life. Esperanza realizes that Marin is waiting for someone, a man, to come along and take control of her life. She refuses to accept responsibility for her life herself; she places that responsibility with the unknown man for whom she is waiting. As Esperanza imagines, Marin is "waiting for a car to stop, a star to fall, someone to change her life" (27). Unlike the movie actress in the story "Beautiful and Cruel," whatever feminine power Marin possesses she gives away.

But in "Red Clowns," Esperanza tells of her discovery that a "Spanish girl" does not possess any power and that whatever is desired of her will be taken from her by force. Ignorance of her own helplessness is what Esperanza most resents: the deliberate falsehoods that lead her to believe she has a power that always has been denied her. The adults into whom children like Esperanza mature are deceived by their culture about who they are and what they can achieve in their lives. Esperanza's mother uses her own life to warn her daughter of the danger of the ideology of personal beauty. She tells how she left school because she had no nice clothes to wear and only when it was too late did she see the mistake she had made. The lives led by her parents represent for Esperanza the discrepancy between the promises made by her culture and the reality of the life that is actually delivered. Her parents believe that hard work will be rewarded in material ways. They live in the expectation that life will become easier and their next house will be bigger and better. Eventually Esperanza stops believing them and the mythology they believe. She refuses to accompany the family on Sunday afternoon drives to admire the houses and gardens of rich Anglo-Americans—the people for whom her parents and neighbors toil. America promises its citizens more than it is willing to deliver; but Chicano culture promises its little girls less than they are capable of achieving— a life of drudgery, servitude, and self-denial.

Cisneros's treatment of sexuality is divided between a celebration of the power of a demythologized feminine sexuality and a powerful awareness of misogyny and the control of women through the control of their sexuality. The control of bodily appearance, how the female body is represented in words and in flesh, is a powerful strategy for the control of women's minds. In the language of patriarchy, femininity is defined closely with the female body. It is because she is a woman that Alicia must rise before dawn to do her dead mother's work before she goes to school. Alicia is told that "a woman's place is sleeping so she can wake up early with the tortilla star" (*Mango Street,* 31) to begin another day of cooking, cleaning, and serving her family. Female identity is inscribed upon the feminine body, as the girls speculate about the true function of women's hips: "They're good for holding a baby when you're cooking, Rachel says. . . . You need them to dance, says Lucy. . . . You gotta know how to walk with hips, practice you know—like if half of you wanted to go one way and the other half the other" (*Mango Street,* 49). It is in terms of feminine usefulness to men—as entertainment (dancing), bearing and raising children, cooking, appearing sexually attractive—that the female body derives its usefulness, not as the

representation of individual or feminine subjectivity. So the feminine is defined in objective terms, as women appear to men, rather than the subjective terms of feminine experience.

Many women are trapped within these cultural constructs. They find their femininity represented in a language that serves the interests of men and the masculine view of the world. Consequently, these women are unable to describe, even to themselves, the reasons for their suffering. The title story of *Woman Hollering Creek* tells of the young woman Cleófilas, who is brought to Texas from Mexico by the husband she hopes will transform her life into the kind of romance she knows from magazines, novels, and telenovelas. "Cleófilas thought her life would have to be like that, like a *telenovela,* only now the episodes got sadder and sadder. And there were no commercials in between for comic relief. And no happy ending in sight" (52–53). She discovers instead a life of neglect, abuse, beatings, loneliness. This is until a nurse introduces her to an entirely different kind of woman—someone who will help her leave her violent husband and return to Mexico, someone who suggests that the "hollering" for which the creek is named does not have to signify only sadness or anger but perhaps also defiance, a bold assertion of femininity and the will to self-determination. This woman, Felice, introduces Cleófilas to a whole new perspective on femininity and a range of previously unthinkable possibilities for living her life. Felice fractures the patriarchal narratives of womanhood that have constrained Cleófilas's thinking about herself and her potential.

Cisneros devotes much of her work to this effort of fracturing the powerful narratives of femininity that serve the interests

of the patriarchy. Not limited to deconstructing patriarchal gender definitions, Cisneros also devotes her energies to telling
about her sexuality but from her own feminine point of view,
which is emphatically not a male point of view. This is the significance of Cisneros's "wicked, wicked ways," the title of her
1987 volume of poems. She is "wicked" in that she has reappro-
priated, taken control of, her own sexuality and the articulation
of it—a power forbidden to women under patriarchy. Her
wickedness is that of defying a patriarchally constructed boundary separating that which is legitimate for a woman from that
which is not. The "loose woman," described in the poem of the
same name, assumes mythological proportions as a consequence
of her subversive powers: "They say I'm a beast. . . . a bitch. / Or
witch. . . . the woman of myth and bullshit. . . . By all accounts I
am / a danger to society. / I'm Pancha Villa" (*Loose Woman,*
112–13, 2.1, 4–5, 24)—come to save the women! This loose
woman breaks laws, disregards religion, terrorizes men; "In
other words, I'm anarchy" (*Loose Woman,* 114, l.47).

The poems collected in *Loose Woman* enact a defiant recla-
mation of feminine sexuality—for example, "I Let Him Take
Me," "I Am So in Love I Grow a New Hymen," "Black Lace Bra
Kind of Woman," "Down There," "A Man in My Bed Like
Cracker Crumbs," and "Loose Woman." Titles such as these are
indicative of the boisterous humor, the earthiness, the extrovert
energy of these poems. All are short, all set a scene and implic-
itly tell a tale, and all speak in powerful images that celebrate a
demythologized femininity. A "black lace bra kind of woman" is
a "loose woman," a woman who defies the polite rules governing feminine behavior, a woman who has "rambled / her '59

Pontiac between the blurred / lines dividing sense from sense-lessness" (*Loose Woman,* 78, 2.7–9). She is dangerous, the kind every girl's mother warned against: "Ruin your clothes, she will. / Get you home way after hours" (2.10–11). This kind of woman is reckless in her enjoyment of her life, her self, her body, and the poem celebrates this vibrant state of being: "And now the good times are coming. Girl, / I tell you, the good times are here" (2.17–18).

In the poem "Down There" Cisneros creates a vocabulary with which to write poetry about the reality of women's bodies. She does this not only to make of feminine sexuality a legitimate subject for poetry but also to challenge the decorum governing the ways in which the female body has been represented in poetry. The poem begins by administering a shock to poetic decorum: "Your poem thinks it's *bad*. / Because it farts in the bath. / Cracks its knuckles in class. / Grabs its balls in public" (*Loose Woman,* 79, 2.1–4). The poem is characterized initially by a sequence of "bad" macho habits: farting, peeing in the pool, picking one's nose, spitting, and swaggering like a macho John Wayne or Rambo. Then the tone shifts slightly and the poem is likened to objects rather than behaviors: a used condom, testicle skin, a lone pubic hair, a cigarette stub "sent hissing / to the piss pot" (2.59–60), half-finished beer bottles—in short, "the miscel-lany of maleness" (1.64). In these stanzas the poem is deliber-ately offensive, the images deliberately shocking, an outrageous violation of poetic decorum. But then comes Cisneros's ironic twist: as she turns to the central (the real) subject of her poem, the language assumes a more serious, decorous, "poetic" tone, yet the subject itself is an outrageous violation of patriarchal poetic decorum—"men-struation": "Yes, / I want to talk at length about Men- / struation. Or my period" (2.88–90). The ironic hyphenation of "men-struation" draws attention to the gendered fashion in which women's and men's bodies enter poetic discourse. Cisneros goes on to describe this feminine blood as the link between sexuality and creativity: "I'd like to dab my fingers / in my inkwell / and write a poem across the wall. / 'A Poem of Womanhood'" (2.120–23). But this poem is not just made of a woman's experience and produced by a woman; it is also for women and of them; it is representative of the commonality of all women: "Words writ in blood. But no, / not blood at all, I told you. / If blood is thicker than water, then / menstruation is thicker than brother- / hood" (2.125–29). It is in the true and authentic representation of feminine experience, including the reality of feminine sexuality, that women will find the solidarity that comes from shared gender experiences. Only by casting off the poetic stereotypes of patriarchal discourse will women overcome the divisive effects of those stereotypes and discover the potential for joy in their own bodies that is denied them.

Cisneros describes the discovery of this potential for joy, this subversive enjoyment of one's own sexuality, as a source of power for women: "Sexyness [*sic*], I think, it's a great feeling of self-empowerment."[11] She has been criticized both by other women and by men for some of the forms taken by this celebration of her sexuality, such as the highly suggestive photograph of Cisneros as "vamp" that adorns the cover of *My Wicked, Wicked Ways*. Cisneros describes that photograph: "The cover is of a woman appropriating her own sexuality. In some ways, that's also why it's wicked; the scene is trespassing that boundary by saying 'I defy you. I'm going to tell my own story.'"[12] Cisneros goes on to describe her dismay when women failed to perceive the transgressive meaning of her gesture. She reports the following encounter, when "some feminist asked: 'How could you, a feminist, pose like lewd cheesecake to sell your book?' And that offended me. At first I was hurt, then I thought about it and said: 'Wait a second, where's your sense of humor? And why can't a feminist be sexy?'"[13] The breaking of sexist stereotypes cuts both ways in Cisneros's work, against both the male and female limits that can be placed upon feminine sexuality. The transgression of patriarchal taboos is an important aspect of Cisneros's work as a Chicana writer. Sandra Cisneros is under no illusions about the power of feminine sexuality as a weapon used against women. She recognizes that in the context of the barrio, or any poor neighborhood, feminine sexuality is equated with vulnerability: "I was writing about it [the barrio] in the most real sense I knew, as a person walking those neighborhoods with a vagina," she says in reference to her subject in *The House on Mango Street*.[14]

Cisneros is not coy when it comes to articulating clearly the reasons why women become trapped in situations of extreme oppression. Fear of violence, sexual violence especially, is one of the prime strategies by which women are kept under control. Poverty, illiteracy, inability to speak English—these reinforce and exaggerate the coercive effect of patriarchal violence by limiting the mobility and opportunities of women. In poetry Cisneros carves out a space for these subjects and the words with which to articulate them. In "Still Life with Potatoes, Pearls, Raw Meat, Rhinestones, Lard, and Horses Hooves," for example, she contrasts the myth of genteel poverty with the reality of life in Mexican San Antonio: "poverty's not quaint when it's your house you can't escape from. / Decay's not beautiful to the decayed" (*Loose Woman,* 109, 2.37–38).

Although Cisneros does not flinch from depicting the squalor and deprivation of the life lived by many Chicanos, she does not dwell upon these hardships. Mexican history and mythology offer a rich vocabulary of poetic allusions with which to represent the complexity of a dual cultural heritage. In particular Cisneros addresses the issue of Mexican role models: "We're raised in a Mexican culture that has two role models: La Malinche y la Virgen de Guadalupe. And you know that's a hard route to go, one or the other, there's no in-betweens."[15] The virgin and the whore—these categories of "good" versus "bad" women are complicated by the perception, shared by many Chicana feminists, that they risk betrayal of the people if they pursue an alternative construction of femininity that is perceived to be Anglo. In her 1986 essay "Cactus Flowers: In Search of Tejana Feminist Poetry" Cisneros questions the playful tone of some Chicana feminist poetry that dares to criticize Chicano men only to a certain point, a point from which the poet can "slip back into the safety zone and say 'just kidding.'"[16] She asks of the poet under discussion, Angela de Hoyos, in her collection *Woman, Woman:* "Why is de Hoyos afraid to fall out of the graces of the males whom she is obviously angry with? Is she afraid of being labelled a Malinchista by them, corrupted by gringa influences which threaten to splinter her people?"[17] Threats to Chicana self-definition come, then, from *Angla* America as well as from the machismo of Chicano culture.

As a Chicana feminist Cisneros needs to revise aspects of her hybrid culture as a woman: that is, both by using her power as a woman and by challenging those aspects of her double cultural inheritance that prescribe what she as a woman can be. In order to do this Cisneros claims a symbolic vocabulary of Aztec allusions in her poems and in stories such as "Never Marry a Mexican," which is discussed above. For instance, the poem "You Bring Out the Mexican in Me" works through a frenetic list of all those things that comprise "Mexicanness." Throughout the poem this notion of Mexicanness has encompassed multitudes, including the most radical opposites (*Loose Woman,* 4–6). From "the filth goddess Tlazolteotl . . . the swallower of sins . . . the lust goddess without guilt" to the Virgin, this poem and the subjectivity it describes aspire toward a kind of unity that can never be unitary, that is always predicated on conflict, the "Aztec love of war," the "pre-Columbian death and destruction," the "rain forest disaster, nuclear threat . . . Mexico City '85 earthquake," extremes of passion. In poems such as this Cisneros claims her right to the inheritance passed down to her by Aztec women, the conquered women who survived despite the Virgin's people. Catholicism is a powerful legacy, but the pagan legacy is just as potent. In poems such as "You Bring Out the Mexican in Me" Cisneros uses this pagan force to resist the gender stereotypes of Catholicism and the guilt with which they are enforced.

Traces of these stereotypes are to be found in every household, in every Chicano/a community. Cisneros's commitment to the *cultura y raza* is represented by the extension of the family to encompass the entire community. In her stories family members are often evaluated for their effectiveness as role models in the ongoing effort to resist oppressive patterns of behavior. This is especially true of female relatives: mother, aunts, comadres, girl cousins, *abuelitas.* The lives that make up the family are subjected to a subtle ideological analysis to reveal the conditions of their entrapment. An ironic commentary on this analytical watchfulness is represented in the story "Barbie-Q." The title itself is a pun—signifying both the universal attraction of Barbie dolls for all little girls and also the fact that the dolls our narrator can afford to own are those salvaged from a warehouse fire: "So what if our Barbies smell like smoke. . . . And if the prettiest doll, Barbie's MOD'ern cousin Francie with real eyelashes, eyelash brush included, has a left foot that's melted a little—so?" (*Woman Hollering Creek,* 16). The narrator has absorbed the merchandising rhetoric together with the values represented by the doll. Consequently the vignette is presented in a tone of naive defiance of those socioeconomic pressures that will ensure these little girls never can meet the standard of feminine beauty signified by the doll. The doll is both role model (in terms of body image, at least) and evidence of the exclusion of Chicanas from governing Anglo definitions of femininity.

In *The House on Mango Street* Esperanza learns first what she does not want to be and then learns what she has the potential to become. She is named for a great-grandmother who was dominated by her husband and spent her life sitting at her window looking out, thinking of all the things she might have been. There are the characters Marin, the neighbor who has been brought from Puerto Rico to baby-sit her young cousins and look for a husband; Minerva, who writes poetry but is trapped physically in an abusive marriage; Esperanza's mother, who speaks two languages and sings opera but is too scared to go downtown because she cannot speak English; and Sally, who marries to escape her violent father. But then there are the comadres, the three sisters, who tell Esperanza that she must escape in order to come back for those who cannot find a way out themselves; it is for them she must always remember: "A circle, understand? You will always be Esperanza. You will always be Mango Street. You can't erase what you know. You can't forget who you are" (*Mango Street,* 105). And Alicia repeats this lesson: if life on Mango Street is ever to improve, then it will be because people like Esperanza have made it better. In response to Esperanza's insistence that she does not belong and does not want to belong, Alicia insists that not only is Esperanza shaped by the culture of Mango Street, but she will return to change it because, she asks, "Who's going to do it? The mayor? And the thought of the mayor coming to Mango Street makes me laugh out loud" (*Mango Street,* 107). It is as a writer that Esperanza must struggle to make that difference, because politicians will not. No one else will do it.

It is as an artist that Esperanza discovers how she can make a difference to life on Mango Street. But the altruistic aspect of her writing is slow to dawn upon her. This is because the Chicana artist needs to be selfish in order to have the time to write. Cisneros has written of her mother who let her read and study in her room rather than do her chores; later it was her family who provided financial assistance when she needed it.[18] The Chicana writer needs to resist the traditional lifestyles available to Mexican American women: marriage and children would leave no time and no energy for creativity. Cisneros tells how even a regular job can threaten the concentration of energy necessary for writing. "I would like a wife, instead of a husband, because then he could take care of the kids," she jokes.[19] For the woman writer, marriage means a burden of housework with which creative work cannot compete. The solitary time needed for thinking and writing is incompatible with marriage—but this is the traditional lifestyle for the Chicana who is expected to move from the father's house to that of the husband. The private mental space in which the creative process occurs is crucially related to physical space and interpersonal space.

It is no accident, then, that the house provides a controlling metaphor in *The House on Mango Street* and that Esperanza's growing awareness of herself as an artist is tied to her need to discover a space of her own; a place to think her own thoughts and to write them down in an appropriate silence. The characters Aunt Lupe and Minerva in *The House on Mango Street* seek in poetry both a refuge from their oppressive lives and an authentic kind of freedom that resolves rather than simply eludes the conflicts that characterize their experience of subjectivity. But these women have no space to call their own. Esperanza experiences the house in which she lives as a metaphor for her entire sense of self. In the first vignette she describes the shame evoked by a nun's words: "You live there? The way she said it made me feel like nothing. There. I lived there" (*Mango Street,* 5). From this humiliation comes a determination to live in a "real" house. And with this real house will come a firm and stable sense of being, in place of the nothingness evoked by the nun. Esperanza sees an image of herself reflected in the nun's face and in her words; as a poet Esperanza is able to use words to construct both a means of escape and a means to return to the house on Mango Street.

Poetry, writing, becomes in Cisneros's work much more than words on a page. Poetry is the real business of living because the writing process engages the poet in the difficult business of contesting all those cultural pressures that are placed upon the ethnic woman. To live in freedom and to be free to write are complementary aspects of the same effort at self-liberation. As a consequence, Cisneros writes many poems about poetry, poems that deliberately confuse poetry with other passionate engagements. "I Let Him Take Me," for instance, misleads the reader by using the language of romantic love in such a way that the poetic muse is personified as a lover. But we are aware only of the lover—until the final line. Then the love which is sneered at by others, the love at which the poet labors and which she nurtures, and the lover who "never disappointed, / hurt, abandoned" is dramatically identified as "Husband, love, my life—/ poem" (*Loose Woman,* 11, 2.15–16, 17–18).

The discovery and protection of a space in which to be alone is one of the threads that unifies the vignettes of *The House on Mango Street.* The narrative sequence develops as a Kunstlerroman—a portrait of the artist as a young Chicana. In their instructive essay "Growing Up Chicano: Tomás Rivera and Sandra Cisneros" Erlinda González-Berry and Tey Diana Rebolledo contrast the characteristics of the male coming-of-age narrative with Cisneros's narrative style in *The House on Mango Street.*[20] Esperanza first learns to see herself as an artist and then realizes how to be an artist by discovering a mission that is defined by what she can do for all the women, not just herself. Her escape from the barrio must be instructive, for then it can be true freedom based on acceptance rather than self-denial. Esperanza wants not simply to escape or transcend her surroundings, for however brief a time; she embraces literature as a potent opportunity to take control over her own life's story. Agency, in the determination of her self and her life, is what writing offers. Speaking as a Chicana, Cisneros explains: "None of us wants to abandon our culture. We're very Mexican, we're all very Chicanas. Part of being Mexican is that love and affinity we have for our *cultura.* We're very family centered, and that family extends to the whole Raza. We don't want to be exiled from our people."[21]

Though many of her characteristic themes and subjects are shared in both her poetry and fiction, the two forms appear quite distinct to Cisneros—opposed almost: "Poetry is the art of telling the truth, and fiction is the art of lying. The scariest thing to me is writing poetry, because you're looking at yourself *desnuda.* You're always looking at the part of you that you don't show anybody."[22] But at the center of that self-scrutiny is the core of truth that Cisneros identifies as the poem itself. In radical contrast fiction is as extroverted as poetry is introverted: "the definition of a story is something that someone wants to listen to. If someone doesn't want to listen to you, then it's not a story."[23] Cisneros's poems do tell stories, but in a compact, economical, and highly imagistic fashion. Her poetry is a kind of storytelling; it can be narrative in this way. But more striking is the highly poetic and evocative quality of Cisneros's fiction.

Several commentators have remarked upon the richly

poetic, allusive quality of Cisneros's prose, and she, remarking upon the formal indeterminacy of *The House on Mango Street,* describes how she wanted to create stories that read like compact and lyrical poems, formed into a collection that could be read at any point in the sequence or as a single narrative.[24] The literary structures Cisneros uses are as multifaceted as her cultural identity. In seeking to forge a language that will express but not misrepresent her experiences Cisneros, like many Chicana writers, encounters a number of difficulties. First, there is the question of language and the competing claims of English and Spanish to prominence in her work. Second, many of the canonical literary styles within the American tradition were created to express the realities of masculine experience. Even those forms suited to feminine expression manifest an Anglo vision of the world. Cisneros, along with many of her Chicana sisters, confronts the twin difficulties of writing as a woman and as a Chicana every time she begins to write. The patriarchal bias of Chicano culture and the Anglo bias of American women's culture represent the twin obstacles of sexism and racism that Chicanas must negotiate in order to write authentically. American English is commonly perceived as a language of duplicity, the language of treaty violation, the voice of the master. English threatens to corrupt Chicana expression just as Anglo-American cultural values corrupt the Mexican American community. Cisneros writes mostly but not exclusively in a hybrid English that is required to accommodate Spanish words and phrases. She describes in a witty bilingual fashion the choice she made to write in English as resulting from her lack of familiarity with the nuances of a Spanish-language culture: "I never write in Spanish, y no es que no quiero sino que I don't have that same palate in Spanish that I do in English. No tengo esa facilidad. I think the only way you get that palate is by living in a culture where you hear it, where the language is not something in a book or in your dreams. It's on the loaf of bread you buy, it's on the radio jingle, it's on the graffiti you see, it's on your ticket stub. It must be all encompassing."[25] But Cisneros's command of idiom is most striking. The narrative voice of *The House on Mango Street* captures the nuances of a child's expression, balanced against the demands of the vocabulary of adulthood into which Esperanza is entering. Cisneros favors the first-person mode of address, and it is this quasi-confessional, seemingly autobiographical style that lends her work (in fiction and poetry) such immediacy and such power.

Power is a word that recurs constantly when describing Sandra Cisneros's writing. She has described the Chicana writer as someone who is necessarily an obsessive. By virtue of who she is and the circumstances of her birth, the Chicana writer has no leisure to pursue the aesthetic just for its own sake. She is motivated not so much by inspiration but by the need to articulate pressing issues and to give expression to the ghosts that haunt her.[26] "Night Madness Poem" describes this compulsion to seek relief in the crafting of words. The poem that seeks expression is likened to "A pea under twenty eiderdowns. / A sadness in my heart like stone" (*Loose Woman,* 49, 2.3–4). As the poem continues, we realize that the words Cisneros wants to speak are to the absent lover she cannot telephone, but these are also the words of her poetry. Frustrated love and frustrated writing merge and are confused, so the poem ends with a challenge: "Choose your weapon. / Mine—the telephone, my tongue" (2.30–31).

The struggle for language in which to represent the realities of her experience is the subject of poems such as "By Way of Explanation," in which she uses geography to describe her body: her knees, "devout Moroccans," her hands "twin comedies / from Pago Pago," "The breasts / to your surprise / Gaugin's Papeete" (*Wicked Ways,* 92, 2.23, 24–26, 30–31). Cisneros deliberately includes the physical body in her poetry in order to contest the assumption that bodily existence is not an appropriate subject for poetry and also to challenge the idea that the body and bodily functions ought not to be spoken of.

This silence is a form of ignorance that oppresses women in particular by keeping them from knowledge of the power they can access through their physical femininity and by promoting feelings of shame and guilt about their sexuality. In the essay "Guadalupe the Sex Goddess" Cisneros discusses her own inherited ignorance of her body and her sexuality. She exclaims, "No wonder, then, it was too terrible to think about a doctor—a man!—looking at you down there when you could never bring yourself to look at yourself. *¡Ay, nunca!* How could I acknowledge my sexuality, let alone enjoy sex, with so much guilt? In the guise of modesty my culture locked me in a double chastity belt of ignorance and *vergüenza,* shame."[27] Many of the poems in *My Wicked, Wicked Ways* address and affirm the poet's transgressive sexuality: in poems about adultery (for example, "For All Tuesday Travellers" and "Amé, Amo, Amaré"), about sexual obsession (such as "Drought"), and about her sensuality and sexual attraction to men (in "Sensuality Plunging Barefoot into Thorns").

The 1992 preface to the reprinted collection is itself a poem that establishes the context for the poems and introduces the primary themes: the difficult choice to become a writer, the transgression of family and cultural expectation: "A woman like me / whose choice was rolling pin or factory / An absurd vice, this wicked wanton / writer's life" (*Wicked Ways,* x). The poem "His Story" develops this theme by presenting the father's view of his nonconformist daughter. He searches among family precedents for women who have trespassed across the borders of approved feminine behavior, trying to find an explanation for his sorrow. The poem concludes with the poet's reflection on her father's explorations: "An unlucky fate is mine / to be born woman in a family of men"; and her father's lament: "Six sons, my father groans, / all home. / And one female, / gone" (*Wicked Ways,* 38–39, 2.33–34, 35–38). The poems that follow this preface are then presented as the offspring of her union with the poetic muse: a brood of "colicky kids / who fussed and kept / me up the wicked nights" (*Wicked Ways,* xii). And in poems such as "The Poet Reflects on Her Solitary Fate," Cisneros describes the compulsion to write, the need to express her creativity: "The house is cold. / There is nothing on TV. / She must write poems" (*Wicked Ways,* 37, 2.13–15).

Though this poem, like all of Cisneros's work, is intensely personal she has discovered how to uncover the subtle and intricate web of connections that bind the personal with the cultural. Cisneros begins with personal experiences, feelings, and thoughts and suggests the complex ways in which these attributes of the private self have been shaped, prescribed, and monitored by cultural, racial, political, and economic forces. Her sense of responsibility as a writer is conceived in terms of these social and cultural influences. She explains that she is the first woman in her family to assume a public voice through writing, to take upon herself the power to speak and find that she is heard.[28] This privilege brings with it a responsibility to witness the lives and to register the worlds of those who remain invisible: the powerless, the silent. Cisneros tells of how she admires the poetry of Emily Dickinson and what she took to be Dickinson's ability to live both domestic and artistic lives simultaneously. Then Cisneros discovered Dickinson's housekeeper, the woman who performed the routine chores to keep the household running, freeing Dickinson to pursue her intellectual work. Cisneros describes how Emily Dickinson's housekeeper helped her to recognize the enormous contribution her own mother made to enable the young Sandra to read and write when instead she should have been washing dishes.[29]

In a sense, then, Cisneros's work is dedicated to her mother and to Emily Dickinson's housekeeper, the women who are forgotten but who made possible the lives of other literary women. In her essay "Cactus Flowers" Cisneros describes the courage it takes to define oneself as a Chicana writer: "To admit you are a writer takes a great deal of audacity. To admit you are a feminist takes even greater courage. It is admirable then when Chicana writers elect to redefine and reinvent themselves through their writing."[30] To be a writer is, for Sandra Cisneros, to have the opportunity to do something for the silenced women and for all women by inventing new paradigms, by defining new Chicana voices, and by living as a liberated feminine subject of the story she has written for herself.

CHAPTER FIVE

Denise Chávez

Denise Chávez is an accomplished novelist, dramatist, and short-story writer. Her work is regional in its setting and characterization, though her subject is diverse and universal. With characteristic exuberance she writes: "Naturally I write about what I know, who I am. New Mexico. Texas. Chicanismo. Latinismo. Americanismo. Womanismo. Mujerotismo. Peopleismo. Worldismo. Peaceismo. Loveismo."[1] This is echoed by Rudolfo Anaya in his introduction to *The Last of the Menu Girls:* "Denise's novel reflects her particular sense of place, revealing the depths of the worlds of women and the flavor of southern New Mexico."[2] The culture and geography of the Southwest are crucial to all of Chávez's work.

Denise Chávez was born on 15 August 1948 in Las Cruces, New Mexico, the second of three daughters. Her father was a lawyer, educated at Georgetown University; and while her father "beat the Anglos at their own game" ("Heat and Rain," 31), her mother studied in Mexico for thirteen summers and was immersed in Mexican culture. Her parents divorced when she was ten, and Chávez describes her childhood as growing up "in a house of women. That is why I often write about women, women who are without men. My father divorced us early on. . . . [My parents'] minds were compatible, their spirits and hearts were not. I grew up knowing separation as a quality of life—and this sorrow went hand in hand with extensions—for despite the fact that my parents were apart, both families were an everpresent part of my life. So I grew up solitary in the midst of noise, a quality I didn't know then was essential to my work as a writer" ("Heat and Rain," 27–28). The experience of living in an extended but fractured family is represented in the opening chapters of her novel *Face of an Angel* (1994). The Dosamantes family is introduced as far back as the narrator's great-grandparents and even back that far, as the narrator reflects, "the stories begin with the men and always end with the women; that's the way it is in our family."[3] In 1974 Chávez obtained a master's degree in theater arts from Trinity University in San Antonio, Texas, and in 1984 she earned a master's degree in creative writing from the University of New Mexico. She has taught and worked as writer-in-residence at numerous universities in the Southwest, including a period as visiting professor of creative writing at the New Mexico State University in Las Cruces. She is currently based in the English department at New Mexico State University. She also works as artistic director of the annual Border Book Festival, a nonprofit event founded in 1995 by a group of writers, artists, and community people to celebrate the literature of the southern U.S./northern Mexico region.

Chávez has won the 1986 Steele Jones Fiction Writing Contest. The title story of her first book, *The Last of the Menu Girls,* won the *Puerto del Sol* fiction award for 1985. In addition she was awarded a Creative Writing Arts Fellowship from the Arts Council of Houston in 1990; she won the 1994 *Premio Aztlán* award; and her novel *Face of an Angel* won the 1995 American Book Award. She is currently working on a second novel, "Loving Pedro Infante."

In addition to her fiction Chávez has written poetry and also plays including *Novena Narrativas y Ofrendas Nuevomexicanas* and the one-woman show "Women in a State of Grace." Support of Chávez's writing for the theater includes the award for best play from New Mexico State University in 1970 for her play *The Wait,* a National Endowment for the Arts InterArts grant to produce her play "Hech en México," and a Rockefeller playwright grant in 1984. Her plays have been produced throughout the United States and Europe, including the Edinburgh Festival and the Festival Latino de Nueva York, and selections from her work have been widely anthologized.

As a writer Chávez emphasizes the importance of spirituality; she describes imagination as a friend in her youth, "later a lover, a guide, a spirit teacher." Writing demands honesty: "I have said to writers I have taught: Don't lie. And to myself: You may lie in other things, but never in this. It's a sacred covenant I have with myself. Honesty. And no meanness" ("Heat and Rain," 30). She goes on, "I could never lie to those voices, to those spirits, to those voices I hear clearly" (31). The first chapter of *Face of an Angel* tells of the beginnings of the novel in the recollection of the narrator, Soveida Dosamantes, of her grandmother warning her that while she can still remember them she should record the stories of all the people around her. They all have a story to tell; each life is worth remembering (*Face of an Angel,* 4). The writer, then, is witness, recorder, and scribe; Chávez watches, notes, and represents the extraordinary everyday lives of those who people her beloved Southwest. She describes her love of popular culture, "what everyone else considers pedestrian, sub-mainstream culture. Director John Waters calls Baltimore the Hairdo Capital of the world. New

Mexico/Texas was and is Character Capital of the Universe. Unbelievable stories, lives" ("Heat and Rain," 30). In *Face of an Angel,* for example, these extraordinary characters include the Holy Ones, the high school janitor, his wife, the accountant at the Border Cowboys Truck Stop, and her husband, who form a "Travelling Prayer Team" to go about "casting off the chains of the oppressed, shining God's blessed light on the darkest of sorrows, and, in general, easing and consoling the troubled" (*Face of an Angel,* 89). The power and attraction of popular culture are explored in the short story "Grand Slam," a monologue spoken by Omega Harkins to her friend Mozetta as she tells about her first boyfriend, Acton, who has appeared as a contestant on the television game show Grand Slam.[4] All of Chávez's work is based on the re-creation of character, and she creates outrageous, ordinary, and interesting characters to tell their stories.

The role of the writer is to record the experiences of people such as Omega Harkins, just as Soveida Dosamantes, the narrator of *Face of an Angel,* records the lives of the people around her. Rocío Esquibel, the primary narrator of *The Last of the Menu Girls,* resolves to remember the people she met when she was a lowly menu girl, even after she has left the hospital to go to college; though she turns away from the faces, the voices, she recalls, "I'd made a list on a menu of all the people I'd worked with. To remember. It seemed right" (*Menu Girls,* 37). Chávez describes the subject of her writing in terms of her characterization: "I write about characters, not treatises, about life, not make-believe worlds. If my characters don't work, I go back and make them work. Without them, robust and in the living flesh, there is no story" ("Heat and Rain," 31). The type of character she represents or re-creates in her writing belongs to a distinct sociocultural group: the marginalized. She writes, "My work has always been for alternative groups, the people who never get much, for the poor, the forgotten. My writing as well is about the off-off Main street type of characters. My short stories are really scenes and I come from the tradition of the travelling *cuentista* [storyteller]. I believe stories should captivate, delight, move, inspire, and be downright funny, in a way. The 'in a way' is what I try to do with all my heart" ("Heat and Rain," 32).

Chávez's work is set on the U.S.-Mexico border, a region which Renato Rosaldo describes as "peopled with multiple subjectivities and a plurality of languages and cultures."[5] In a piece about the life, murder, and surprising anonymity of the Tejana singer Selena, another celebrity of this border zone, Jerry Adler and Tim Padgett write: "On the border, Chávez says, 'exteriors are crumbling, unpainted, ramshackle, but inside is a realm of magic.' She is entranced by the folk religion: the curanderos who heal with holy water and herbs, worshipping before altars that look like religious garage sales; the local saints like El Niño, a faith healer who died in 1938 in Espinazo, Mexico, and has been canonized by acclamation, not Rome; the sacred tortilla on which appeared an image of Christ's face, and which can be viewed, partially eaten, in a glass-fronted shrine in someone's living room. But mostly, she loves belonging to a place that is neither Mexico nor America, but some of both.[6] But in "The State of My Inquietude" the existence of the border is a source of anxiety. The poem is based upon a contrast between the poet's travel, "Española bound / and los," and the unhampered freedom of the moving clouds: "My sorrow sings of traveling mile / of soul / flung to cloud equivalent."[7] The poem "Artery of Land" describes the sense of belonging to the border region that is more than social or cultural or even familial. Chávez's use of imagery draws together the human and the natural features of the landscape. Images such as the "pore-red valleys" and the "vision line" of the shimmering New Mexico heat relate the human to the natural so as to make them converge in the final image of small children resting, pretending to sleep, in airless rooms: "They recall / tiny beads of sweat: / Home."[8] Home, then, becomes associated profoundly with the sensations of heat and sweat, the human moisture that like water is able to quench "certain / desert thirsts." This southwestern desert scenery provides the imagery of happiness in the otherwise bleak poem "Cuckoo Death Chime." In this poem images of death are associated with cold, silence, darkness; in contrast, the heat and light of the desert symbolize love and the free sharing of words and thoughts: "we sat in the sun like lizards / our hands touched the sky / our words were fused / in a night-blue room of loving."[9]

Tey Diana Rebolledo, writing of the importance of the southwestern border country in the work of contemporary Chicana writers, lists the following as distinctive characteristics of the region: "perceptions of the desert and its plants, domesticated flowers and gardens, the cactus, and the figure of the curandera (healer) as the mediator between nature and human beings."[10] Orelia is the healer, the unofficial curandera, in *Face of an Angel*. The mestiza character Juana in the play *Novena Narrativas* remembers her grandmother who was a curandera: "She taught me the healing life of herbs, what to do with cota and osha, como sobar con aceite while praying." As she says these words, Juanita dons a medicine wheel necklace (a native bead necklace with spiritual significance), and she lights cedar and gathers up the macaw feathers in preparation for the chant she will sing to La Virgen and to the four winds.[11] In Chávez's work, Rebolledo observes, the desert reflects the struggle to define the self; she quotes Chávez as saying of her early play "Mario and the Room María" that "the characters have a land inside and outside that is still unchartered, unpredictable and disquieting."[12] The natural landscape functions as mother/teacher, spiritual guide and informant, like the curandera who mediates this power to human society.

In *Face of an Angel* Soveida begins her "Book of Service" with the observation: "*When you grow up in the Southwest, your state is your country. There exists no other country outside that which you know*" (*Face of an Angel,* 105, Chávez's italic). Region, and the Southwest specifically, also appears as a prominent theme in *The Last of the Menu Girls.* In the section "Willow Game" the child Rocío is represented as politically naive, unaware of the significance of national regions. Nonetheless the narrative voice places herself within a clearly defined region: "I was a child before there was a South. That was before the magic of the East, the beckoning North, or the West's betrayal" (*Menu Girls,* 41). In the culture of the barrio, to go down the street was to travel in the direction of family, "the definition of small self as one of the whole, part of a past," but to travel up the street was to move in the direction of town, a move filled with dread and alienation (*Menu Girls,* 41). Early in the narrative Rocío introduces the prejudiced perceptions of the significance of the border among Anglos, especially in relation to immigrants. In the section titled "Juan María / The Nose" Rocío describes the reactions of the Chicana nursing staff to the casualty of a barroom fight: Rosario dismisses him as an illegal alien; Esperanza claims that immigrants like him "ain't human . . . he don't speak no Engleesh!" *(Menu Girls,* 32, 33); only Erminia dares to interject that her mother's maids were nice, except for those who stole; and it is only Rocío who notices the man's name: "'His name is Juan María Mejía,' I ventured" (33).

Rocío's father expresses contempt for the "wetbacks" he believes are moving into the neighborhood and his outrage that the welfare he pays for should subsidize them. In *Face of an Angel* Chicanos/as also make disparaging remarks about Mexicans. Soveida is advised repeatedly not to marry a Mexican, and Chata the cleaning lady prefers to work for "las americanas" because her own people, as she describes them, will not pay her what she is worth. Rocío is uncomfortably aware of her own situation as occupying a border space between Mexican and U.S. cultures. This consciousness is represented by the interlinked images of immigrants and college students getting food stamps: Esperanza exclaims in disgust, "It's a disgrace all those wetbacks and healthy college students getting our hard earned tax money. Makes me sick. Christ!" (*Face of an Angel,* 36). This sense of being an alien, of occupying an indeterminate cultural border zone, is emphasized by her experience when she leaves home, and the barrio, for college. There, in the North, she is cold, her name is constantly mispronounced, she is mistaken for Filipino, and her childhood culture is alien and incomprehensible.

Among Chávez's most urgent themes is the exploration of the possibilities for a Chicana girl's life: metaphors of serving dominate in *Face of an Angel* (Soveida writes, "As a child, I was imbued with the idea that the purpose of life was service," 171); and nursing is featured in *Last of the Menu Girls,* which begins with the words, "I never wanted to be a nurse" (13). In both texts the notion of service is redefined from what initially is demeaning to an involvement in the life of the family and community that is deeply meaningful and fulfilling. The poem "I Am Your Mary Magdalene" addresses this idea of feminine service but from the perspective of masculine definitions of servitude as a female subject position. Men require of women service as a means of apology, as a form of abasement and submission. The poem begins, "I am your Mary Magdalene / come, let me wash your feet / stroke your brow / can we undo the past / throw it away . . . ?"[13] The first two lines are repeated to form the conclusion of the poem, but before that Chávez asks two questions: she asks when, or under what circumstances, she has had to become some man's Mary Magdalene; and she also asks what happens when she refuses to adopt this apologetic and submissive posture. The alternative is banishment, "that high tower / I can see all the way into the chambered heart / I am back at that place / overlooking blue land / surrounded by gargoyles," which is no alternative, and so these lines are quickly followed by the refrain, "I Am Your Mary Magdalene." If there is no alternative, it is important, then, that the poet discovers how these gender positions are constructed. She must study "the chambered heart" into which she can see. There she finds that men project onto women their own weaknesses, especially their sensual weaknesses, so that the guilt or shame attaching to these feelings can be blamed on women: "Often I have had to apologize / to men /

for passions," she writes. She is accused by needy men, "You want too much"; and men with "chained libidoes" express concern "about how *you* are oversexed." Her response, as a woman, must be "I Am Your Mary Magdalene." In *Face of an Angel* the young Soveida confesses, "I identified with Saint Mary Magdalene, the supreme woman saint, ultra-whore, no cloying virgin, the top sinner among all the saints, except Saint Augustine" (*Face of an Angel,* 57).

In the first section of *The Last of the Menu Girls* the potentiality of Chicana life is represented in terms of a contrast with the opportunities available to white women. Rocío asks, "What was I to do then, working in a hospital, in that place of white women, whiter men with square faces?" (*Menu Girls,* 17). This is twinned with the rejection of the women in her own family: her mother with her tired, ugly feet; Great Aunt Eutilia and Doña Mercedes both dying of cancer; her fastidious sister Mercy. Images of women appear in succession in this section, "The Last of the Menu Girls." These women represent a wide diversity of feminine experience: old and young, rich and poor, white and Chicana, of the past and of the present. They offer a gallery of portraits against which Rocío can measure her own potential; she considers emulating these images and sees aspects of herself reflected in them. Rocío looks at the portrait of Florence Nightingale hanging near the hospital cafeteria and sees "a dark-haired woman in a stiff nurse's cap and grey tunic, tending to men in old-fashioned service uniforms. There was beauty in that woman's face whoever she was. I saw myself in her, helping all of mankind, forgetting and absolving all my own sick, my own dying, especially relatives, all of them so far away, removed"

(17). Arlene, Rocío's fellow menu girl, remarks on a likeness between Rocío and the portrait; but the similarity is intangible: Rocío will learn to serve, but it will be as a writer who gives voice to all those women, especially the relatives, from whom she has distanced herself. During her summer at the hospital Rocío is still searching for a feminine role model who will set her on that learning curve. Her mother; Great Aunt Eutilia; Doña Mercedes; her older sister Ronelia; Arlene; Dolores, the nurse's aide; patients such as Elizabeth Rainey, in whom Rocío says, "I saw myself, all life, all suffering" (27); and Mrs. Daniels, who vents all of her life's bitterness and hatred as she dies—all reveal to Rocío feminine lives and different ways of defining femininity. In the later section "Shooting Stars," Rocío observes, "For most of us, choice is an external sorting of the world, filled with uncertain internal emptiness." And she asks, "Who was I, then, to choose as a model? . . . Something seemed to be lacking in each of them. The same thing that was lacking in me, whatever that was" (62). Asked what it is that she does want to be, Rocío answers, "I want to be someone else, somewhere else, someone important and responsible and sexy. I want to be sexy" (34).

The strength that derives from the community of women in the family, the extended family of comadres, and Chicanas more generally is a theme that recurs in Chávez's work. Early in *Novena Narrativas y Ofrendas Nuevomexicanas* the narrator tells how she derives strength and courage from the knowledge that the spirits of her mother, grandmother, and "all the women who have come before me" are "always near, watching over me, guiding me, constantly teaching me." And so in the individual women she encounters in daily life she can perceive what she calls the "thread that connects me to all women, everywhere" (*Novena Narrativas,* 88). In this play the imagined presence of all these women inspires the creation of the diverse femininities represented by the dramatic characters: Jesusita Rael, the store owner; Esperanza González, the wife of a Vietnam veteran; Minda Mirabel, foster child; Magdalena Telles, the mother of seven children; Tomasa Pacheco, the nursing home resident; Juana Martínez who works in a factory; Pauline Mendoza, Chicana teenager; and Corrine "La Cory" Delgado, a bag lady. As the brief description of these characters indicates, they represent the various life stages of women (child, teenager, worker, mother, elderly grandmother) and a diverse range of Chicana lives (schoolgirl, spinster, wife, mestiza, factory worker, shopkeeper).

The strength that each of these female characters shows is the strength of endurance, the survival of pain, suffering, deprivation through an unfoundering commitment to the idea of love represented by the Madonna. Each scene consists of a monologue addressed to the statue of La Virgen of Guadalupe, from which these characters derive a strong sense of love, acceptance, and comfort. The only exception is the teenager Pauline, whose monologue is actually her part of a dialogue with an unseen, unheard teacher. In this scene the image of La Virgen appears as a tattoo Pauline is drawing on her own flesh. She confesses, "It's my art work. I'm working on my tattoos and my drawings. I'm gonna be an artist" (*Novena Narrativas,* 98). What enables this hard Chicana delinquent to soften, to give up drunkenness and violence, and begin to see some value in herself is the influence of the invisible teacher who forces her to stand and speak. This teacher introduces Pauline to alternative ways of being and opens her mind to the possibilities for her life: "She's Chicana," Pauline says, "I never known anybody . . . a lady and a chicana and an artist . . . It surprised me, you know?" (98). Whereas Pauline's earlier teachers had encouraged her preference for silence and withdrawal from the class, Isabel Martínez forces her to find a voice and use it. In this way Pauline is brought into the community of women.

For other women, it is La Virgen who acts as mediator, linking them to a wider network of feminine love and caring. Juana recalls, "I remember my abuelita telling me, 'Acuérdate que eres india, y que la Virgen María, la mestiza, es tu madre querida. The Mother's Mother is your mother as well. Never forget that. You are a child of many worlds: say your prayers, praise the sun, glorify the moon, and send your spirit in the wind'" (*Novena Narrativas,* 96). The tough, aged bag lady Corinne finds shelter and comfort from La Virgen. She asks, "¿Quién sabe?" and answers herself, "Mi Madrecita sabe, no?" (100). Though Magdalene's monologue is addressed to her recently returned lover, Miguel, she explains why she must leave to make her annual pilgrimage for La Virgen. She tells how she has made the pilgrimage for each of her children and for their fathers and how this day she will go for him and their unborn child. Her generosity of spirit and her love of life and desire to help people have brought her seven children. Like her namesake, Mary Magdalene, she sacrifices herself for others. When she addresses the altar, it is to ask forgiveness: "Que la Virgencita me perdone. She understands everything. Everything. And she forgives everything" (94). At the end of the play the narrator Isabel returns to her own self and her own voice to describe her sense of life—these lives—as a song, "the song of childhood, the song of love, the song of parting, the song of death," each of which is part of a greater chorus, an "unending song of love and life" (100). The Virgen offers a source of peace and strength for the times when life is so hard that it is difficult to go on singing; and in the same way, Isabel offers the writer's "total love and acceptance and friendship" (100) from which the strength to go on is inspired.

The life-sustaining power of women is the theme of the poem "Tilt-a-Whirl," in which Emilia, the mestiza servant, is described: "your great tortilla-hands / sustained me / you folded me up / like dough / set me back down / . . . as easily as flipping / a tortilla from the heat."[14] The figure of Emilia with her "squat heavy hands, her Saviour's hands" appears incidentally in *The Last of the Menu Girls,* as an image of comfort and safety; like the Anglo woman who stayed with them awhile, Emilia is "one of the many who passed through our youthful lives, as servers or served" (*Menu Girls,* 72, 73). This theme is explored extensively in the novel *Face of an Angel:* the culture of women, feminine traditions, history, the generations of women. In the early stages of the novel Soveida perceives service as the servitude of women, like her mother, who still washes her father's dirty laundry although they have been divorced for years. Later she learns that to serve is to love and that to serve well is to serve oneself; her mother realizes this as she tells Soveida, "All my love mistakenly went to someone else when it should have come to *me.* Nobody can love us the way we need to love ourselves. Especially for women like us" (*Face of an Angel,* 373). These women are those who have loved destructively, allowing men to dominate and violate them, accepting brutality in place of love and domination in place of caring. What Soveida learns from the mistakes made by the women around her is that service can be a way of expressing her love positively for herself and for others. This lesson she learns most fully from Chata, the cleaning lady, and Oralia, her grandmother's maid, both of whom are women who have devoted their lives to serving others. In *The Last of the Menu Girls* Rocío sees her older sister as a kind of mirror, reflecting an image of her grandmother, her mother, and her younger sister, Rocío herself. Later she is able to hear the voices that tell her, "We are the formless who take form, briefly, in rooms, and then wander on. We are the grandmothers, aunts, sisters. We are the women who love you" (*Menu Girls,* 85).

The physical experience of femininity is explored in both *The Last of the Menu Girls* and *Face of an Angel.* Early in *Face of an Angel,* Soveida tries to talk about menstrual bleeding with her mother and is called "escandalosa!" The importance of talking about the female body grows as Soveida discovers that Mara's mother died because she was too embarrassed to consult a doctor about the complications she suffered after the birth of her daughter. Gradually she identifies her own peculiarly feminine sufferings, her infections and discharges and bleeding, as her body's expression of rage and bitterness provoked by her husband's infidelities and maltreatment of her. In this novel, then, Denise Chávez uses the full vocabulary available to her to represent in its fullness the experience of femininity.

The beauty of the female body is questioned hard. Early in *The Last of the Menu Girls,* Rocío associates femininity with pain, suffering, and death, and so she comes to question the nature of feminine beauty, to ask, "What did it mean to be a woman? To be beautiful, complete? Was beauty a physical or a spiritual thing, was it strength of emotion, resolve, a willingness to love? What was it then that made women lovely?" (*Menu Girls,* 53). Bodily experience is represented as a constraint within which women must live: like the suffering women Doña Mercedes, Elizabeth Rainey, and Mrs. Daniels in *The Last of the Menu Girls,* and in *Face of an Angel,* Soveida's mother, appropriately named Dolores, who is trapped within a large-breasted body that her husband finds appealing: " 'My harness,' that's what she always called her brassière" (*Face of an Angel,* 19). Female destiny is linked with female disease in *The Last of the Menu Girls,* as Rocío looks at her mother's scarred legs and listens to her Aunt Eutilia's dying. In *Novena Narrativas* the child Minda links femininity with death; she remembers being told, "The female thing won't kill you, or your mother being dead. All things have to die. It's natural" (*Novena Narrativas,* 92). But Minda wonders why at her birth she lived and her mother died. As she grows, the abused child associates sexuality with suffering and death. She confides her secret only to her doll, and only then by attributing to her imaginary friend Jennifer her sexually abusive father: "This is a secret for always and forever. You can't even tell God, understand? Jennifer's father hurts little girls. He beats her and does ugly, dirty things to her. What he does is bad! And he told her if she ever told anybody, he would kill her!" (91). Femininity is associated with pain, suffering, and death; masculinity is associated with violence and abuse. Even Jesusita remarks that what Minda needs is a mother and, laughing nervously, "to be close to God, if God's not a man!" (90).

God the Father appears rarely in these father-absent, women-dominated households, and it is La Virgen who is the reigning deity: characters such as Esperanza invoke her as "mi Reina." In *Face of an Angel* first Soveida and later Chata insist that God must be a woman.

The search for one's own femininity is represented in Rocío's unfolding search for her own authentic subjectivity. The discovery of her own integrity is the main unifying theme of *The Last of the Menu Girls.* At the beginning of the section "Evening in Paris" young Rocío wanders the aisles of Woolworth's searching for the perfect Christmas gift for her mother and seeing reflected about her confused images of potential selves. This theme is matched by an awareness of the danger and difficulty of self-definition, the fear of what she will find and the temptation to hide from painful discoveries. Young Rocío is haunted by the images of aging, decay, and dying that she sees in the women around her, knowing that this will be her fate too: "I never spoke of growing old, or seeing others grow older with any sense of peace. It was a subject that was taboo, a topic like Death" (*Menu Girls,* 64). The personal authenticity Rocío seeks is difficult to obtain, based on a complex balance of freedom within limits. This dynamic, described by her mother, appeals to Rocío in her search for a way of living as herself and yet part of the *familia* and la raza. Her mother describes to Rocío the ethic of *compadrazgo* (cofather): "having to do with the spiritual well-being and development of one of God's creatures." This is a system of mutual obligation, of support and love that are not identical with the immediate family relation. Her mother explains: "The warmth of a family is something you can't deny, but compadrazgo is different, Rocío. It allows the best of a family's qualities to shine through, yet there's a certain honest detachment. To be a *compadre* is to be unrelated yet related, and yet willing to allow the relationless relation absolute freedom within limits" (168). It is this relationless relation, this critical distance from all that is familiar, that allows Rocío to pursue her quest for self-definition, and to find it in her writing. Her role as a writer depends upon the distance that permits her to write with honest detachment and the love born of familiarity about the family and community that shaped her.

The difficulty and necessity of writing are explored in the short poem "Silver Ingots of Desire." In this poem the image of a pillow is used to convey the comfort and relief that only literature can bring; when those valuable but burdensome silver ingots of desire weigh the poet down, she can only call, "Bring me a pillow / a story / upon which to lay my head."[15] The writing is addressed to all those who do not know about the existence and experience of the marginal people, the forgotten, who comprise Chávez's literary subject. This is the theme of the love poem "Tears," but here the forgotten person remembered through writing is the poet's own younger self. In this love poem the poet confesses her need of the absent lover, a need to share, to tell, to communicate honestly and in full: "I tell you stories no living man has heard, / stories of locked-in sighs, / wandering stories of other lives, / myself as a young girl."[16] The effect of these stories will be an understanding of her now as she was then—a history that will make her larger, more sophisticated, and more simple. In *Novena Narrativas* the narrator, Isabel, describes finding a letter from her dead mother and the sensation she experienced that her mother was alive and addressing her: "Isabel, Isabel, what are your priorities? Mija, you need some lipstick, you're so pale, are you wearing a bra? It was as though she was right here next to me telling me how much she loved me, how proud of me she was, and to keep on working" (*Novena Narrativas,* 88). *Face of an Angel* is prefaced by a series of questions:

> *My grandmother's voice was rarely heard, it was a whis-per, a moan. Who heard?*
>   *My mother's voice cried out in rage and pain. Who heard?*
>   *My voice is strong. It is breath. New Life. Song. Who hears?* (Chávez's italic)

Writing can bring life to the past, to forgotten people and experiences, but authentic, effective communication is difficult to achieve. When Rocío recalls the trauma of the willow tree's death in *The Last of the Menu Girls,* she remembers her painful solitary struggle to articulate her feelings: "To carry pain around as a child does, in that particular place, that worldless, grey cor-ridor, and to be unable to find the syllables with which to vent one's sorrow, one's horror . . . surely this is insufferable anguish, the most insufferable" (*Menu Girls,* 49). The necessity to find words, to end this anguish by articulating it, is complicated by the difficulty of discovering an appropriate vocabulary and form of expression. Forms and the filling in of forms is Rocío's job at the hospital. She offers a bureaucratic communication channel that limits the possibilities of communication but nonetheless makes communication possible. The dietician Mr. Smith tells her proudly that some patients write on their menu cards compliments about the food, but when she returns to the hospital as a patient no one takes her menu order; the food she eats is nameless, and her experience as a patient is largely anonymous.

In Denise Chávez's work, writing represents both freedom and responsibility: "writing is defined as the act of meaningful communication from a particular, isolated point of view, as transgression of the borders of the individual self, as a service to oneself and the community, and as a territory of freedom checked by responsibility."[17] In *The Last of the Menu Girls* Rocío finds in writing an answer to her need both to balance affirmation of herself within her racial and gender relations and also to break free of stereotypes that oppress and paralyze by limiting her opportunities. The ethic of *compadrazgo* and *comadrazgo* (comother), mentioned above, extends family relations out from the immediate family unit to encompass the community. This principle of mutual responsibility and caring is expressed in a variety of ways: Rocío's mother explains that she is bound to help her compadre in any way she can; as the *madrina* (godmother) to his child she has a spiritual obligation to guide and protect that child's soul, to feed and shelter her should she find herself in trouble, to take the place of her parents if they should die. The basis of compadrazgo as she explains it to Rocío is loving acceptance of the other, her compadre: "a union truer than family, higher than marriage, nearest of all relationships to the balanced, supportive, benevolent universal godhead" (*Menu Girls,* 169). This explanation prefaces the story of Regino the handyman, in the section "Compadre" and Nieves's decision to employ Regino to build her fountain, despite his slow and shoddy work. Rocío finds in this explanation not only the answer to her mother's behavior but also an explanation for her own service to the community. Through her writing, by writing the stories that become *The Last of the Menu Girls,* Rocío is able to express her own loving acceptance of the people who are her extended family and of her own place together with them.

As has already been noted, Chávez's language is designed primarily to capture the authentic voices of her characters: "I really write according to what I hear—sometimes English, sometimes Spanish, sometimes both. As a writer, I have tried to capture as clearly as I am able *voices,* intonation, inflection, mood, timbre, pitch" ("Heat and Rain," 31). This point is repeated by Rudolfo Anaya in his introduction to *The Last of the Menu Girls,* where he notes that "her eye for detail is sharp; the interior monologues of her characters are revealing; and Denise's long training as a dramatist serves her well in creating intriguing plot and dialogue."[18] The story "Grand Slam" takes the form of a single dramatic monologue spoken by Omega Harkins as she talks on the telephone to her friend Mozetta. Mozetta's part in the conversation is not reported, and we know only those responses that Omega repeats or that we can deduce from answers Omega gives to questions we do not hear. The structure of the conversation rambles, as Omega digresses into subjects she suddenly recalls or into explanations and judgments of characters she mentions.

In combination with this emphasis on the realistic re-creation of voice, Chávez uses complex patterns of imagery to express the hidden emotional, psychological, cultural, and spiritual meanings of the experience represented by mundane voices. For example, in *Face of an Angel* the image of breasts recurs in conversations and reported stories throughout the narrative to express themes of feminine sexuality, women's bodily experience, social and cultural attitudes toward femininity, individual self-image and self-esteem, maternal nurturance and care, and so on. The discontinuous narrative technique of *The Last of the Menu Girls* requires that the distinct sections be unified through the loose semantic linkage of image patterns. A set of images recurs throughout the stories, and indeed throughout all of Chávez's writing, lending coherence in terms of the developing meaning of the text in the absence of a single continuous plot. For instance, the themes of death, dying, and disease are associated with the seasons. For example, early in the text Rocío reflects upon her experience of working at the hospital: "I had made that awesome leap into myself that steamy summer of illness and dread—confronting at every turn, the flesh, its lingering cries" (*Menu Girls,* 36). Much later, when she is ill, depressed, cold in the northern winter, and surrounded by images of death and decay, she writes in her journal a poem which recalls "Texas in April" as an image of impalement, "Sorrowed death trance of fear" (122).

Darkness is associated with the unknown, with mystery and the excitement of discovery: young Rocío's dreams and fantasies she describes as being "stuffed in dark corners" (*Menu Girls,* 87) like her mother's old photographs hidden in her closet. Rocío describes Regino as the man who periodically emerges "from the darkness" to fix the things that Rocío's father is never there to fix. This "darkness" is the darkness of a mysterious masculinity, a man's space, which Rocío likens to a hardware store, "a place dark and full of mysteries" (149). The conjunction of darkness with mystery and discovery is found in Chávez's poem "The Study," in which the darkness and deep redness of the room become the terms of comparison that make the room comparable to the poet's own creative mind: "the hue of that room / encarmined stillness / dusty red my dear / and oh so dark, / your pages."[19] It is only in the final line of the poem that the dark mystery of the room, the dusty books it contains, and the still redness of the interior are revealed as the symbolism of the poetic consciousness, "your pages." Throughout *The Last of the Menu Girls* the image of the house sustains a distinction between inside and outside, the private domestic world versus the public world. The comfort represented by the domestic space is symbolized by the closet, in the section of that name, "the heart and spirit of the house" (*Menu Girls,* 91). The outside world is symbolized by baking heat and staring eyes; Rocío "felt the heat, saw the faraway street leading where? To town. . . . I could see someone outside, passing our house. . . . Someone in a crowded car passed slowly down the street" (147). The masculine gaze is located in the street, outside this "house of women," as Rocío calls it; and this masculine look traps her, standing there in the heat in a moment of paralyzing self-consciousness.

Rain and heat are images closely associated with the Southwest in Denise Chávez's writing. She titled her *testimonio* "Heat and Rain" and describes her first recollection as "the burningly beautiful intensity of my dry, impenetrable land. . . . The heat, then the rain, and the water were my first friends" ("Heat and Rain," 27). Rain and heat are linked with the representation of strong emotions in the poem "Door," in which the colors of the scene are evocative of Chávez's New Mexico landscapes. The setting of the poem is set by the poet's directions: "evening: the brilliancy of white house against navy sky / afterimaged thunder lay still // A woman stands / her lust / treelike / with spaces."[20] The rainstorm that threatens represents the woman's emotional turmoil; the "impending rain" expresses her uncertainty, and the lightning flashes express her longing. When the storm finally breaks, "She rages across the sky / her thunder / a thing diffused / a hidden bruise / beloved one, your touch" (78). In contrast, in the poem "Chekhov Green Love" gentle rain represents a kind of love that soothes powerful emotions, a spiritual balm that "eases the raging" (1.12), and like music it works to achieve the "fine tuning / of our spirits in the rain" (2.18–19).[21]

Specific feminine figures are used as images to emphasize the theme of self-discovery or self-definition, which was discussed above. In the story "The Last of the Menu Girls," the first story of the discontinuous narrative, Florence Nightingale is linked with Rocío—"Her look encompassed all the great unspeakable sufferings of every war" (*Menu Girls,* 37). It is this knowledge of suffering that Rocío will acquire in the course of the narrative. Her growing maturity is represented as a deepening knowledge of the wars that are fought for reasons of race and gender and class but are waged invisibly. In *Face of an Angel* the narrator Soveida observes that in her family frightening images of women such as the skeleton La Sebastiana or La Llorona—the dispossessed woman, the woman who has drowned her children and who haunts rivers as she searches endlessly for them—were not used to intimidate the children of her family into good behavior: "Our ghosts were real. There was no need for the wailing Llorona or the demented Coco. Our ghosts haunted us in a way no fantastic demons ever could" (*Face of an Angel,* 52). The sexual abuse her cousin Mara suffered at the hands of Soveida's father, the beatings her grandmother Lupita endured from her husband, her Tío Todosio's pederasty—these were the silent ghostly presences haunting her childhood. As Mara confides to her, "Dolores and Mamá Lupita were my bogeywomen, Soveida" (52).

La Llorona is the unseen and silent presence in the poem "This River's Praying Place." The woman who prays by this river "is thread of me: / cactus crossed storm of wandering discontent."[22] The image of the silent woman, unable to give voice to the words she has to say, governs the poem. She describes herself stretched out to rest on the river bed, "my head on these future words." But she is permitted no rest: "Those black ones prodded me still. / I jumped up, flowing with words, / flung to me from the sideways river / of that other place." The poetic voice and the figure of the unnamed "her" become confused as the poem reaches its close, as if the poet is now possessed by La Llorona, "tangled in her hair / exultant now—/ downcast later with her silent words" (67). The words flung from the "other" river of "that other place" are the words of suffering and longing that La Llorona would articulate if only she had access to voice.

The acquisition and articulation of voice is an important theme in Denise Chávez's work, but the issue of voice also influences the style in which she writes. The narrative style of both *Face of an Angel* and *The Last of the Menu Girls* is based upon the experience of the first-person narrator who is telling her own story in her own words. Chávez's style is also heavy with dialogue that is not reported by the narrator but is included directly so that, again, the characters can speak in their own voices, rather than allow the narrator to "speak for them." This authenticity is significant; the narrative respects the diversity of voices represented by the characters of the southwestern border country and refuses to alter them in any way. In *The Last of the Menu Girls* Rocío remains the primary narrator and governing consciousness of the narrative, but she allows the characters to express themselves in their own words, just as Chávez allows Rocío to tell her own story in her own words. For this reason Spanish words and phrases are blended with English. In *Face of an Angel* the narrator Soveida explains why it is important to have access to the Spanish language: "Spanish, my father's little-used language, he having grown up at a time when children were punished for speaking Spanish on the playground. Spanish, my mother Dolores's language of intimacy and need. Spanish, Doña Trancha's shrill, invective language of complaint and horror without ceasing" (*Face of an Angel,* 215). The use of language conveys a silent freight of personal, cultural, and family history.

The Last of the Menu Girls uses linguistic code-switching between Spanish and English variably across the different sections that comprise the narrative. The mixing of English and Spanish is especially significant in the final section, "Compadre," which concerns Rocío's discovery of her artistic role within the community of her family and friends. But the preceding section, "Space Is a Solid," uses English exclusively. It is in this section that the narrative "crosses over," in Renato Rosaldo's phrase, by using a second and then a third Anglo narrator.[23] In this section Rocío's narration and her voice break up as the narrative deals with the circumstances of her emotional and cultural alienation. As Rocío descends further into illness, anxiety, and finally a nervous breakdown, the burden of the narration switches back and forth from Rocío to her student Kari Lee, then to Kari Lee's mother, Nita Wembley, then to Rocío's boyfriend Louden. In this way the fracturing of Rocío's sense of self and the increasingly fragile hold she has on her emotions, her body, and her mind are represented in a partial and fragmentary style of narration that lacks a unitary point of view. We only ever obtain subjective and partial views of the trauma Rocío undergoes in this section of the narrative.

This idea of fragmentation as a narrative strategy informs the style of the entire text of *The Last of the Menu Girls.* Annie Eysturoy, in her study of the contemporary Chicana novel, describes the necessarily subversive nature of the literary genre to which this text belongs, the female bildungsroman, which seeks to represent the process of feminine maturity, self-discovery, and self-definition:

When the female "I" is the central consciousness of a *Bildungsroman,* the rendering of the female *Bildungs* process is based on a female experiential perspective: the oppositional nature of the interaction between the female self and socio-cultural values and gender role expectations is not presented by an external and distanced omniscient narrator, but based on and interpreted by the complex subjectivity of the female *Bildungsheld.* By assuming the role of the narrator/protagonist, the female "I" becomes the conscious subject of her own *Bildungs* story who, through the act of narrating, actively participates in the process of her own self-formation. When the female "I" takes on narrative authority, she gains authority over her own life and her own story, an act which in and of itself subverts patriarchal confinement of the female self.[24]

This subversion is emphasized by the disruption of the continuous first-person narrative that is the preferred form of the male bildungsroman for the representation of the coherent development of a mature, masculine subjectivity. Denise Chávez, like Sandra Cisneros, uses a discontinuous form in order to represent the fractured perception of subjectivity by the maturing Chicana consciousness. These discontinuous narratives subvert both the content and the literary form of the inherited patriarchal literary genre of the bildungsroman. Discontinuity is a powerful narrative device allowing Chávez to shift the focus of some of the sections, as in "Space Is a Solid" and also in "Compadre," where both the viewpoint and the narration change. As Marcienne Rocard notes, this is a way for Denise Chávez to give voice to a "diversity of human experience, [representing] the importance of community and the web of interindividual relationships extending beyond the family unit."[25] So discontinuity becomes a technique that serves the interests of Chávez's literary compadrazgo, making space for all the voices of her extended familia.

The narrative style of *Face of an Angel* is more homogenous, consisting as it does for the most part of Soveida Dosamantes's first-person narration. There are, however, some significant breaks, as in chapter 5 where both her mother and her father tell the story of their failed marriage in two narratives placed side by side on the page. Chapter 32 is narrated by a third-person omniscient narrator who tells the story of Albert Chanowski, who has the distinction of being the only customer of El Farol ever to harass Soveida. This character represents the conjunction of several kinds of prejudice: racial, sexual, class; he also represents the snobbish superiority of a cultured person from the East living in the Southwest. In these respects he is paradigmatic, and for this reason we do not read Soveida's subjective representation of him but the objective assessment of an unnamed, external narrative point of view. Soveida's narration also breaks in the chapters that record the assignments she completes for her course in Chicano culture: her oral history of Oralia's life in chapter 41 and her essay, "Mothers, Teach Your Sons," in chapter 42. Each of these chapters also records the comments of her teacher upon her work; in each case she is criticized for the emotive nature of her language and the lack of scholarly rigor of her presentation. These chapters, then, provide a compelling motivation for the writing of the novel itself, which represents those worlds of experience—of Soveida, her family, and those she loves, such as Oralia, who are otherwise excluded from the written record. Interspersed throughout the novel are the chapters of Soveida's own book, "The Book of Service," addressed to all aspiring waitresses. These chapters, which are numbered independently of the novel's chapter numbering, serve a number of functions. They offer a commentary on Soveida's own developing philosophy of service and her maturing sense of personal integrity; they reflect on the significance of incidents occurring at that point in the main narrative plot; they deepen our understanding of the motivations of characters other than

Soveida; and sometimes they reflect in a humorous self-reflexive style upon the main narrative.

As discussed above, the disconnected or discontinuous narrative form, like that of Cisneros's *The House on Mango Street,* with which *The Last of the Menu Girls* has been frequently compared, effectively represents the pressures of race and gender and the sense of subjective fragmentation that results. Individual narrative units and the experiences they represent are autonomous, but the narrative derives its continuity or coherence of meaning through the unity of setting, character, time, and genre (the Kunstlerroman), all of which represent the development of the child into the writer. Chávez uses temporal discontinuity to structure the narrative so that we see the early influences that shape Rocío's artistic sensibility and sense of self: the central sections take us back in time and then leap forward to the more mature Rocío who writes the book we have been reading.

The literary technique of Chávez's writing is sophisticated, innovative, and highly skilled; perhaps above all, this technical ability is largely invisible, disappearing behind the thematic richness it serves. Technique serves the interests of representation, and in Chávez's work the representation of the Chicano/a culture of the Southwest, and of New Mexico in particular, is paramount. Sandra Cisneros has said of the author of *Face of an Angel:* "Denise Chávez is a *chismosa* par excellence—a gossip, a giver away of secrets, a teller of tales our Mamma told us not to tell. That's why these stories are delicious; so wacky, tender, hilarious, and *terrible,* they must be true. Chávez serves us the stories of those condemned to serve, the workers our ancestors, those citizens who have served others yet too seldom people the center of the page."[26] In her writing Chávez gives voice and literary presence to these people whose absence from the pages of American literature Cisneros regrets, and she re-creates in literary form the voices in which they must speak if we are genuinely to hear them.

CHAPTER SIX

Alma Luz Villanueva

Anger, rage, and sadness are the negative tones of Alma Villanueva's work as she explores themes of violence, poverty, sexual abuse, racism, imperialism, and militarism in her poetry and her prose. Cutting right across this negative aspect, however, is a profound commitment to the values of spirituality and feminine powers of nurturance and survival. Her autobiographical poem *Mother, May I?* represents this assessment of a woman's life as rich with spiritual potential despite the realities of suffering and deprivation. The philosophy of eco-feminism informs her work in a variety of ways, from themes to imagery and style. Elizabeth Ordóñez writes: "Villanueva's poetry is dynamic, vital, and personal, but her 'I' is almost always a 'we' as she speaks of women's common experience, and contributes significantly to the enrichment of a common female literary culture, as well as to the creation of a renewed and transformed society."[1]

Alma Luz Villanueva was born on 4 October 1944 in Lompoc, California, and raised in the Mission District of San Francisco in a family of mixed Yacqui, Spanish, and German ancestry. In the poem "Mestiza" from *Desire* (1998) she writes: "I'm a Mestiza, a mixed-blood: / Yacqui, Spanish, German, English— / my people from the four corners / of the Earth."[2] She was raised in this neighborhood by her Mexican grandmother until the age of eleven. The relationship between grandmothers and their granddaughters, and the absence of loving mothers and fathers, is a recurring theme in Villanueva's writing. Many of the

ALMA LUZ VILLANUEVA

details of her life enter into the texture of Villanueva's writing; frequently her poems are dedicated to members of her family— most often her daughter, sons, and grandmother—and key situations and events, such as the sexual assault she suffered as a child, recur throughout her work. She has a master of fine arts degree from Vermont College of Norwich University and has taught fiction and poetry at various colleges and universities, including Cabrillo College in Aptos, California, and most recently the University of California at Santa Cruz, the University of California at Davis, and the Naropa Institute. She has served on the National Endowment for the Arts fiction panel. Her volume *Poems* won the University of California at Irvine's Third Chicano Literary Prize in 1977, her novel *The Ultraviolet Sky* (1988) won the American Book Award of the Before Columbus Foundation, and her poetry collection *Planet* (1993) was awarded the 1994 Latino Literature Prize. Her collections of poetry include: *Bloodroot* (1977); *Mother, May I?* (1978); *La Chingada* (1985); *Life Span* (1985); *Planet,* a volume which includes the reprint of *Mother, May I?;* and *Desire* (1998). Her second novel, *Naked Ladies* (1994), won the PEN Oakland Josephine Miles Award and was followed by a collection of short fiction, *La Llorona and Other Stories* (1994). Alma Villanueva's work, especially her poetry, has been widely anthologized.

Villanueva's political and philosophical views are closely allied to her views of the role of the feminist writer in contemporary society. She is a declared feminist and eco-feminist, concerned to explore in her work both the impact of racism, sexism, and masculine violence upon women and the planet, and also strategies with which to counter these destructive energies through feminine strength and spirituality. The role of the feminist writer, then, is to expose the brutal reality of issues such as poverty, sexual abuse, domestic violence, militarism, and racism. In Villanueva's writing these harsh subjects are pursued within the context of her poetic quest for a universal female community. In the poem "a poet's job" she writes that a poet must see "the contours of the / world" and with this vision make "a myth to share / for others to see."[3] But this myth and this world are not abstract and transcendent; instead they are grounded in our present experience, "right here." As has been discussed in preceding chapters, Chicana writers have developed a tradition of writing that focuses on the transformation of deprivation, pain, and suffering. The Kunstlerroman form used by Cisneros and Chávez, for example, represents this transformation through the symbolic maturity of the young Chicana into the adult writer. With the transformation of pain through the transfigurative power of the literary imagination comes the rebirth of the writer into a voice that is able to express defiance of patriarchal gender roles and inherited modes of thinking, feeling, and living. Writing strengthens and supports personal identity by transforming the wounds inflicted by poverty, racism, and sexism into the power to speak and act.

Villanueva makes of her early childhood suffering, her abandonment by her parents, her experience of sexual violence, and her poverty subjects for literature, and she speaks of these in a voice that is not the adopted voice of male literary decorum but rather a voice grounded in her experience as a woman and a Chicana. This discovery of the power of self-expression is the unifying theme of Villanueva's acclaimed poem sequence *Mother, May I?,* her novel *The Ultraviolet Sky,* and poems such as "(Her) Desire," in which she describes dreaming of an old woman clothed in all creation and in that symbolism the poet discovering "Words, my desire. Words, my death" (*Desire,* 6), and "it is my nature," in which she describes her compulsion, as a woman and a poet, to engage always in rebirth and self-creation (*Bloodroot,* 33). In *Mother, May I?* concrete experience becomes a kind of personalized myth through the transformation of a woman's cyclic changes and emergence into wholeness and hope. Marta Sánchez calls this poem sequence a "sustained narrative sequence in lyric form."[4] *Mother, May I?* is a sequence of twenty-nine poems, divided into three parts, but some of the poems are given titles that mark significant moments in the life the poet is chronicling—which is her own. "The Dead" introduces the adults around a young child who have lost their capacity for joy; "Playing" recalls her mother and "Dreaming" her sense of separation between her spirit and bodily self. The repetition of the title in the second poem called "Dreaming" ironically ushers in a brutal period in the child's life: first, she is the victim of a vicious sexual assault; next her mother gives her up for fostering (she "gives me away // to strangers"); and then her grandmother is taken away to a nursing home ("they give her away / to strangers // too") where she dies.[5]

The poems in part 2 continue the theme of suffering, represented by the growing child's eating disorder, the pervasive sense of threat in the project where she lives, her pregnancy and rejection by the child's father, and the violence of her marriage. The first named poem in this section is "Birthing," which is placed after the description of her children's births; the poem refers to a spiritual or metaphoric birth of the self, which has yet to happen. Instead the poet describes the loss of her voice: "my mouth locked tight. / and a loneliness grew // that I couldn't name" (*Planet,* 109). The sense of having lost herself is dissipated only by the discovery of her grandmother's unmarked grave; in the tears she is finally able to shed, in this grief, the beginnings of self-creation emerge. She is able to leave the husband who is negating her and listen to a tiny voice, "and her mouth opened slightly / and a word spilled out. The word // was 'I'" (112). The poem named "Inside" gives voice to this nascent sense of identity; it tells her "I am here. Birthing / (yourself) is / no easy task" (112). The poems of part 3 begin with the poet's discovery of her place in the world and her complete feminine power in "Her Myth (of creation)" and move on to explore the relationship between generations of women—her mother, grandmother, and daughter—in "Life Cycle (up to 32)," The Proof (about 33)," "The Thread (the amputation)," "Mother, May I?," and the "Epilogue," which explains the importance of her discovery of her woman's poetic voice.

The interconnectedness of all life on the planet, which has been knocked out of balance by the technological, rational, and scientific impact of a dominant and violent imperialistic masculinity, is Alma Villanueva's most fundamental subject. The poem "The Planet Earth Speaks" expresses the love that drives all natural processes; here Villanueva represents the love of the planet for all the life it supports by using the image of gravity: "I spin through time / and darkness: I glue // you to me with love" (*Planet,* 13). Each section of the poem except the last ends with the word "*Unconditionally*" (Villanueva's italic). The first section concerns the love expressed by and required by the planet: "I made you to / love me whole, small / echo of my womb: / to love me as I // love you. / *Unconditionally.*" The next section catalogs the richness of the natural world and the variety of life the planet supports and makes available for human use, "*Unconditionally.*" The third section laments the lack of love, the absence of respect, the hate and destruction, and "the loneliness / of those who are / born and die / without loving. / *Unconditionally.*" Finally, the poet shifts away from a human perspective to articulate the planetary view that sees change but not death and views Earth itself as mere dust caught in a celestial spiral.

The integration of the human, natural, and elemental is represented in the poem "Encounter" where the poet's encounter with the one perfectly shaped tree is followed by the encounter with an eagle, which with the poet and her two companions make four living beings in correspondence with the four elements of nature in a dramatization of the realization they share: "realizing Libra (the / balancer) was in our // births. Birth, life, / death, and rebirth" (*Planet,* 50). The poems in the sequence "Dear World," written throughout 1994 and concluding with poems sent to President Clinton in 1996, address the destruction of this global balance by the operations of the military-industrial complex. Many of the poems address the horror of the war in Bosnia and focus on the mothers' loss of their children, the violent killing of children that stains the purity of the natural world, like the blood-stained snow of the slope where children played before the bombs exploded in the poem of 26 January 1994 ("Dear World, 26 January 1994," *Desire,* 119). Villanueva relates this physical killing to the destruction of the spirit, what she calls "the Spirit of the World," that would inspire individuals to fight for their lives and for life itself.

This destruction is found not only in war zones like Bosnia and Africa but also in the inner cities of the United States, in "Mexico, Central America, Brazil, / Korea, Thailand, Tibet, Israel," wherever there is a border over which to fight ("Dear World, 14 May 1994," *Desire,* 125). The poem concludes with the ironic observation that the only border that counts is the one that separates the earth from the sea, the "Mother of us all, / the only true borders, / Her Womb, the land masses / One, once" (126). The second of two poems sent to President Clinton also addresses the domestic situation of the United States. The first expresses her reaction to a photograph of the president inspecting troops preparing to leave for Bosnia, and noting the tears in his eyes and her own revulsion at the reports of death, rape, and torture, the poem concludes: "I am proud that my / president wants to weep" ("Dear World," "Winter Sun, December 3, 1995," *Desire,* 137). In the later poem Villanueva asks the president to empathize with, to imagine, that he is a small boy raised by a single mother on welfare, living in a project, always hungry, always surrounded by violence and death, never having enough of anything. She admits her own experience of living on welfare with her three children, hating it and needing it but refusing to allow herself to become dependent upon it: "Me, I'm too angry / to be the sacrificial lamb at the altar // of our national abundance; those bleeding / lambs make our (fed) lives possible; / we don't even bother to honor their still / beating hearts to the rising sun. Imagine" (140). Villanueva invokes here the image of ancient ritual sacrifice, which honored and valued the sacrifice made by those who, in her America, make their sacrifice unheard, unseen, and unvalued.

The poems collected in the volume *Bloodroot* seek to counter these destructive energies with a vision of the feminine voice unified with the elements of nature to create a primal, mythical feminine consciousness of the world. The empathy between woman and nature is represented by the discovery of a natural counterpart to every stage of a woman's life in poems such as "I wait" (*Bloodroot,* 6). The poet identifies with nature, especially the process of growing and the connection with the earth, in this poem and others such as "i dreamt" (29). The experience of birth, described in the poem "watching the natural slope" (18), is both the defiance of death ("I see / death grin between my legs") and a dissociation from the communion with nature that the female poet enjoys. At the moment of giving birth she feels that she contains multitudes. All of creation is contained within her until the moment of individuation as the child emerges and begins to breathe independently: "your breathing / startles me." Nature is depicted as in harmony with a feminine universe in the poems "bloodroot" (1), "ZINZ" (2), and "you must forgive" (26).

The feminist poet celebrates the creative power of women because men willfully forget, fear, and deny this feminine power. In "(wo)man" she writes, "I celebrate the absence of mystery of / the 'eternal mystery of woman': / we are" (*Bloodroot,* 4). The power of femininity to create and re-create is clear to see by those who are able to see. Nature provides examples of living things creating or becoming themselves, and these are depicted in poems such as "to a friend with deer/eyes" (*Bloodroot,* 9) and "I Remember When You Held the World in Your Pocket, or, the Healer . . . ," in which crystals change, grow, "and what they must become is whole" (*Planet,* 39). Images such as these contrast sharply with the artificial, plastic re-creation of nature in the poem "Friction" where a "hard, black, plastic chair, // under a leafy tree unvisited / by birds, wind, sun and / rain" offers the poet the only shelter she can find in a crowded airport (*Planet,* 56). In the novel *The Ultraviolet Sky* Rosa must move from the city into the wilderness of the mountains in order to discover her own feminine and artistic powers there, in communion with the spirits of the land.

In Villanueva's work there develops, then, a conflict between images of feminine nature and lifeless masculine imitations of nature. In this connection she represents the violent imposition of masculine will on nature; this is captured in the controlling image of "View from Richmond Bridge" (*Bloodroot,* 9): in a littered city lot a dead tree trunk has been carved with the face of a man. The link between masculine domination and male sexuality is the subject of the poem "I sing to three sons." In the section addressed to "3rd Son" she exclaims, "you fly into the world / with a hard-on, red & furious . . . / you eclipse yourself in your / appetite for life" (*Bloodroot,* 40). The will to dominate, to possess, is identified with masculine sexuality in "to my brothers," in which she asks, "why must men / always yearn to create new universes / (having worn the last one / to a frazzle) / and then proceed to make it in his image" (*Bloodroot,* 15). This poem, which responds to Gregory Corso's imperative "Be a Star-

Screwer!," is Alma Villanueva's response to the aggressive masculinity and misogyny of Beat poetry.

The misogynistic patriarchal conception of feminine subjectivity is defined in a Chicana context by the heroine of *The Ultraviolet Sky.* Rosa explains to her husband about the character she
calls "Mexican Man": "He's the man I never wanted to marry.
He's the man I've seen women make the endless piles of tortillas
for, as he grows fat and stupid while his brain shrinks to fit his
narrow mind that dictates boys are better than girls, boys become
men, girls become wives, men have moments of freedom,
release, women count tortillas and the children. Men have
affairs, women become whores. Puta. La Puta."[6] Masculine violence, like the femininity that is its target, is seen only by those
who have the understanding to perceive it. The denial of violent
masculinity by those around her is the subject of the poem "I saw
a unicorn the other day" (*Bloodroot,* 7), in which this mythical
creature impales a young girl upon its hard metallic horn of silver. In the poem "The Lady of Longing" she asks, "Must / the
only embrace // between men be / the attitudes of war, death?"
(*Planet,* 23).

The nurturing of self-love or self-esteem is empowering for
women, but feminine self-loathing serves the interests of patriarchy. This is the scene set in the opening of Villanueva's novel
Naked Ladies. Alta expresses the self-loathing, the desire to kill
herself as the ultimate expression of her own sense of worthless-
ness, that is her response to her husband's violent machismo.[7]
Her case is not isolated; all the women Alta knows have been
victimized by male violence: her mother who is viciously beaten

by Alta's stepfather; her friend Jackie who finally leaves the husband who habitually beats her; the Anglo woman named Katie whom she rescues from a mugger and who is constantly humiliated by her husband; the sister of her friend Steve who was raped as a child.

The contempt with which Alta's husband Hugh regards her is not motivated by misogyny alone, though Alta makes her first move toward understanding him when she realizes, "Hugh hates my womb. . . . And it isn't because I'm Mexican; it isn't even because I'm me. It's because I'm a *woman*" (*Naked Ladies,* 117, Villanueva's italic). Alta's black friend Steve tells her, "'He's a white man, Alta. The man hates his *own* guts, man. When're you ever goin' to *understand that*?'" (94, Villanueva's italic). Hugh is hostile and contemptuous of all women, but his aggression is fueled by the racism his parents taught him, to despise all Mexicans, including Alta, as "spics," and also by the homophobia and his own repressed homosexuality that causes him to experience ambivalent sexual feelings toward Alta. The first major conflict between them that is reported in the narrative is sparked by Hugh's demand for anal intercourse, which Alta refuses. She does not perceive that Hugh's arousal is linked to the idea of sodomy, and our attention is drawn to this link only later by the narrator's observation that Hugh is aroused by the idea of "making it" with his workmate Tony and the passing reference to Hugh's lover.

As the narrative reveals more about the homosexuality that Hugh is unwilling to acknowledge, this disclosure is set within the context of Hugh's relationships with his parents. His rage against Alta's growing assertiveness and independence fuses with his hatred of his mother: "for a moment he was a boy of five tied up in a chair, screaming his lungs out to a shut kitchen door" *(Naked Ladies,* 74–75). To assuage this anger Hugh decides to visit his lover Bill, but their sexual relation is confused in Hugh's behavior and his words as a paternal relationship: "As Hugh came, spurting in wide, wild circles, splattering the walls, the floor, and Bill with his hot, stinging life, he cried, 'Daddy, Daddy! I love you, Daddy'" (77–78). And as Bill prepares to penetrate him, he whispers, "Daddy needs to love you too. Daddy needs to love you" (78).

The second part of the novel focuses on the issue of sexual abuse, beginning with Jade's confession to Alta first of her rape by her father when she was an adolescent and then her more recent abduction and rape by two men. The abortion she must undergo some weeks after the attack is represented as a second, mechanical violation or rape. Alta has to place Jade's disclosure within the context of her work as a counselor and the abused children with whom she works. Even the apparently innocent green eyes of Alta's black lover Michael are explained as the result of an event in which "some white guy over a hundred year ago raped some scared shitless, young black girl," as he explains (225). The narrative of *Naked Ladies* culminates in the confrontation of Jade, Michael, and Alta with the men who raped Jade: Ray and Jim. It is the exchange between the two men as they threaten and torture Jade and Michael, under the pretext of intimidating Jade so she will drop her case against them, that reveals the true motivation of their violence and cruelty. The leader, Ray, unwittingly reveals to his accomplice the violence with which he keeps his wife compliant and his sexual abuse of his young children: "Ya jus' be breakin' ''em in for mankind, the way I see it. . . . She [his wife] knows an' she knows what's good fer 'er. Put a fear a God in 'er right away. Ahm the man, ain't I?" (265–66). But it is for the narrator to make the connection between Ray's sexual violence, his lack of mercy, and his own repressed childhood trauma: "There was no inkling of mercy, no memory of mercy. Jade's cries, horrible to hear, were like his own when he was two, three, four, five, but he had no memory, none at all, of his father beating him, raping him. It had stopped when he was five when his father left" (268). This, then, offers an explanation for his preference for raping in gangs: it makes him feel close to his buddies, close to his father in the shared sexual violence of these moments, just as Hugh cries out for his father at the moment of sexual climax.

Masculine violence is twinned with the will to dominate throughout the narrative. For example, Katie's husband Doug holds her face until she cries or he hits her, and Hugh hits Alta and also uses sexual aggression bordering on rape in the attempt to make her submissive, making her wonder, "How many times can I back down and just let him fuck me to get it over with" (*Naked Ladies,* 44). She advises Katie to bite the hand that humiliates her, to fight back; in return, Katie persuades Alta that her fantasies of suicide are born of a similar unwillingness to fight back. At the thought of Alta camping with her friends and without men Hugh becomes enraged and "had an overwhelming urge to punch her right in the face, to knock her down, to make her bleed. *To make her*" (58, Villanueva's italic). When Alta is finally able to confide this to Jackie, her friend immediately sympathizes: "That's how they break your spirit. Makes you feel like week-old hamburger, doesn't it? The old total control bit" (91).

ALMA LUZ VILLANUEVA

In this novel the most effective male strategy to ensure feminine submission is to convince women that they are to blame for the mistreatment they suffer. When Jackie confronts Rita with the fact of her husband's infidelity it is to reassure Rita that she is not to blame for her husband's faithlessness; in Steve's account of his young sister's rape her parents blamed the girl for somehow inviting the attack; Doug blames Katie for contracting breast cancer like his mother did; Alta wonders whether she is to blame for Hugh's violent hatred of her. These individual men articulate the attitudes and prejudices of a misogynistic society, which Villanueva represents in the form of contemporary technological medicine. Rita's mastectomy and her growing sense of herself as an amazon lend her the strength finally to confront Carl about his infidelity; she refuses to remain complicit or to accept blame for his betrayal of her, and she finally reveals her father's sexual abuse of her as a child. But Carl simply accuses her of being hysterical, and this is supported by the doctor's view as he tells Carl, "Most women are weak, impressionable and, ultimately, hysterical: poor things. We men have to help . . . give her the tranquillizer" (*Naked Ladies,* 174). In *The Ultraviolet Sky* Rosa encounters the inherited misogyny of modern medicine; in the hospital where she is to give birth she is drugged and ignored, and when a doctor attempts to harness her she finally gives in to her rage and literally kicks out against this anonymous yet invasive treatment. In order to fight back, women have to break the cycle of complicity and self-hatred; in *Naked Ladies* this is Alta's fundamental insight, and she tries to explain to Michael, "in our culture, patriarchal culture, as you know, that meeting [between women is] discouraged, mainly because the feminine tends to be crippled. They cripple her and women, many women, continue to go along with the crippling. . . . A woman getting her own power breaks that agreement between women" (222). The refusal of complicity and the nurturing of feminine intimacy are twin strategies in the fight against patriarchal domination and masculine violence.

The alternative to patriarchal destruction is imagined in Villanueva's work through feminine power and wholeness, as "birthing, re-birthing / from the heart of // woman" in the poem "The Lady of Longing" (*Planet,* 23). In this poem Villanueva sees herself as one woman who could facilitate this rebirth but only through the power of her feminine sexuality, the power of her "monthly blood, my / web of words, my / healing." But this will work only if she can find the man for whom she is longing, the "gentle man" in the phrase that is repeated throughout the poem. Those longings are difficult to answer because of the long history of hostility, aggression, and misogyny that have characterized gender relations. The poet uses her line breaks artfully and wisely to explain: "I am trying, from a his / story of distrust, to / remember a gentle, // gentle man."

Villanueva's first novel, *The Ultraviolet Sky,* represents this necessary feminist struggle. The main character, Rosa, is a painter who throughout the narrative persists in trying to paint a lilac sky that resists her efforts. Until she discovers her own wholeness and fixes the dysfunctional relationships that cause her to doubt herself and her power, Rosa cannot complete her painting. As the novel opens, she is engaged in conflict with her husband who wants to possess and dominate her; her son is debating with his pregnant girlfriend whether she should have an

ALMA LUZ VILLANUEVA

abortion; her best friend refuses to see the truth about her faithless, domineering husband and forbids Rosa to speak this truth;
and most seriously of all, none of the people close to her will
respect her decision to retreat to the mountains in order to redis-
cover her own integrity. Rosa rejects the conventional answers to
her spiritual and emotional crisis offered by patriarchal culture
and tries instead to assert her own self and fulfill the terms of the
quest she knows she must pursue.

Rosa faces strain in all her relationships, but she knows that
when the conflicts are resolved, then her painting will be complete. Even at the beginning she is aware that "what she'd started
was destined to be beautiful; a black, lace shawl suspended in a
lilac sky with deep, purple orchids blooming in a circle, magi-
cally, without stems" (*The Ultraviolet Sky,* 23). But she cannot
satisfy herself that the color of the sky is correct; the painting
refuses to be right, to be complete. As she works on the other elements, the shawl and then the orchids, she feels the painting
speaking to her. What it demands is that she leave it for a while
and "simply let it exist" (64). During the time that she resists the
temptation to work on the lilac sky, Rosa undergoes a process of
spiritual education and self-growth. This begins with her tattoo,
a wild rose outlined in lilac, and proceeds through her move from
the city. The color of the sky she sees from the cabin at Lupine
Meadows helps her decide to move to the mountains, thinking
that there she could perhaps complete the painting. The discovery of her pregnancy only makes the lilac sky even more elusive;
Rosa's thoughts are focused on the polluted and violated world
into which this child will be born, and she asks aloud, "You will
be a child of the Earth, a native Person of the Earth. . . . Will we

survive this century, Luzia?" (232). Her pregnancy does give her the opportunity to sketch the face of her unborn child and to see it as continuous with the faces of her female ancestors; this experience leads Rosa to wonder about the face of Quetzalpetlatl, the goddess whose black shawl protects the earth. The birth of her daughter, the murder of her friend, and the death of her dog at her own hand after he savaged and killed another dog show the proximity of life and death, and destruction and creation finally conspire in the place where Rosa has buried her placenta and her dog to reveal the truth of the lilac sky. In that place Rosa realizes that the sky always appeared too pale or too dark because it is dynamic, not static; it is an ultraviolet sky: "That's the color of the lilac sky. That's why I can't see it. I'll never be able to *see* it. I can only witness what it does. The way it births us, the way it kills us . . . like love" (378). What Rosa finally understands is that evil has no part in the essence of the creation but rather is made by humans, by choice; this is the flaw in the sky and its beauty, and the love that inspires the goddess Quetzalpetlatl to love and protect and constantly remake this flawed creation is the vision that Rosa has sought.

The power of creation, the capacity to give birth, is a significant source of Rosa's feminine strength. In the poem "witches' blood" Villanueva uses women's natural process of menstruation to represent feminine power. She uses this natural process to retaliate against patriarchal images of women's blood as being unclean and unholy in the opinion of men and priests alike: "Power of my blood, your secret / wrapped in ancient tongues / spoken by men who claimed themselves / gods and priests and oracles— / they made elaborate rituals / secret rituals and extolled the cycles, / calling woman unclean" (*Bloodroot,* 31). In this view feminine inferiority is represented by women's natural and biological cycles, but Villanueva suggests that the menstrual cycle symbolizes woman's part in the very cycles the priests extol. Villanueva goes on to describe men as being hungry for the blood shed in war, some counterpart to the "patience of pregnancy / the joy of birth— // the renewal of blood." Women possess the power to "rebirth" themselves every month; in the poem "to my brothers" Villanueva addresses the masculine denial of this power and their responses to it: "I know men have always / turned up their noses at the smell of / The Rag and so they've / taken refuge in their brain / and think the universe runs on sperm" (15). The creative power of femininity is usurped by this patriarchal contempt for women, their bodies, their sexuality. Women who not only affirm their creative power but use it to rebirth themselves are demonized: "Call me witch / call me hag / call me sorceress / call me mad / call me woman." Ordinary women all possess this power; all women participate in the universal cycle of birth and rebirth. For those reasons the poet rejects the notion of herself as a goddess. It is her participation in the natural cycle that lends her the power she possesses, and the symbol of that participation is her "witch's blood."

The powerful woman is integrated, whole, and accepting of the feminine and the masculine aspects if her own subjectivity, like the male voice that speaks inside the poet's head in the poem "Presumption" (*Planet,* 44) and prompts her to request of men that they listen to the voice of femininity that speaks inside them. In the poem that speaks of her death, "Empty Circle," Villanueva concludes, "All I ask for in this / life is the sun" (*Desire,* 32); the sun symbolizes here the fusion of masculine and feminine, all the change and diversity and contradictions that make life a dynamic process. The preceding poem in the collection *Desire,* "Sweet Stranger," makes clear this unchanging fact of constant universal change: "nothing is familiar— / everything is newly born— / the Earth has changed from yesterday" (30).

Images of metamorphosis, transformation, birth, and rebirth recur throughout Alma Villanueva's work. In the poem "in your body" the daughter's coming into adulthood is both a second birth for the mother and also the daughter's self-birth: "you must push / yourself / alone / into the world," the poet writes (*Bloodroot,* 37). In *The Ultraviolet Sky* Rosa's quest takes her into what Geneviève Fabre calls a realm where "private memory interacts with the collective memory, history encounters myth, and . . . personal truth merges with some global truth."[8] Villanueva represents the process of transformation and rebirth through her use of myth: mythical language, mythical figures, and the mythical quest upon which characters such as Rosa embark. In the poem "to my daughter, bringer of life" Villanueva suggests that the truths that are expressed in metaphor and myth originate in the blood that mothers share with their daughters. The singing of the poet's daughter as she plays her flute creates a conjunction of music or song with myth and suggests that the poet is inspired by the inherited wisdom of her feminine ancestry:

I wonder how the most ancient
myths,   told and retold before my
grandmother's mother's mother spoke

through her mother's blood, truly speaks
my questions—

(Bloodroot, 43)

Alma Villanueva appears to share Alicia Ostriker's notion of
"revisionist mythmaking" as a strategy for appropriating the
patriarchal images of women that are perpetuated, inherited cultural myths. The feminist poet must formulate in her poetry a
feminine figure of mythical stature who represents appropriate
values and standards for a postpatriarchal culture. Villanueva
uses images from Aztec and Mexican mythology—Coatlicue, La
Virgen de Guadalupe, La Soldadera, La Abuela—to construct
this exemplary figure. In his 1980 essay "Terra Mater and the
Emergence of Myth in *Poems* by Alma Villanueva" Alejandro
Morales explains the ways in which the Earth Mother image
informs the poetic mythicization of the abuelita figure in Villanueva's *Poems*.[9] His work is taken up and developed by Elizabeth Ordóñez, who adds the crucial feminist dimension to the
interpretation of Villanueva's work.[10] While Morales analyzes
the ways in which the power of myth is attributed to the developing figure of the abuelita, he does not attend to the significance
for the ensuing generations of women of this accumulation of
feminine power. Resistance to Anglo-American masculine culture is one aspect of the legacy handed down in a matrilinear
fashion from grandmother to mother to granddaughter through
the generations. A mythical female community based upon
matrilinear inheritance is the object of Villanueva's poetic quest.
Marta Sánchez sees in this emphasis upon feminine community

and gender identification a rejection of Villanueva's Chicana identity: "She chooses a mythical community of women because she is thereby permitted to speak to alienated women everywhere, regardless of race. The consequence of her choice is the silence of her poetry on the subject of Chicana experience. In a curiously paradoxical way Villanueva shows that the search for a female identity is especially complex when considered in relation to a Chicana self-definition. She challenges readers to discover how to include a Chicana identity in a female identity."[11] It is through the strength of her feminist voice that Villanueva achieves resolution of the personal conflicts between her sense of herself as a woman and as a poet. The shared alienation of Villanueva with all women overcomes barriers of race, class, and culture. In *Mother, May I?* she expresses what Sánchez calls "conflict between a longing to reach an audience of alienated women everywhere, regardless of race, and a longing to communicate with a more particularized Chicano readership."[12] But Villanueva's expression of Chicana subjectivity is powerfully represented in her use of images derived from her mestiza inheritance, which are discussed below. The absence in her childhood of the formative influences of both her mother and her father leads necessarily to the act of self-creation. In the poem "I was a skinny tomboy kid" her adoption of a masculine persona to disguise her own feminine vulnerability is one stage in her self-creation: "transforming my reality / and creating a / legendary/self" (*Bloodroot,* 50). The image of the caterpillar becoming a butterfly captures this transformation of the self in the poem "a question of longevity" (*Bloodroot,* 65).

Villanueva's efforts at transformation are not only personal, but they are also feminist attempts to reinterpret feminine figures that have been maligned and despised in patriarchal culture. For example, the figure of the Medusa is revised in the poem "Medusa and I," in which instead of turning men to stone, the effect of Medusa is to turn a hard man into a tender man. Only a brave man can approach a woman who possesses such power, and Villanueva describes Medusa "waiting for the man brave / enough to fuck her, discovering // he could die of tenderness, this fucking / not turning him to stone, but turning / him into a loving man" (*Desire,* 48). The Earth Mother or Goddess figure is an image of profound inspiration that recurs throughout all of Villanueva's work. The Goddess in the poem "The Object" is variously identified with the crystal, with the spirit of the earth, and with the poet's own creativity and her feminine strength (*Planet,* 59). In "Splendid Moments" the poet speculates that the "Goddess, God, It" exists in and through the experience of love: "oh yes—I would like to / think we are coaxing her into / being as we become" (*Planet,* 63). This "It" is comparable with the spirit "It" of "The Mango Poems." The creative power of femininity is identified with the natural processes of creation and the Earth Mother/Goddess, and the creative imagination of the poet who affirms the power of her femininity in the act of writing.

Images of women appear in Villanueva's writing variously as mothers, grandmothers, daughters; as goddesses; as witches or *brujas.* In each case Villanueva seeks to affirm the value and power of these diverse feminine images. In the poem "witches' blood," discussed above, the image of blood is a symbol of strength, as the poet suggests in the opening line, "Power of my blood" (*Bloodroot,* 31). For her, there is strength in the history of her bloodline. Her monthly bleeding is a reminder of her power and her recognition that she too has witches' blood. In contrast to men, who must commit murder and kill in war "for blood to flow . . . naturally," the blood that women draw is the blood "once a month" that represents a woman's ability to create life. Villanueva uses the inherited image of the witch in the poem "The Last Words," which is dedicated to "Anne and Sylvia / and all those that burned before them / in Salem and other places" ("The Last Words," 117–18). Villanueva uses her mestiza inheritance in her choice of imagery by drawing on her Indian as well as Mexican and Anglo or European cultural inheritances. She represents the witch as a phoenix rising from the flames, rebirthed and re-created. One of the key figures in *The Ultraviolet Sky* is Quetzalpetlatl or Feathered Serpent Woman, who, like the phoenix, survives burning. *The Ultraviolet Sky* represents Rosa's halting attempts to paint the black lace shawl with which Quetzalpetlatl protects the world. In the course of her quest for the truth of this Goddess, Rosa learns the power of feminine love to create life and to forgive the destruction, death, and cruelty that flaw the Goddess's otherwise perfect creation. While Rosa struggles with her painting, her friend Sierra struggles against her husband's hostility to write her poems. The "Witch Poems" that Sierra sends to Rosa, subtitled "Canto de Mujer: Song of the Woman," include a poem called "Of/To/Man," which Rosa quotes. In this poem Sierra expresses the power of woman through the imagery of pregnancy and birth, but rather than use the figure of a witch she uses the image of Eve to symbolize the patriarchal representation of feminine sexuality. She begins by accusing the man of the poem's title, "You, man, are the snake in / my garden," and goes on, "Everyone since Eve & Adam's / been blame ME / for The First Fuck—and it was / ME who got knocked up! Well, / hell, I'm not sorry" *(The Ultraviolet Sky,* 170). This defiant representation of woman as a source of joy, power, and strength, who discovers these resources in her own sexuality, attempts to redress the negative patriarchal image of women that is perpetuated in canonical texts.

The mythical figure of La Llorona, like the biblical image of Eve, is reinterpreted in Villanueva's stories collected in *Weeping Woman: La Llorona and Other Stories.*[13] These fictions address the various forces of patriarchal culture that oppress women and children. La Llorona is used as an empowering figure throughout the stories, though they are often disturbing in Villanueva's stark portrayal of the many ways in which children are lost in contemporary America: through abduction and murder (in "The Burden"), rape (in "The Edge of Darkness"), incestuous abuse (in "Birth of a Shell"), poverty (in "Real Rainbows"), and abandonment (in "There Was a Time"). These children are not murdered by their mothers, though their mothers search for them emotionally and spiritually as well as literally. It is in this search that La Llorona is an empowering feminine force. The focus of the stories shifts as the volume progresses, away from the lost children and toward the mothers who ceaselessly search for them. The resources of love, caring, and sheer will to survive that sustain these women become Villanueva's subjects.

Villanueva strives to use a feminine language, especially a feminine literary language, that is not based on contrast with the masculine phallocentric tradition but is woman-centered and takes its inspiration from the female body. Writing is described as giving birth in *Mother, May I?* In *The Ultraviolet Sky* the meaning of the narrative is expressed through Rosa's paintings and Sierra's poetry. The feminine body is identified with elements of language; the body becomes language in the poem "Siren": "her body a / dictionary dying / to define life, / growth, a / yearning."[14] Language is inseparable from feminine consciousness in the poem "in your body," published in *Bloodroot,* and woman is represented as her own muse in "Of Utterances," in *Poems.* Elizabeth Ordóñez sees Villanueva's work as exemplifying the call in recent European and American feminist theory for a feminine textuality that is grounded in the materiality of the female body—by affirming the natural and physical power of women and by subverting patriarchal oppositions such as those between male and female, body and spirit, experience and its literary inscription.[15] The feminine body provides the mediating power for the synthesis of sexuality and spirituality. The language of feminine sexuality, of sexual passion, is complemented by Villanueva's vocabulary of maternal sexuality; in *Mother, May I?, The Ultraviolet Sky,* and elsewhere in her work Villanueva uses the language of the child and the language of the mother talking to her child to transgress the boundaries of patriarchal literary decorum.

Villanueva deliberately breaks with patriarchal decorum in poems such as "duck 2," which begins "go fuck a duck" (*Bloodroot,* 61). The notion of literary decorum is the subject of Villanueva's transgressive poem "I know," in which she admits, "I know / there are subjects that / 'don't lend themselves to art'" (*Bloodroot,* 44). But she goes on to write a poem about defecation, observing that were she a baby she would be cleaned and petted, but "as things / stand, I'll wipe my / own hairy ass." The closing lines, however, shift the focus away from the distinction between the innocence of a baby to the learned shame of an adult and introduce a parallel between the poet's subversive expression in poetry and her bodily evacuation, as she vows to "be careful the next time / I fart, / write a poem, / my tongue at the ready." Her tongue that she sticks out at the literary "good taste" she defies is the tongue that speaks her defiant words in poetry. In "Sassy" she wonders whether the most valuable lesson children can learn is how to fight for what they want and how to dare to love themselves. To do these dangerous and necessary things they must learn to transgress, to cross repressive boundaries and to subvert the taboos upon which society insists: "To / get there you must sass back / God and fight him for the door" (*Planet,* 27).

Literary language is creative, and Villanueva identifies the power to give birth and to re-create with the creative power of language in the poem "Resound" (*Planet,* 6). In this poem music, linked both to sound and words, banishes the darkness, causes it to die, and at the same time brings light into being, into life. Transgression is sometimes needed to expose the connection between language and creativity; I have discussed Villanueva's treatment of menstruation as a literary subject, in conscious defiance of patriarchal literary standards, and her preference for the imagery of pregnancy to represent spiritual rebirth is pronounced in her novels *The Ultraviolet Sky* and *Naked Ladies.* Women's physical sexuality offers the inspiration, vocabulary, and symbolic lexicon for Villanueva's renovation of the patriarchal literary tradition. Another important aspect of Villanueva's transgressive poetics is her use of autobiographical forms, such as the journal or confession. She admits that she is an "escandalosa": "a woman who says too / much, too loudly" (*Life Span,* 30). Marta Sánchez emphasizes the importance of the autobiographical in *Mother, May I?:* "Since autobiography necessitates a retrospective look at a person's life and an explanation of how authors arrive where they do, such an endeavor offers Villanueva the opportunity to confront some compelling questions about her personal formation that stand in the way of a desired poetic vision."[16] These include the absence of her mother and her unknown father but also her poetic debt to Sylvia Plath and Anne Sexton, who are influences behind her use of what Sánchez calls the "confession mode to disclose the private and intimate details of her life."[17]

Like that of Plath and Sexton, Villanueva's work depends heavily upon the development of an imagistic language to convey her meaning. The following will explore the role of some of these images in Villanueva's writing. The rose symbolizes the discovery of self and personal integrity in the final poem of *Mother, May I?* and the original poem from which this is excerpted, "legacies and bastard roses" (*Bloodroot,* 62). The rose is the shape of the tattoo on the poet's shoulder in "The Flagrant Mala Puta" (*Planet,* 28) and also in "Promise" (*Planet,* 32), where it is linked to the idea of "the child within" who holds out hope and optimism for the planet and for life, who believes in promises. The dead rosebush in the poem "The Great, Great Tide" represents the triumph of the destructive power of the sea (*Planet,* 36). In "A Cat Named Mozart" it is a rose that captures the poet's attention while her cat is so free of preconceptions as to be able to admire a single blade of grass (*Planet,* 68); the rose is named the Peace Rose, but the cat actually knows the experience of peace. The perfection of a rose, whole and integrated, is likened to the attempt to live one's masculine and feminine aspects, androgynously, in the poem "Crazy Courage" (*Desire,* 72); and this same idea of integration and acceptance informs the image of the rose as life in the poem "Dear World, Why?" (*Desire,* 129).

In keeping with the emphasis upon nature, Villanueva repeatedly uses images of flowers, shells, and the sea. The imagery of flowers, in conjunction with bird imagery, represents freedom and the freedom of thought in "Changing Woman" (*Planet,* 46). "The Orchid" likens the beauty of the exotic flower to a woman's sexuality; a women opens to love as the flower blossoms (*Planet,* 66). The title of the novel *Naked Ladies* refers literally to the wildflowers found by Alta's daughter: "a long, dark, mauve stalk with a delicate pink flower on its tip. The pink was the color of the most tender, innermost flesh: of womb or heart. Or soul" (*Naked Ladies,* 39). But symbolically the "naked ladies" are the women whose lives are laid bare in the narrative—Alta, Katie, Jackie, Rita—and the beauty and delicacy of the flower which springs up wherever there is opportunity represents the indomitable will to survive all the suffering of their lives and through love to prevail. The shell is a symbol of feminine integrity in the poem "in your body" (*Bloodroot,* 37), and the feminine shell is opposed to the masculine inflexibility of stone and rock in "Deity" (*Planet,* 41). A motif that connects the stories of *Weeping Woman* is the fragile seashell that features in every story and represents the hard-won integrity of feminine identity in a violent, patriarchal culture. The sea from which these shells emerge symbolizes a threatening, powerful masculinity in the poem "in your body" (*Bloodroot,* 37).

Villanueva also uses a pattern of celestial imagery of moon, sun, earth, and rainbow; these images are employed characteristically in the poem "Backpackers": "the only journey is into the sun, / by the light of the moon, / by the pull of the earth, / rainbows as our garments" (*Planet,* 79). The sun represents the wholeness of life, the moon the power of feminine imagination, the earth's gravity the love that unifies and sustains life, and the rainbow is the experience from which we learn how to see and accept life in all its diversity. The rhythms of the moon are likened to a woman's biorhythms; in the poem "Simplicity" the moon "never dies, but journeys into / silvery waters of her cratered / womb" (*Planet,* 4). In the poem "No One's Child" the moon and sun, darkness and light, are conjoined by the rainbow of experience in a process that "is never easy, but that's / the way joy is born— / wild child of the sun and moon" (*Planet,* 7). The sun appears as the source of both life and death in "The Politics of Paradise," in which the poet observes, "Heal, harm, heal, harm— / the sun is like that— / but without the sun; / nothing" (*Planet,* 17). The stars in the poem "Planet" are represented as the backdrop to the blazing light of the North Star. The North Star is symbolic of all that which is completely Other, outside human comprehension, unlike the stars that are "almost // human, soft and twinkling" (*Planet,* 3). The image of a rainbow at the center of the sun appears in the poem "Simplicity" (*Planet,* 4); in "The Harvest" the rainbow image is set in opposition to the pervasive cement of the urban setting (*Planet,* 10). The transformative power of the rainbow is likened to Villanueva's poetic voice that helps her to escape her confinement within everyday existence; just as the prisoner imagines the earth and the pregnant woman burdened by her heavy body imagines the child soon to be released, so the poet must imagine her voice, "there among the / stones, gathering / rainbows." The rainbow also symbolizes her mixed ancestry and her desire to be everything, to gather up all of life in herself, as in the poem "Witness" (*Desire,* 75).

To speak on behalf of the women who are oppressed not only by men but also by other women within the context of a violent, misogynistic patriarchal society is Alma Villanueva's motivation. The cycle of feminine complicity with the destructive energies of patriarchy, in which the feminine power to create is put to the service of death, is the basic subject of Villanueva's Chicana feminist writing. She writes as a poet, even in her fiction, with a heavy emphasis on imagery and symbolism in order to create the feminine poetic vocabulary she needs and to contest the devaluation of women, of mythical feminine figures and real women alike, in the misogynistic cultures that comprise her mestiza identity. Marta Sánchez argues that Villanueva is a feminist poet before she is a Chicana poet, and in some respects this is true; but the elements of Aztec, Mexican, and Anglo cultures that inform and empower her work are unmistakably Chicana in conception and representation. Villanueva speaks as a Chicana, but in doing so she speaks for the devalued, the victims, the dispossessed everywhere.

CHAPTER SEVEN

Lorna Dee Cervantes

Lorna Dee Cervantes has received perhaps the most critical attention of all contemporary Chicana writers. Her two slim volumes of poetry, *Emplumada* (1981) and *From the Cables of Genocide: Poems on Love and Hunger* (1991), betray a highly sophisticated poetic talent. Cervantes's work is characterized by her angry use of language, her passionate expression of emotions, and a complex interweaving of imagery to represent a feminist view of Chicana life in contemporary America. Cervantes shares Alma Villanueva's adversarial attitude toward the agents of oppression: men, whites, the affluent, the complacent; and she also shares Bernice Zamora's careful use of symbolism and technical poetic skill to translate that anger and outrage into enduring works of art. Marta Sánchez, in her study of contemporary Chicana poetry, describes Cervantes's work as being divided into two predominant types of poems: "the narrative, discursive, 'hard' mode to communicate the real, divisive world she knows as a Chicana; [and] the lyrical, imagistic, 'soft' mode to evoke contemplative and meditative moods."[1] This view of the technical character of Cervantes's poetry arises from Sánchez's description of Cervantes's work as primarily concerned with the struggle between her identities as poet and as Chicana. Race and gender are inextricably bound in Cervantes's sensibility, according to Sánchez; any issue of poetic voice, then, concerns the tension between her poetic voice and her voice as a Chicana. This judgment is a bit formulaic, and in the pages that follow it will be suggested that Cervantes's poetic achievement is rather more complex than in Sánchez's representation.

Lorna Dee Cervantes was born in a Mexican barrio of San José, California, on 6 August 1954 to a family of mixed Mexican and Chumasch Indian ancestry. She grew up, with her brother, in a single-parent, woman-dominated household managed by her mother and grandmother. Marta Sánchez emphasizes the significance for Cervantes's work of her upbringing in a father-absent family living in an urban, working-class environment under the formative influence of two generations of women. Certainly in the poems in *Emplumada,* such as "Under the Shadow of the Freeway," Cervantes confirms the importance of this early experience. In the 1970s she attempted to live solely as a writer and publisher; to this end she established the small press Mango Publications to publish the work of Chicano writers and founded and coedited the highly respected Chicano literary review/chapbook series *Mango.* Cervantes received several small grants from the National Endowment for the Arts to work on her own poetry, and her 1981 collection, *Emplumada,* was awarded the 1982 American Book Award of the Before Columbus Foundation. She is the recipient also of the Fine Arts Work Center, Provincetown Fellowship and the London Meadow Fellowship. In the 1980s Cervantes followed many Chicano/a writers into a professional/artistic life defined in part by the academy. She graduated from California State University at San José in 1984 and in 1990 obtained her doctorate in the history of consciousness at the University of California at Santa Cruz. She has taught creative writing at the University of Colorado in Denver and at the University of Colorado, Boulder. Her editorial work continued with the coediting of the multicultural magazine *Red Dirt.* Her second volume of poetry, *From the Cables of Genocide,* has won the Latin American Writers' Institute Award and the Paterson Poetry Prize, and she has been the recipient of a Lila Wallace/Readers Digest Foundation Award. She is currently working on two new collections of poetry, *Bird Ave* or *Bird Avenue* and *How Far Is the War.*

Cervantes's political and philosophical view of the world is fundamentally a radical Chicana perspective; she describes how "when I was 18, 19 years old I got involved in the Chicano movement, and specifically the Chicano cultural movement. I see myself as a cultural worker. And I was, well, I am very political, that is, an activist."[2] This conception of herself as an activist, as a "cultural worker," informs her poetry at the most basic level. The act of writing poetry, the claim to "be" a Chicana poet, as well as the poetry itself all possess an urgent political significance. Particularly in Cervantes's early work men are represented as the enemy; Cervantes's attitude toward men and the patriarchal culture that shapes masculinity is adversarial. In the first poem of the collection *Emplumada,* "Uncle's First Rabbit," she represents men as being trained to exploit nature in an abusive attitude toward life, which leads them also to abuse women. Sexual and domestic violence are the themes represented in poems such as "Lots: I," "Lots: II," and "For Virginia Chávez." Women, then, are forced to become strong, self-reliant, and autonomous; feminine autonomy, which some blame for the breakdown of family structures, is clearly a response to this rather than a cause; within the Chicano/a community it is the ethnic pressure upon men to be macho, the ethic of machismo itself, that threatens the family and the community. Machismo is represented as an expression of the colonized mind. Cervantes calls upon the double colonization of Chicano/a culture—first by Spain and then by the United States—to express the common experience of oppression that cuts across gender positions. So Anglo prejudice and racism are seen to be at the bottom of this pressure upon Chicanos to preserve and assert their masculinity at the expense of their women. But Cervantes could also be seen to endorse, in part, Octavio Paz's interpretation of machismo as the Mexican male response to the threat of emasculation. The absent Father and the degraded Mother of the nation create a psychic symbolism that underlies the masculine compulsion to assert a powerful sexual self-image. In order to resist racism, the unity of the community must be preserved against these colonialist threats. In Cervantes's representation harmony between the sexes, and by extension within the family and the wider community, can be achieved only through feminine efforts to learn to live with men, to make them cooperate rather than oppose, to transform the adversarial relationship into an alliance. As Juan Bruce-Novoa observes, in poems such as "Beneath the Shadow of the Freeway," Cervantes invokes the older female oral traditions to suggest the possibilities for this kind of uneasy harmony, based upon balancing strength with tenderness and caution with openness, sincerity, and reserve.[3]

Betrayal is an ever-present possibility against which Cervantes can never relax her guard. Many of the poems collected in *From the Cables of Genocide* express a negative, at times despairing view of the chances for enduring relationships with men. Constant vigilance is then required, not only because of the antagonism between men and women but also because there is a fundamental conflict between the worlds of human society and nature. Nature and civilization are always opposed, always warring, even when peace seems to prevail. And so the transcendence of strife and the harmony of warring opposites she struggles to achieve in her poetry must always be won again; it cannot endure.

Cervantes has a clear view of her poetry as a form of resistance. What she is resisting is multifaceted: the oppression of women; the racist oppression of Chicano/as and other minorities; class oppression and exploitation; and the colonization of minds that accompanies these forms of oppression. Sometimes it is only the psychological effects of oppression, the self-denial, the internalized violence, the hatred, that is the subject of her writing. For example, in the poem "Visions of Mexico While at a Writing Symposium in Port Townsend, Washington," which is an angry poem, the object of her anger is unknown, but the consequence of this is that the anger itself becomes the entire subject of the poem: "Our anger is our way of speaking, / the gesture is an utterance more pure than word" (2.25–26).[4] The resistance inspired by such a powerful expression of anger motivates a range of secondary themes, but these remain secondary.

Resistance and subversion are essential aspects of the work of a Chicana feminist writer. Cervantes describes her role as a self-described Chicana poet as being in itself a subversive act: "I chose the tag 'Chicana.' In the barrio when you 'call' somebody 'out,' they put the label on you and call you out. But if you have the power of self-definition, it leads to self-determination. And so for me to say, 'OK, I'm a Chicana writer, I am a feminist

quote

writer, I am a political writer. Y que?' is what we say. And what of it. And now I can do all sorts of things. I do all sorts of things. To me poetry is an exercise in freedom. That's what's at stake. I choose the label. For me it's an act of subversion."[5] Self-definition offers an alternative to the stereotypes prescribed by a racist and sexist culture; the freedom of self-definition extends well beyond the freedom to name, as Cervantes suggests, and enables the poet to engage in actions and behaviors that are otherwise prohibited. As a self-declared outsider, the poet can claim the power to do and say things that simply cannot be said or done by one who "belongs" fully to the community and expresses this belonging through conformity. This is an ambivalent and difficult position for the poet to adopt: being both outside and yet within, both of the community and yet apart from it, the poet is the analyst of the very conditions to which she herself is subject. The designation of poet does not bring immunity; on the contrary, the poet remembers more and records in often painful detail the collective and individual histories of her people.

The poet performs an important cultural function as the collective memory of the community. She recalls and gives voice again to all that has been silenced by the patriarchal erasure of the feminine voice and the racist silencing of the Chicano/a people. In the poem "Poema Para los Californios Muertos" she recalls the dispossession of her Californio ancestors and does not avoid the bloody violence of this history: "Californios moan like husbands of the raped, / husbands de la tierra, / tierra la madre" (*Emplumada,* 42, 2.8–10). The violation of Californio culture, the violent colonization of this territory by the United States, is expressed as violence against nature ("tierra la madre") that has a gender as well as a racial element. Thus, Cervantes analyzes this moment of historical trauma as she recalls it as part of the Chicano/a legacy of oppression. In the poem "For My Brother" Cervantes remembers not so much a collective experience but a personal memory that is paradigmatic of Chicano/a experience. She recalls the common poverty of the childhood she shared with her brother: she remembers the bickering over the purchase of a "new used car," how there was no money left after the bills had been paid, how each evening even the sun resembled less than a penny as it disappeared behind the smog. These recollections are not specific to women, but they are formative of Chicano/a subjectivity. Imagination and the resources of one's own intellect were what they had in place of material goods. Cervantes does not romanticize this lack. She regrets the deprivation of her childhood, but she will not allow herself or her brother to forget what it was really like. The poet's individual and collective memory is a form of testimony and a confrontation with originary moments, moments from which elements of contemporary Chicano/a experience originate. The first poem of *Emplumada,* mentioned above, offers a clear example. In "Uncle's First Rabbit" Cervantes describes a kind of masculine initiation ritual. The first successful hunt is a moment of transformation as a boy enters the patriarchal world of men. Far from a celebration of dawning maturity, Cervantes's poem laments the loss of innocence in this first moment of violence. The rabbit is intended for his grandfather's supper, and its death reminds him of his father's drunken violence that killed his baby sister; in these ways Cervantes links this one remembered event with a pattern of inherited masculine behaviors. And she generalizes from

I'm not sure I agree w/ there being an enemy."

domestic violence to military violence, identifying the same inherited valuation of death and domination through violence. Through her refusal to forget key traumatic moments, the Chicana poet is able to identify and analyze the oppressive practices that characterize contemporary Chicano/a experience.

As well as a keeper of memory, a translator, and scribe, the Chicana poet is also necessarily a warrior; she seeks fulfillment through her imaginative struggle with the "enemy." Her antagonist is represented by the natural incarnations of spiritual forces that can be brought into harmony by the imaginative power of the poet, but if they are not controlled, then they can become immensely destructive. In the poem "Caribou Girl," as in other poems in both *Emplumada* and *From the Cables of Genocide,* these forces are represented through the imagery of water. The girl of the title is the object of the poet's admiration and love; this girl desires a voice with which to express "her own mythology, her own sanity" (*Emplumada,* 21, 1.13). At the end of the poem her halting, struggling attempts to find this voice and to find her poetic way are represented by the image of walking on water: "She slips from the rocks / and I know she will drown" (2.61–62). She cannot save herself because she has traded the feathers of the spirit powers that might have rescued her. Cervantes invokes the indigenous deities Wankan Tanka (of the Sioux people), Manitou, Quetzalcoátl, Ometeótl, and the Aztec gods. But in her invocation they are incarnated as birds: Wankan Tanka is the mockingbird; the others are "four great hawks and a speckled bird" (2.25, 31). These powers assist the poet to discover fulfillment. They also lend her the power to save her friend, the beloved "caribou girl." Cervantes aims to create a personal relationship of peace and harmony with nature through the power of imagination to harness spiritual energy and with it to contest the antagonism that prevails between the human and the natural worlds. It is this desire that Marta Sánchez sees as divisive of both Cervantes's work and her sense of herself as a poet. But the reconciliation of these divisions is precisely the demonstration of Cervantes's poetic power and the legitimation of her function as a poet. Cervantes acknowledges the difficulty of her task in poems such as "Four Portraits of Fire" (*Emplumada,* 28–29). In the first of the four sections Cervantes describes the poetic access to spiritual power through imagination: "I find a strange knowledge of wind, / an open door in the mountain / pass where everything intersects" (2.1–3). But this secret access to harmony and universal reconciliation is no easy solution to the problems of Cervantes's world. With a play on the word "pass," which is placed at the beginning of line 3 and so breaks the phrase "mountain pass" into its constituent words, Cervantes brings into play the two meanings of the word: the noun meaning "access; and the verb meaning "to go by." In the following lines, then, she reminds us that the ills of the human world will not easily disappear or go by: "Believe me. This will not pass. / This is a world where flags / contain themselves, and are still, / marked by their unfurled edges" (2. 4–7). In this poem, as elsewhere in her work, images of nature can reflect both positively and negatively in relation to human culture: holding up a contrasting positive image to show what we should be doing, and also reflecting the negative images of destructive human behavior.

Cervantes's work consistently represents her vision of life

LORNA DEE CERVANTES

as continual struggle— and without conflict there can only be defeat. The desire for spiritual transcendence of human conflict is not so much the desire for escape (poetry as escapism) as it is the expression of the highest achievement of harmony and reconciliation. Consequently, there is no divorce between Cervantes's lyrical poems, such as "Caribou Girl," and those poems that address explicitly her social commitment to the struggle against gender, race, and class oppression. In one of the most accomplished of these "political" poems, "Poem for the Young White Man Who Asked Me How I, an Intelligent, Well-Read Person Could Believe in the War between Races," the antagonists against whom Cervantes struggles are Chicano machismo and patriarchy in general, Anglo-American dominance and racism, and the Anglo forms of expression that articulate the terms of her struggle (*Emplumada,* 35–37). Gender oppression in this poem is represented within the context of racial prejudice and class deprivation. For all that, Cervantes's vision is not all bleak: women share a unity based on common experience and the challenging of common enemies; likewise, Chicanos all share the experience of racial prejudice and economic exploitation, and these commonalties provide the basis for coexistence even if that coexistence is not necessarily peaceful and is always subject to the possibility of betrayal.

gender oppression by racial prejudice.

"Poem for the Young White Man . . ." contrasts two opposed views of life in the United States: that of the Anglo and that of the mestiza. Only those who experience no boundaries, no constraints by virtue of race or gender, and who do not go hungry can afford the luxury of being apolitical. And correspondingly, only they can express distaste for what they call "political poems." The poetic voice claims that she can occasionally escape the political condition of her life, but this escape is only fleeting; it is escapism rather than transcendence. What is a constant reality in her life is the violence directed against those she loves—her family, her friends. She knows herself to be a casualty of the race war that rages around her; the scars she bears are from wounds inflicted on her sense of self. Though she may try to write apolitical poetry, the reality of racial conflict is too close, too deeply inscribed on her mind and soul. The speaker alludes to her condition as a citizen of the borderlands—caught between two cultures, belonging to neither but situated within the terms of both: "Every day I am deluged with reminders / that this is not / my land // and this is my land" (36–37). Cervantes here again uses the historical double colonization of the Chicano/a people to articulate the experience of dispossession. Her ancestors lived in California long before it was a part of the United States; her family lived through the trauma of annexation; and she continues to live in a colonized space belonging culturally neither to the United States nor to Mexico. Thus, although she may not "believe in" war, she cannot keep from involvement in it; seen from the perspective of the colonizer she is the "enemy" by virtue of the color of her skin. In this world there are no innocent bystanders, and to hold oneself apart from this conflict is then to condone the violence, the killing, the maiming.

The personal, confessional mode of this poem contrasts with the rhetorical flourishes and exhortation to political action of much of the male Chicano movement poetry. Cervantes participated in the Chicano movement but, like many Chicanas, found herself marginalized by reason of her gender. She describes the resistance to her work, to the whole idea of Chicana literary expression, as her motivation to write: "*Emplumada* was directly a result of some of that resistance to those [male Chicano] essentializing ideas as far as what is Chicano literature, what it sounds like, what themes it deals with. Not only was it male-dominated, but it was considered counterrevolutionary to criticize this. You don't talk bad about your own *familia*. So 'Beneath the Shadow of the Freeway' came out of the need to document my experience, a woman-centered experience, and to counteract this expression of what the Chicano family was, with this patriarch, and mama's in the kitchen slapping tortillas. The whole book was in reaction and resistance to that."[6] This is a theme we have seen recur in contemporary Chicana literature. The denunciation of Chicana writing as a form of cultural betrayal is the theme of early poems such as "Para un revolucionario" and "You Cramp My Style, Baby." In these poems Cervantes contests the idea that to demonstrate concern for women's issues, to be active on women's behalf, was to be a traitor, a Malinchista, to the people. But the alternative for Chicanas was effective exclusion from a movement that expressed the values of machismo and of masculine experience and culture. Tey Diana Rebolledo's interpretation of the poem "Para un revolucionario" focuses on Cervantes's expression of desire for equality between men and women rather than the promotion of women's issues at the expense of men.[7] The emphasis Cervantes places on the word "carnal," however, raises the whole issue of the identification of the feminine with the body, at the expense of women's intellectual capacity. This could be seen to underlie the patriarchal justification of women's exclusion from political activism, on the grounds that men are more intellectual. In this connection Cervantes may be playing upon the relationship between the word "carnal" and the concept of *carnalismo* (brotherhood) to point ironically to women's exclusion from the political "brotherhood" by reason of her body/sexuality/gender.

Feminism is an unquestioned source of Cervantes's poetic and political inspiration. She describes herself as having been a feminist ever since she was old enough to know what that was, and she has been an activist since she was sixteen. For her, feminism is inseparable from being Chicana; she says, "I think that the culture is inherently feminist. Certainly matricentric."[8] However, the literature of the Chicano canon, developed as the cultural expression of the Chicano movement, was far from "matricentric" in its early formulations. The masculine domination of this literary canon was expressed not only in terms of the male authors whose work dominated it, but also in terms of the literary forms that confirmed the legitimacy of the texts that were deemed canonical. This meant that women were excluded from the Chicano literary canon by a subtle double bind: first the canonical language was best suited to the expression of male experience, and then the literary forms that were adapted to represent authentically and powerfully the Chicana experience were deemed "unliterary." Thus, the subject of the Chicana condition and the language of Chicana experience were judged unsuited to the cultural role of Chicano literature. Lynette Seator explains the implications of this situation for Cervantes's poetry:

Together, the poems of *Emplumada* tell the story of a coming-of-age in which time-honored "great expectations" are necessarily altered. The rites-of-passage of a Mexican-American woman will not fit the formula of the nineteenth-century *Bildüngsroman,* nor will her rites be consonant with stereotypic sex roles in Chicano coming-of-age novels. As long as the achievement of an identity through a temporal process in which the child struggles to adulthood is male-identified, a discussion of the struggle toward an autonomous female identity will be viewed as feminist; and within the closely held values of ethnicity "feminism" is likely to be equated with subversion. Thus the poems of *Emplumada,* speaking as they do for a Chicana coming-of-age, heighten awareness of human as well as artistic complexities.[9]

Seator's explanation accounts for the multiple subversions enacted by Cervantes's work: she subverts the European canon (of Bildüngsroman) as well as the canon of Chicano coming-of-age novels (such as Rudolfo Anaya's *Bless Me, Ultima* and Tomás Rivera's . . . *y no se lo trago la tierra*); and in addition to this literary subversion, she subverts the patriarchal exclusion of Chicana experience from the category of "Literature." So in her poetry Cervantes is engaged in proving her own worth as a poet at the same time that she is proving the value and legitimacy of the Chicana condition as a literary subject.

The poems of *Emplumada* relate to each other to form a poem sequence. (The similarity in structural style is one of the reasons why Cervantes's work is often compared to Bernice Zamora's poem sequence *Restless Serpents.*) As mentioned above, in these poems Cervantes seeks harmony with nature,

[handwritten margin note: Critic natural harmony = escapism]

with the world, through the exercise of her poetic imagination. She contests a variety of enemies, who are essentially all the same enemy; through these encounters she is guided by the mother figure, eventually to triumph through the feminine strength from which she develops true wisdom. This harmony is expressed in a number of poems that are lyrical meditations on the natural world—for example, "Shells" and "Starfish." Marta Sánchez, in her analysis of Cervantes's lyric work, wants to argue that the representation of natural harmony offers an escape from cultural activism, that these poems are escapism: "Cervantes' lyric poems express a desire to be free from the pressure of social commitment and responsibility. Spoken by disembodied lyric speakers, they reveal her need to speak in a voice that deliberately tries to avoid claiming a social consciousness."[10] These poems express a sense of harmony with nature; the human poetic consciousness is at home in nature, and in this way Cervantes expresses both her capacity as a pure poet and the power of the wisdom that the women in her life have taught her. Images in the poem "Shells," such as the orderly stringing of shells (*Emplumada,* 59–61) and the lines "I find in shells / the way I live / everything I touch // is fragile / but full of color" (2.4–8), suggest the delicacy as well as the beauty of the harmony she can achieve. There is a political significance to images such as these, but it arises from the context in which the poem exists. Cervantes's claim to be a poet, a Chicana feminist poet, is staked just as much on poems such as these as on explicitly political poems. As she writes in "Emplumada," "These are warriors // distancing themselves from history" (*Emplumada,* 66, 2.14–15). We must also be aware of the place of a poem such as "Shells" within the sequence of *Emplumada:* it is one of a number of poems late in the collection in which Cervantes shows the range of her poetic skill. "Shells," the poem about the natural world, is accompanied by love poems, "For John on the Cape" and "Moonwalkers," and poems addressed to Chicanas, such as "Before You Go" and "Oranges." The ability to write about many subjects, to be many things, and to escape the cultural stereotypes to which minority writers are subjected—all of this is part of Cervantes's resistance poetry.

It is against the concept of machismo that Cervantes is able to give expression to her own experience of ethnicity because her experience as a Chicano/a is complicated by her condition as a woman. Machismo is described by Lynette Seator as "the cult of masculinity that sets women apart from an existential process of becoming something in the world."[11] As already indicated, particularly in earlier discussions of Octavio Paz, machismo defines the traditional gender relations of Chicano culture. It is against this that Cervantes defines an experience of femininity that does not conform to these expectations and conventional relations, though she warns in the closing line of the poem "Macho," "remember: the word for *machismo* is *real*."[12]

The opening poem of the collection *Emplumada,* "Uncle's First Rabbit," discussed above, describes machismo in the form of a masculine "coming-of-age" ritual. By beginning the collection in this way Cervantes announces that one of her primary themes will be the operations of patriarchy; she does this, as Bruce-Novoa argues, in order "to confront the masculine paradigm with a protest, critique and negation" and to suggest an alternative feminine paradigm with "its roots and strength in women themselves, whose experiences the poetry seeks to give voice to."[13] There is no single moment of maturity in this feminine paradigm with which to compare the masculine moment of first killing. Instead, in poems such as "Beneath the Shadow of the Freeway" and "Crow," Cervantes describes the slow process by which she has learned from her mother and grandmother the ways of feminine autonomy and self-reliance within Chicano/a culture. In the poem "Crow" she tells how "Women taught me to clean // and then build my own house" (*Emplumada,* 19, 2. 6–7). This construction of a private space of one's own perhaps marks the achievement of feminine maturity, in contrast with the public ritual that signals the achievement of masculinity in "Uncle's First Rabbit." The image of the house as a representation of subjectivity is used negatively in *From the Cables of Genocide* in poems such as "The House He Falls in Love With," in which the empty house reflects the emptiness of the prospective buyer, and "Hotel," in which the anonymity of the place mirrors the poet's alienation and despair.

These two poems are indicative of the urban perspective from which Cervantes writes in contrast to many of the canonical Chicano writers mentioned, who situate themselves and their writing in the countryside, the llano, in nature, reflecting the origin of the Chicano movement in land and labor issues. Juan Bruce-Novoa goes on to argue that Cervantes uses the idea of nature in order to represent her experience of patriarchy as the principle of imposing the masculine will through violent means. "Nature in Cervantes is the other violated by man," he argues.[14] This is certainly true of poems such as "Uncle's First Rabbit," "Shooting the Wren," and "Buckshot," which begins: "My man wants to kill. He longs to shoot his gun into the air" (*From the Cables of Genocide,* 67, 2.1–2). But Cervantes's use of nature to articulate the double oppression of Chicanas by reason of race and gender is much more complex than this. And in her writing the issue of race is inseparable from gender issues and other forms of social oppression. For example, she addresses the experience of dispossession in the poem "From Where We Sit: Corpus Christi." In this poem the relation of the Chicano/a to the tourist is the same as the seagulls feeding from the crumbs offered them. It is not the human world, the First World of the tourists, that the Chicana speaker identifies with. Rather, she identifies with the natural scavengers, with whom she shares a common language. It is the language of subservience that the seabirds "speak as they beg" (*Emplumada,* 33, 1.4). These birds represent nature tamed and corrupted; Cervantes suggests that racism has attempted to tame the Chicano/a people in the same way.

Tey Diana Rebolledo describes how in poems such as "Beneath the Shadow of the Freeway," Cervantes uses the image of urban encroachment to capture the experience of living within multiple borders. "In large urban areas, freeways were often built in the barrios—the Chicano residential areas—destroying not only older houses and sections but cultural traditions as well."[15] The erasure of existing social structures to make way for the new is a powerful image set in a region where the Spanish culture that predated its annexation by the United States was placed under erasure by the conquering power. The attempts to deny and destroy the cultures of the "virgin land" of the Spanish Southwest are evoked by Cervantes's powerful image of the barrios

modernity of her home — Cx'hc

erased to make way for the technological development of the modern United States. In this poem, then, Cervantes highlights temporal borders between the historical past and the present, her family past and present, the community past and present. These historical divisions reflect ethnic divisions, between Chicanos/as and Anglos, and class divisions as well. The border between dominant and minority cultures is reinforced by the sense of a generational division, with Cervantes representing the future as opposed to the continuity with the past represented by her grandmother, and her mother's ambivalence about tradition versus modernity. The modern world is the world of patriarchy, bureaucracy, and male government, a public world which, as mentioned above, the poet learns to translate for the private female world of her family.

The indigenous past is represented in Cervantes's work through her subtle use of references to the indigenous inheritance of the mestiza. Cervantes invokes this historical context through her use of symbolism rather than by invoking some essence of the Chicana that is to be found in the mythological past. So in the poem "Caribou Girl" the symbolism of indigenous deities is described as infusing the natural world with power that is available to the poet through her exercise of artistic imagination. The indigenous figures themselves offer no direct role model or spiritual advice. This is quite a distinctive characteristic of Cervantes's writing, in view of the extensive use of inherited images such as La Malinche and La Llorona by other Chicana writers. Cervantes expresses a painful awareness of her separation from Mexico as a Chicana; she is no more Mexican than she is an Anglo. This cultural history emerges as a painful and humiliating experience in the poem "Oaxaca, 1974." The poet describes her search for the Mexico that will match her consciousness with her body: "My brown body searches the streets / for the dye that will color my thoughts" (*Emplumada*, 44, 2.6–7). But to the Mexicans she meets she is worse than a stranger; the old women see her as representing an indictment of her ancestors who gave her a Mexican name that fights her mestiza self—she is a "pocha," Americanized, and little better than a whore: "México gags, / ¡Esputa! / on this bland pochaseed" (2.8–10). The past is associated with death, defeat, and decay in "Poema Para los Californios Muertos," in which she, as a Chicana poet, is witness to the past and the inheritor of its legacy. Here the roots of her identity are buried. In the poem "Freeway 280" a dialectic between the past and the present is reflected in the dialogue between the past (the poet's ancestors and her younger self) and her present self.

The search for an authentic self is an ambiguous and difficult task for the mestiza. Cervantes's mixed cultural inheritance is expressed in part by the poetic images she chooses to give a particular cultural emphasis. For example, the much-remarked-upon usage of the word *pluma* in the title of her first poetry collection is a complex play on Spanish and indigenous words. *Pluma* in Spanish means both "pen" and "feather," so to be *emplumada* is to be armed with a pen or to be feathered like Cervantes's own native ancestors. The mestiza is of necessity a cultural translator, operating in the linguistic domain of more than one culture. But the relations between Chicanas and Mexican or Latina women is complicated by the stereotype of the Anglicized or Americanized woman, as *la pocha*. This is the theme explored

[margin annotation: soft and had dialect]

in the poem "Oaxaca, 1974," as indicated above. The double rejection of Mexican and United States culture leaves the mestiza in an alienated position.

The poem "Refugee Ship" explores the identity crisis of a woman who is caught between the conflicting demands of these two cultures. Her self-image has been consciously formed within the racist prescriptions of United States culture, but her face is that of the mestiza. Subjective and objective experiences of herself are in conflict; nature is in conflict with nurture. This theme appears also in other poems, such as "Poem for a Young White Man. . ." This woman has no self-conception of her hybridity, and yet her hybrid racial inheritance is visible on her physical self. The images of her grandmother and her religion are cultural icons representing the traditions and cohesion from which the woman feels alienated. She is a refugee in multiple ways: from cultural tradition, from Mexico, from her own Spanish name, from her sense of what and who she is. She finds disconnected traces of herself both at home and abroad, but these traces will not be united in a single psychological and emotional space that she can call home. Rather than experiencing herself as multiple, as hybrid, with the power to be many things, she experiences her self as fragmented and powerless, crippled by self-denial, the denial of her Spanish half. Her assimilation, then, is represented in terms of loss. The Spanish counterpart to "Refugee Ship" is the poem "Barco De Refugiados." Ada Savin notes: "In only one instance throughout the *Emplumada* poems does Cervantes surrender to despair, to apathy, and that is the only time when she chooses to write the same poem twice, in Spanish *and* in English,

creation of two selves
only poem in 2 languages .

as if only the juxtaposition of the two versions could possibly convey her existential plight."[16] The repetition of the poem in two languages does have the effect of including the poet, Lorna Dee Cervantes, in the plight expressed by this refugee mestiza. Cervantes addresses this poem to both her Spanish and English readers and in this way dramatizes her own double self.

The creation of multiple selves, the adoption of an identity by putting on a mask—"haciendo caras / making face" in Anzaldúa's term—is represented in the poem "Visions of Mexico. . ." In this poem the manipulation of physical appearance is used to transcend ethnicity. The poem consists of two parts: the first tells of the poet's self-perception when she is "south" in Mexico; the second tells of her self-image when she is "north" in the United States. In neither place does she feel at home. In Washington she hears the dismissal of Mexico as "a stumbling comedy," and as she looks around she sees evidence for this attitude: "at the bar, two Chicanas / hung at their beers. They had painted black birds that dipped beneath their eyelids"; and she notices "the bubbles of their teased hair" (*Emplumada,* 46, 2.48, 51). The black birds that are the heavily mascaraed eyelashes of the two Chicanas echo in the final image of the poet gathering her feathers to make the quills with which to write. Cervantes suggests through this use of imagery that the creation of identity through writing is not so different from the self-creation with mascara in which the Chicanas sitting at the bar engage. But the analogy between writing and makeup breaks down; the poet uses words to explore the many facets of her mestiza identity, to discover the full extent of what she is. The women in the bar use makeup in order to make themselves conform to a sexual image or object, and they are motivated by the desire to "be better than" they are, to escape their hybrid ethnicity.

The ending of "Poem for a Young White Man. . ." is positive, despite the anger expressed in the poem. The imagery of feathers, used for writing quills, represents the construction of a border consciousness and a genuinely hybrid identity in the northern land of her birth but with the benefit of the wisdom she has inherited from her Spanish ancestry. Quills signify both writing and traditional native artistry, especially in conjunction with the image of native feathers (pluma). The link between indigeneity and spiritual synthesis or harmony represented in the poem "Caribou Girl" has been mentioned above. What was not emphasized is the way in which Cervantes describes the disruption and reinvention of inherited myths. The girl of the poem expresses her own mythology, rather than repeating the words from books, and these words of her own: "She wants to give them to the world / con un abrazo. / She wants to speak them like her father / Who lives them" (*Emplumada,* 21, 2.16–19). The weakness of this girl is her relative lack of ambition: she wants to speak her words but does not challenge her father's sole authority to act on the words he speaks. However, she does imagine and create alternative mythologies, and she does struggle to articulate her own subjective experience. It is left to the poet to extend this subversion into the world of action.

Positive images of women who refuse to be confined to passive roles are balanced in Cervantes's work by negative images of women, images that divide a woman against her own subjectivity. These images identify women exclusively with reproduction, with physical beauty that does not last, with passivity and acceptance of suffering. Cervantes contests these images, but transgression of them is difficult when the boundaries between genuine subversion and rebellious gestures are blurred and the breaking of rules can only be self-destructive. The poems "For Virginia Chávez" and "Abortion" explore this difficulty. "Abortion" presents a series of images of dead ends, of blocked communications, of arrested movement (*From the Cables of Genocide,* 36). "For Virginia Chávez" begins with the recollection of adolescent daring as the poet and her friend rebel against the constraints of their Chicana upbringing by acts of sexual daring: "We could utter / the rules, mark the lines / and cross them ourselves" (*Emplumada,* 16, 2.16–18). But sexual rebellion is not a genuine form of rebellion when it opposes limited definitions of feminine sexuality. Virgin versus whore are the alternatives for feminine sexuality within which these girls make their choices. For the poet, this means abortion; for her friend, early marriage and entrapment in a life of domestic violence. The limited models of feminine sexuality offered these girls result in their unwitting exploitation, even as they believe they are rebelling against "the rules."

Genuine subversion of patriarchal definitions of femininity is represented by Cervantes's questioning the traditional value attached to virginity and feminine innocence in the poem "Lots: II." This poem exists in counterpoint with the previous poem in the *Emplumada* sequence, "Lots: I." The first poem is headed "The Ally," and the ironic opening lines read: "He told her / shut up and die" (*Emplumada,* 8, 2.1–2). The actual ally to which the poem refers is the voice echoing in the rape victim's head, the voice that "would not be / silent and still" (2.20–21). The second poem, "Lots: II," is headed "Herself" and is articulated by the victim herself. She tells how she gathers herself after the attack, makes a mental list of everyone who could help her, and then erases each one: "I scratched / each one" (*Emplumada*, 9, 1.6). She recognizes that they will be unable to hear or to understand what she has to say; instead, she takes note of herself, of her body, for the first time: "my used skin glistened / my first diamond" (2.10–11). This diamond image, expressing here the new value she has discovered in herself, in her power to defeat death, alludes ironically to the diamond engagement ring that would have symbolized the value of her innocence to her prospective husband. The loss of her virginity would in traditional patriarchal culture render her worthless as a bride. The loss of sexual innocence in this poem is accompanied by a loss of all traditional feminine values. This woman has discovered a power, and a voice, that violates patriarchal definitions of feminine passivity and acceptance of masculine domination. It is her resistance, her refusal to obey the violent male voice that demands her death, that gives her power and voice.

Violence is a recurring theme in Cervantes's poetry. Sexual and domestic violence are paired in "For Virginia Chávez," in which the image of "kicks in your belly" refers both to her violent husband and to her unborn child (*Emplumada*, 16, 1.41). In "Beneath the Shadow of the Freeway" the image of the child's fear as the unsteady drunken footsteps stop outside her bedroom door links sexual with domestic violence. Cervantes's confrontation with the brutality of sexual violence is represented in "Lots: I" and "Lots: II" with an emphasis on the masculine power that threatens to silence women by assaulting their vulnerable sense of sexual identity. Brute masculine power is set in opposition to feminine powers of expression and perception in "Lots: II" and in "Meeting Mescalito at Oak Hill Cemetery," in which each night the speaker locks her bedroom door against her abusive stepfather but then settles down to admire the peacock feathers she had found in the cemetery that morning: each "green eye in a heaven of blue, a fistfull / of understanding" (*Emplumada,* 10, 2.20–21). Cordelia Candelaria suggests that Cervantes represents in her work a "biblical interpretation of suffering" as prerequisite to growth and perhaps even transcendence.[17] So the sexual violence experienced by victims of assault and abuse, like the grinding poverty suffered by the poet and her brother as described in "To My Brother," in some way allows access to alternative means of perception and new powers of thinking and understanding.

Cervantes's poetry reveals an acute sense of the importance of geographical and cultural place. Her poetry is grounded in the specificities of life in northern California and the working-class sections of San José especially. In the poem "To My Brother" she does not shirk from describing the grim poverty of the barrio, the squalid conditions of life, but equally she recognizes that imagination lives on in the people of this community nonetheless. The poem presents the sharp contrast between subjective and objective realities: material deprivation in contrast with dreams "like crazy meteors of flying embers: / a glow in the heart all night" (*Emplumada,* 38, 2.23–24). The poems "Beneath the Shadow of the Freeway" and "Freeway 280" both link technological advancement or encroachment upon the cultural space of

[handwritten margin note: ideas of space cultural, personal, political]

the barrio to the defiant persistence of la raza. In these poems Cervantes mourns the loss of self that is associated with the destruction of the cultural space that was the barrio. Other poems in *Emplumada* evoke places that are suggestive of the pre-Columbian period: Michoacán, Oaxaca, and Tenochtitlán were all important places in the Aztec empire; the latter was the Aztec name for Mexico City. Physical place is more closely associated with self-identity and subjective space, rather than cultural and community space, in the later poems such as "Hotel" and "On Touring Her Hometown" in *From the Cables of Genocide.*

The imagery and symbolism used by Cervantes in her poetry build up a complex private lexicon. Recurring images cluster around birds, the sea, seashells, the moon, mountains, and cliffs. As noted above, nature can be used to show the ideal behaviors that humans do not achieve, but nature can also show counterparts to the patterns of cruelty and brutality of human society. Floral imagery, in the form of faded flowers, expresses the theme of time and temporal decay in the last poem of *Emplumada:* only through art can one find escape from the vicissitudes of history and temporal life. In that poem, "Emplumada," the image of two hummingbirds "stuck to each other, / arcing their bodies in grim determination / to find what is good" (*Emplumada,* 66, 2. 11–13) represents the struggle to unite opposites that is the essence of art and poetry. Bird imagery, especially the image of birds in flight, recurs throughout *Emplumada.* Quetzalcóatl, the feathered serpent god, is the symbol of learning among the Toltec gods; as Lynette Seator points out, the Toltec gods Cervantes evokes—Ometeotl, Manitou, Quetzalcóatl—are of ambiguous gender identification, and so they are available for use in delineating the new Chicana identity Cervantes seeks to construct. These figures are unlike the inherited Christian models, such as La Malinche, La Virgen of Guadalupe, and La Llorona, each of which has been subject to extensive patriarchal interpretation.[18]

Migratory birds are symbolic of the Chicano heritage of migration between cultural homes and the experience of dispossession by both Mexico and the United States. Seabirds, like the gulls in "From Where We Sit: Corpus Christi" and "Beneath the Shadow of the Freeway," are scavengers, but they are trusting; they remind the poet of her "soft" grandmother who lived with an abusive man for twenty-five years because she was too trusting and also because she had nowhere else to go. In this connection the birds represent a dangerous image of false security, which is a particular for Cervantes because of the proximity of her grandmother as a family precedent and a gender model. But her grandmother is also one of the women who taught the poet self-reliance and personal autonomy: "She believes in myths and birds. / She trusts only what she builds / with her own hands" (*Emplumada,* 12, 2.35–37), and that last line is echoed in the final line of the poem. The image of the quilt as a symbol of the union or negotiation of oppositions and the affirmation of difference is also represented in "Beneath the Shadow of the Freeway"; the same image takes on additional significance as a source of safe haven and comfort in the poem "Meeting Mescalito at Oak Hill Cemetery." As Elizabeth J. Ordóñez observes, "women salvage the remnants and worn leftovers of even their adversaries, making those discards something wonderful and new."[19]

The power of language.

In the same way that the quilt is constructed from salvaged remnants, so in a way Cervantes's poetic language seeks to create a new voice with which to express a Chicana consciousness that is diverse and hybrid. The control of language is represented as masculine; language belongs to the world of action and power and so is part of the patriarchal world. In the poem "For Edward Long," Cervantes describes how her earliest poetic voice was learned from a man. In this poem the man she describes as "Pardner, Doctor, crazy / mathematician and sometimes / wizard to the child I still am" (*Emplumada,* 15, 2.15–17) encourages her to sing and teaches her to hear more in poetry than she ever has before; as the father and grandfather she never had, he provides male approval of her utterance. Cervantes makes a poetic subject of her struggle to make the English language express her complex cultural inheritance. The need to tame language into "obedient words" and constantly to translate her experience is the theme of "Visions of Mexico. . ." In "Beneath the Shadow of the Freeway" her grandmother's powerlessness is related to her lack of language skills. Cervantes was brought up to be a fluent speaker of English without a Spanish accent, and to this she attributes her acute awareness of the political nature of language: "I grew up speaking exclusively English. It was a big deal in my family. My family on my mother's side, my grandmother's side are Californios and Chumash from Santa Barbara. My parents both spoke fluent English. The racism being what it was and the history of genocide being what it was, it was vitally important for my family to raise me and my brother speaking English without an accent. And it was really enforced. . . . The relationship between language and power was always clear to me. So the language I use as a poet is always for me a political choice."[20]

The theme of migration recurs in Cervantes's work, often together with the image of migratory seabirds. In "Refugee Ship" and "Visions of Mexico. . ." the image of migration is used to signify cultural dislocation. Marta Sánchez comments: "The theme of migration has always had strong implications for a Mexican-Chicano community whose history has been shaped by patterns of migration, both internal (within Mexico and within the United States) and external (between Mexico and the United States)."[21] Migration between homes, between Mexican and "American" selves, is a move between rural and urban, oral and literate, Third World and First World cultures. Migration imagery is used in both *Emplumada* and *From the Cables of Genocide*.

Cervantes chooses to use English rather than Spanish as the primary language of her work; her use of code-switching and Spanish phraseology is even more limited in *From the Cables of Genocide* than in *Emplumada*. The use of two languages in one poem and the use of two languages but in different poems are distinct linguistic strategies, as explained in the introduction. Sánchez explains that both techniques require the reader to move from one language to another: "The difference lies in how the movement takes place. In a bilingual experience the reader must mentally juxtapose poems in English with poems in Spanish; in an interlingual experience, the tensions in syntax, the connotations, the ironies, and the reverberations of words and images interlock, pulling in two directions at once."[22] Cervantes uses both strategies. In *Emplumada* she juxtaposes English and Spanish versions of the same poem, "Barco de Refugiados" / "Refugee Ship." In other poems she shifts from English to Spanish while maintaining the grammatical structure of her expression. In "Poema Para los Californios Muertos" she writes, "What a bastard child, this city / lost in the soft / llorando de las madres" (*Emplumada,* 42, 2.5–7). By using the phrase "llorando de las madres" rather than "the crying of the mothers" Cervantes evokes echoes of La Llorona, weeping for her lost children, as well as recalling the historical trauma of the Spanish people who were dispossessed of their homes and nation.

In both *From the Cables of Genocide* and *Emplumada* Cervantes uses section headings, headnotes, and epigrams to set up symbolic associations and patterns of meaning that are explored in the individual poems. The details of this technique are explained by John F. Crawford in his 1987 essay, "Notes toward a New Multicultural Criticism: Three Works by Women of Color."[23] In these poems Cervantes uses a subjective first-person persona, which, as Candelaria notes, lends her poetry "an intimacy reminiscent of Confessional Poetry."[24] In fact Cervantes's second book of poetry is dedicated to Sylvia Plath, among others. This use of personae is related to Cervantes's strategy of using personal utterance in order to articulate experiences that are of universal appeal and significance. She describes how this strategy is a part of her work as a Chicana poet: "For me as a Chicana poet, there's this sense of responsibility. Especially as a Chicana writer, I think you get a lot of, you know, 'you should write universal themes, this is just the Chicana experience, it's not universal.' So I had this idea that you could go so deep into the personal that you could come out into the other side into the universal."[25] Two voices can be heard in "For Virginia Chávez": those of the poet and her working-class Chicana friend who is the victim of domestic violence. Patricia Wallace notes, "Cervantes reaches for unity, for the power of imagination to close the gap between the poet and the friend, between language and experience. But the conclusion of the poem insists on the difficulty of defining these mobile relations in any way which does not encompass both difference and sameness."[26] I would argue that this is because experience and consciousness cannot be separated from language. In "The Body as Braille" two voices engage in dialogue: one is educated and cultured, the voice of scientific understanding; the other expresses intuitive knowledge and the voice of tradition. These utopian versus realistic perspectives on the world express the central tension in Cervantes's poetry: her desire to transcend conflict through poetry and her recognition that social revolution is needed to overcome injustice. "These two contradictory attitudes shape Cervantes' poetic sensibility," according to Sánchez.[27] Her desire for integration of her poetic and personal voices, her desire to speak to and for the Chicano/a community and also give expression to her own poetic muse—these are the conflicts Sánchez identifies and analyzes, and which she reconciles in her achievement of a distinctive poetic voice.

The overcoming of silence among Chicanas, a silence demanded and enforced by a patriarchal Chicano culture, a racist Anglo-American culture, and a disdainful Mexican culture, is the primary motivation of contemporary Chicana literature. Lorna Dee Cervantes, like Bernice Zamora, Ana Castillo, Sandra Cis-

neros, Denise Chávez, Alma Luz Villanueva, and the many Chicana writers I have been constrained by reasons of space to omit
from close consideration, finds her power and her inspiration in
the lives of the women around her. Her literary voice is their
voice; her subject, their lives; her achievement an achievement
shared by the Chicana community and the developing Chicana
literary canon.

NOTES

Chapter 1—Introduction:
The Contemporary Chicana Renaissance

1. bell hooks, *Ain't I a Woman?* (Boston: South End Press, 1981).

2. Angela Davis, *Women, Race and Class* (1981); rpt. (London: Women's Press, 1982).

3. hooks, *Ain't I a Woman?,* 97.

4. Ibid., 98–99.

5. W. E. B. Du Bois, *The Souls of Black Folk* (1903); rpt. (New York: Penguin, 1996).

6. Sandra Cisneros, "From a Writer's Notebook. Ghosts and Voices: Writing from Obsession," *Americas Review* 15 (Spring 1987): 71–72.

7. Ibid., 72.

8. Richard A. García, *The Chicanos in America, 1540–1974* (Dobbs Ferry, N.Y.: Oceana Publications, 1977), vii.

9. Octavio Paz, "The Sons of La Malinche," trans. Lysander Kemp, rpt. in *Goddess of the Americas: Writings on the Virgin of Guadalupe,* ed. Ana Castillo (New York: Riverhead Books, 1996), 201.

10. Debra A. Castillo, "Border Theory and the Canon," in *Postcolonial Literatures: Expanding the Canon,* ed. Deborah L. Madsen (London: Pluto Press, 1999), 193.

11. Gloria Anzaldúa, *Borderlands/La Frontera: The New Mestiza* (San Francisco: Aunt Lute, 1987), 30.

12. Ibid., 28.

13. Cherríe Moraga, *Loving in the War Years* (Boston: South End Press, 1983), 100.

14. Rudolfo Anaya and Francisco Lomelí, eds., *Aztlán: Essays on*

the Chicano Homeland (Albuquerque: University of New Mexico Press, 1989), 1.

15. Ibid., ii.

16. Anzaldúa, *Borderlands,* 205.

17. Ibid., 2.

18. Bernice Zamora, *Releasing Serpents* (Tempe, Ariz.: Bilingual Press/Editorial Bilingüe, 1994), 25.

19. Anzaldúa, *Borderlands,* 3.

20. Ibid.

21. Ibid., 10.

22. Angela de Hoyos, "Arise, Chicano!," in *In Other Words: Literature by Latinas of the United States,* ed. Roberta Fernández (Houston: Arte Público, 1994), 69.

23. Ana Castillo, *My Father Was a Toltec and Selected Poems, 1973–1988* (New York and London: W. W. Norton, 1995), xvii–xviii; see also Ana Castillo, *Massacre of the Dreamers: Essays on Xicanisma* (New York: Plume, 1995).

24. Castillo, *My Father,* 63.

25. Ana Castillo, "We Would Like You to Know," in *My Father Was a Toltec,* 83.

26. Bernice Zamora, "Notes from a Chicana Coed," in *Making Face, Making Soul: Haciendo Caras,* ed. Gloria Anzuldúa (San Francisco: Aunt Lute Foundation, 1990), 131–32.

27. Anzaldúa, *Borderlands,* 82.

28. Helena María Viramontes, *Under the Feet of Jesus* (New York: Penguin/Dutton, 1995), 150.

29. Yvonne Yarbro-Bejarano, "Chicana Literature from a Chicana Feminist Perspective," in *Chicana Creativity and Criticism: Charting New Frontiers in American Literature,* ed. María Herrera-Sobek and Helena María Viramontes, special issue, *Americas Review* 15, no. 3, 4 (Fall–Winter 1987): 140.

30. Anzaldúa, *Borderlands,* 58.

31. Ibid., 59.

32. See, for example, Carol W. Pfaff and Laura Chávez, "Spanish/English Code-Switching: Literary Reflections of Natural Discourse," in *Missions in Conflict: Essays on U.S.-Mexican Relations and Chicano Culture,* ed. Renate von Bardelben, Dietrich Briesemeister, and Juan Bruce-Novoa (Tübingen, Germany: Gunter Narr, 1986), 229–54.

33. Marta Ester Sánchez, *Contemporary Chicana Poetry: A Critical Approach to an Emerging Literature* (Berkeley, Los Angeles and London: University of California Press, 1985), 21.

34. Lorna Dee Cervantes, *Emplumada* (Pittsburgh and London: University of Pittsburgh Press, 1981), 39.

35. Anzaldúa, *Borderlands,* 54.

36. Ibid., 59.

37. Ibid., 18.

38. Ibid., 19.

39. Cherríe Moraga, *Waiting in the Wings: Portrait of a Queer Motherhood* (Ithaca, N.Y.: Firebrand Books, 1997), 18.

40. Ibid.

41. Cherríe Moraga, "Art in America con Acento," in *In Other Words: Literature by Latinas of the United States,* ed. Roberta Fernández (Houston: Arte Público, 1994), 301.

42. Ibid.

43. Ibid.

44. Ibid., 301–2.

45. Ibid., 306.

46. Helena María Viramontes, *The Moths and Other Stories* (Houston: Arte Público, 1995), 36.

47. Ibid., 42.

48. Edit Villareal, *My Visits with MGM,* in *Shattering the Myth: Plays by Hispanic Women,* ed. Linda Feyder (Houston: Arte Público, 1992), 165.

49. Ibid., 207.

50. Josefina López, *Simply María,* in *Shattering the Myth: Plays by Hispanic Women,* ed. Linda Feyder (Houston: Arte Público, 1992), 130.

51. Ibid.

52. Ibid., 131.

53. Ibid., 132.

54. Ibid., 141.

55. Alicia Gaspar de Alba, "Cimarrona," in *In Other Words: Literature by Latinas of the United States,* ed. Roberta Fernández (Houston: Arte Público, 1994), 411.

56. Ibid.

57. Naomi Quiñónez, "La Llorona," in *In Other Words: Literature by Latinas of the United States,* ed. Roberta Fernández (Houston: Arte Público, 1994), 156.

58. Alma Luz Villanueva, *Weeping Woman: La Llorona and Other Stories* (Tempe, Ariz.: Bilingual Press/Editorial Bilingüe, 1994).

59. Ana Castillo, *The Mixquiahuala Letters* (New York: Anchor Books, Doubleday, 1986).

60. Viramontes, *Moths,* 60.

61. Sandra Cisneros, *The House on Mango Street* (1984); 2d rev. ed. (Houston: Arte Público, 1988), 81ff.

62. Denise Chávez, *The Last of the Menu Girls* (Houston: Arte Público, 1986), 190.

63. Denise Chávez, *Face of an Angel* (New York: Warner Books, 1994), 20.

Chapter 2—Bernice Zamora

1. Bernice Zamora, *Restless Serpents* (Menlo Park, Calif.: Diseños Literarios, 1976); rpt. in *Releasing Serpents* (Tempe, Ariz.:

Bilingual Press/Editorial Bilingüe, 1994). Subsequent page references to this reprinted edition are given in the text.

2. Juan Bruce-Novoa, *RetroSpace: Collected Essays on Chicano Literature* (Houston: Arte Público, 1990), 86.

3. Gloria Elsa Li, "Bernice Zamora: Interview," in *Chicana (W)rites on Word and Film,* ed. María Herrera-Sobek and Helena María Viramontes (Berkeley, Calif.: Third Woman Press, 1995), 284–85.

4. Gloria Anzaldúa, *Borderlands/La Frontera: The New Mestiza* (San Francisco: Aunt Lute, 1987), 17.

5. Juanita Luna Lawhn, "Bernice Zamora," in *Heath Anthology of American Literature,* ed. Paul Lauter (Lexington, Mass. and Toronto: D. C. Heath and Co., 1990), 2: 2492.

6. Li, "Interview," 285.

7. In Roberta Fernández, ed., *In Other Words: Literature by Latinas of the United States* (Houston: Arte Público, 1994), 260. Subsequent page references are given in the text.

8. Li, "Interview," 287.

9. Ibid., 288–89.

10. Ibid., 295.

11. Ibid., 299.

12. Bruce-Novoa, *RetroSpace,* 86.

13. Li, "Interview," 294.

14. Ibid.

15. Ibid., 301.

16. Ibid.

Chapter 3—Ana Castillo

1. Ana Castillo, *Massacre of the Dreamers: Essays on Xicanisma* (New York: Plume, 1995), 12.

2. Ana Castillo, "Introduction," in *My Father Was a Toltec and Selected Poems, 1973–1988* (New York and London: W. W. Norton, 1995), xv.

3. Ibid. xix.

4. Ibid.

5. Ana Castillo, Self-description, http://www.anacastillo.com.

6. Mary Louise Pratt, "'Yo Soy La Malinche': Chicana Writers and the Poetics of Ethnonationalism," *Callalloo* 16 (Fall 1993): 871.

7. Ana Castillo, "My Mother's Mexico," in *Latina: Women's Voices from the Borderlands,* ed. Lillian Castillo-Speed (New York and London: Simon and Schuster, 1995), 26–36. Subsequent page references are given in the text.

8. Alvina E. Quintana, "Ana Castillo's *The Mixquiahuala Letters:* The Novelist as Ethnographer," in *Criticism in the Borderlands: Studies in Chicano Literature, Culture, and Ideology,* ed. Héctor Calderón and José David Saldívar (Durham, N.C.: Duke University Press, 1991), 72–83.

9. Ibid., 74.

10. Ibid., 79.

11. Ana Castillo, *The Mixquiahuala Letters* (New York: Anchor Books, Doubleday, 1986), 30. Future page references are given in the text.

12. Ana Castillo, "Our Tongue Was Nahuatl," in *My Father Was a Toltec and Selected Poems, 1973–1988* (New York and London: W. W. Norton, 1995), 157. Subsequent page references to this volume are given in the text.

13. Ana Castillo, "1975," in *My Father Was a Toltec,* 133.

14. Norma Alarcón, "The Sardonic Powers of the Erotic in the Work of Ana Castillo," in *Breaking Boundaries: Latina Writing and Critical Readings,* ed. Asunción Horno-Delgado, Eliana Ortega, Nina M. Scott, and Nancy Saporta Sternbach (Amherst: University of Massachusetts Press, 1989), 96.

15. Ana Castillo, "The Invitation," in *My Father Was a Toltec,* 115.

16. See Hector A. Torres, "Story, Telling, Voice: Narrative Authority in Ana Castillo's *The Mixquiahuala Letters,*" in *Chicana (W)rites on Word and Film,* ed. María Herrera-Sobek and Helena María Viramontes (Berkeley, Calif.: Third Woman Press, 1995), 137.

17. Ana Castillo, "Extraordinarily Woman," in *Goddess of the Americas: Writings on the Virgin of Guadalupe,* ed. Ana Castillo (New York: Riverhead Books, 1996), 74.

18. Ana Castillo, "Me and Baby," in *My Father Was a Toltec,* 138–39.

19. Ana Castillo, ed., *Goddess of the Americas: Writings on the Virgin of Guadalupe* (New York: Riverhead Books, 1996), 73.

20. Ana Castillo, *Sapogonia (An Anti-Romance in 3/8 Meter)* (Tempe, Ariz.: Bilingual Press/Editorial Bilingüe, 1990). Future page references are given in the text.

21. Yvonne Yarbro-Bejarano, "The Multiple Subject in the Writing of Ana Castillo," *Americas Review* 20 (Spring 1992): 69.

22. Ana Castillo, "An Idyll," rpt. in *My Father Was a Toltec,* 96.

23. Alarcón, "Sardonic Powers of the Erotic," 105.

24. Yarbro-Bejarano, "Multiple Subject," 67.

25. Castillo, "Introduction," in *My Father Was a Toltec,* xviii.

26. Ana Castillo, "A Letter to Alicia," in *My Father Was a Toltec,* 103–4. See Tey Diana Rebolledo, *Women Singing in the Snow: A Cultural Analysis of Chicana Literature* (Tucson: University of Arizona Press, 1995), 197.

27. Ana Castillo, *Loverboys: Stories* (New York and London: W. W. Norton, 1996), 26. Future page references are given in the text.

28. See Alarcón, "Sardonic Powers of the Erotic," 98.

29. Castillo, "Introduction," in *My Father Was a Toltec,* xvii.

30. Ana Castillo, *So Far from God* (London: Women's Press, 1993), 27. Future page references are given in the text.

31. Alarcón, "Sardonic Powers of the Erotic," 94.

32. Cortázar quoted by Erlinda González-Berry, "The Subversive *Mixquiahuala Letters:* An Antidote to Self-Hate," in *Chicana (W)rites Back on Word and Film,* ed. María Herrera-Sobek and Helena María Viramontes (Berkeley: Third Woman Press, 1995), 116.

Chapter 4—Sandra Cisneros

1. Pilar E. Rodríguez Aranda, "On the Solitary Fate of Being Mexican, Female, Wicked and Thirty-three: An Interview with Writer Sandra Cisneros," *Americas Review* 18 (Spring 1990): 64.

2. See Sandra Cisneros, "Ghosts and Voices: Writing from Obsession," *Americas Review* 15:1 (1987): 69–72.

3. Cherríe Moraga, jacket blurb, Sandra Cisneros, *My Wicked, Wicked Ways* (1987); rpt. (New York: Alfred K. Knopf, 1995).

4. Aranda, "Interview," 66.

5. Ibid.

6. Sandra Cisneros, *The House on Mango Street* (1984); rpt. (London: Bloomsbury, 1992), 10. Future page references are given in the text.

7. María Elena de Valdés, "The Critical Reception of Sandra Cisneros's *The House on Mango Street,*" in *Gender, Self, and Society Proceedings of IV International Conference on the Hispanic Cultures of the United States,* ed. Renate von Bardelben (Frankfurt, Germany: Peter Lang, 1993), 293.

8. Sandra Cisneros, *Woman Hollering Creek and Other Stories* (1991); rpt. (London: Bloomsbury, 1993), 69. Subsequent page references are given in the text.

9. Marcela Christine Lucero-Trujillo, "The Dilemma of the Modern Chicana Artist and Critic," in *The Third Woman: Minority Women Writers of the United States,* ed. Dexter Fisher (Boston: Houghton Mifflin Co., 1980), 330.

10. María Herrera-Sobek, "The Politics of Rape: Sexual Transgression in Chicana Fiction," in *Chicana Creativity and Criticism: Charting New Frontiers in American Literature,* ed. María Herrera-Sobek and Helena María Viramontes, speical issue, *Americas Review* 15, no. 3, 4 (Fall–Winter 1987): 178.

11. Aranda, "Interview," 69.

12. Ibid., 68.

13. Ibid., 69.

14. Ibid.

15. Ibid., 65.

16. Sandra Cisneros, "Cactus Flowers: In Search of Tejana Feminist Poetry," *Third Woman* 3:1,2 (1986): 74.

17. Ibid. 74.

18. Aranda, "Interview," 79.

19. Ibid., 71.

20. Erlinda González-Berry and Tey Diana Rebolledo, "Growing Up Chicano: Tomás Rivera and Sandra Cisneros," *Revista Chicano Requeña* 13.3–4 (1985): 109–19.

21. Aranda, "Interview," 66.

22. Ibid., 75.

23. Ibid., 76.

24. See Sandra Cisneros, "Do You Know Me? I Wrote *The House on Mango Street,*" *Americas Review* 15 (Spring 1987): 78.

25. Aranda, "Interview," 74.

26. See Cisneros, "Ghosts and Voices," 73.

27. Sandra Cisneros, "Guadalupe the Sex Goddess," in *Goddess of the Americas: Writings on the Virgin of Guadalupe,* ed. Ana Castillo (New York: Riverhead Books, 1996), 46.

28. See Sandra Cisneros, "Notes to a Young(er) Writer," *Americas Review* 15 (Spring 1987): 76.

29. Ibid., 75.

30. Cisneros, "Cactus Flowers," 79.

Chapter 5—Denise Chávez

1. Denise Chávez, "Heat and Rain: Testimonio," in *Breaking Boundaries: Latina Writing and Critical Readings,* ed. Asunción Horno-Delgado, Eliana Ortega, Nina M. Scott, and Nancy Saporta Sternbach (Amherst: University of Massachusetts Press, 1989), 32. Future page references are given in the text.

2. Rudolfo Anaya, "Introduction," in Denise Chávez, *The Last of the Menu Girls* (Houston: Arte Público, 1986). Subsequent page references are given in the text.

3. Denise Chávez, *Face of an Angel* (New York: Warner Books, 1994), 11. Future page references are given in the text.

4. Denise Chávez, "Grand Slam," in *Latina: Women's Voices from the Borderlands,* ed. Lillian Castillo-Speed (New York and London: Simon and Schuster, 1995), 138.

5. Renato Rosaldo, "Fables of the Fallen Guy," in *Criticism in the Borderlands: Studies in Chicano Literature, Culture, and Ideology,* ed. Héctor Calderón and José David Saldívar (Durham, N.C.: Duke University Press, 1991), 85.

6. Jerry Adler and Tim Padgett, "Selena Country," *Newsweek,* 23 October 1995, p. 77; rpt. http://www.latino.com/selena.html.

7. Denise Chávez, "The State of My Inquietude," in *Chicana Creativity and Criticism: Charting New Frontiers in American Literature,* ed. María Herrera-Sobek and Helena María Viramontes, special issue, *Americas Review* 15, no. 3, 4 (Fall–Winter 1987): 80.

8. Denise Chávez, "Artery of Land," in *Chicana Creativity and Criticism,* 70.

9. Denise Chávez, "Cuckoo Death Chime," in *Chicana Creativity and Criticism,* 76.

10. Tey Diana Rebolledo, "Tradition and Mythology: Signatures of Landscape in Chicana Literature," in *The Desert Is No Lady: Southwestern Landscapes in Women's Writing and Art,* ed. Vera Norwood

and Janice Monk (New Haven and London: Yale University Press, 1987), 97.

11. Denise Chávez, *Novena Narrativas y Ofrendas Nuevomexicanas,* in *Chicana Creativity and Criticism,* 96. Subsequent page references are given in the text.

12. Chávez, quoted in Rebolledo, "Tradition and Mythology," 117.

13. Denise Chávez, "I Am Your Mary Magdalene," in *Chicana Creativity and Criticism,* 66.

14. Denise Chávez, "Tilt-a-Whirl," unpublished poem, quoted in Tey Diana Rebolledo, *Women Singing in the Snow: A Cultural Analysis of Chicana Literature* (Tucson and London: University of Arizona Press, 1995), 114.

15. Denise Chávez, "Silver Ingots of Desire," in *Chicana Creativity and Criticism,* 71.

16. Denise Chávez, "Tears," in *Chicana Creativity and Criticism,* 68.

17. Heiner Bus, "Gender Roles and the Emergence of a Writer in Denise Chávez's *The Last of the Menu Girls* (1986)," in *Gender, Self, and Society: Proceedings of IV International Conference on Hispanic Cultures of the United States,* ed. Renate von Bardelben (Frankfurt, Germany: Peter Lang, 1993), 285.

18. Anaya, "Introduction," in Chávez, *The Last of the Menu Girls.*

19. Denise Chávez, "The Study," in *Chicana Creativity and Criticism,* 72.

20. Denise Chávez, "Door," in *Chicana Creativity and Criticism,* 78.

21. Denise Chávez, "Chekhov Green Love," in *Chicana Creativity and Criticism,* 79.

22. Denise Chávez, "This River's Praying Place," in *Chicana Creativity and Criticism,* 67.

23. Rosaldo, "Fables of the Fallen Guy," 88.

24. Annie O. Eysturoy, *Daughters of Self-Creation: The Contemporary Chicana Novel* (Albuquerque: University of New Mexico Press, 1996), 86.

25. Marcienne Rocard, "*The Last of the Menu Girls* by Denise Chávez: The Emergence of Self as Woman Writer," in *Gender, Self, and Society: Proceedings of IV International Conference on Hispanic Cultures of the United States,* ed. Renate von Bardelben (Frankfurt: Peter Lang, 1993), 89.

26. Sandra Cisneros, *Face of an Angel,* i.

Chapter 6—Alma Luz Villanueva

1. Elizabeth Ordóñez, "Alma Luz Villanueva," in *Chicano Literature: A Reference Guide,* ed. Julio A. Martínez and Francisco A. Lomelí (Westport, Conn.: Greenwood Press, 1985), 415.

2. Alma Luz Villanueva, *Desire* (Tempe, Ariz.: Bilingual Press/Editorial Bilingüe, 1998), 66. Subsequent page references to poems in this volume are given in the text.

3. Alma Luz Villanueva, *Bloodroot* (Austin, Tex.: Place of Herons Press, 1977), 17. Future page references to this volume are given in the text.

4. Marta E. Sánchez, "The Birthing of the Poetic 'I' in Alma Villanueva's *Mother, May I?* The Search for a Feminine Identity," in *Beyond Stereotypes: The Critical Analysis of Chicana Literature,* ed. María Herrera-Sobek (Binghamton, N.Y.: Bilingual Press/Editorial Bilingüe, 1985), 108.

5. Alma Luz Villanueva, *Mother, May I?* (Pittsburgh, Pa.: Motheroot Publications, 1978); rpt. in Alma Luz Villanueva, *Planet with Mother, May I?* (Tempe, Ariz.: Bilingual Press/Editorial Bil-

ingüe, 1993), 99, 100. Subsequent page references to this reprinted edition are given in the text.

6. Alma Luz Villanueva, *The Ultraviolet Sky* (Tempe, Ariz.: Bilingual Press/Editorial Bilingüe, 1988), 243. Future page references are given in the text.

7. Alma Luz Villanueva, *Naked Ladies* (Tempe, Ariz.: Bilingual Press/Editorial Bilingüe, 1994), 12. Subsequent page references are given in the text.

8. Geneviève Fabre, "Leave-Taking and Retrieving in *The Road to Tamazunchale* and *Ultraviolet Sky*," *Bilingual Review/Revista Bilingüe* 16 (1991): 171.

9. Alejandro Morales, "Terra Mater and the Emergence of Myth in *Poems* by Alma Villanueva," *Bilingual Review/Revista Bilingüe* 7:2 (1980): 124–40. See Alma Luz Villanueva, *Poems,* in *Third Chicano Literary Prize* (Irvine: University of California, 1976–1977). Subsequent page references to this volume are given in the text.

10. Ordóñez, "Alma Luz Villanueva," 415–19.

11. Marta Ester Sánchez, *Contemporary Chicana Poetry: A Critical Approach to an Emerging Literature* (Berkeley, Los Angeles, and London: University of California Press, 1985), 84.

12. Ibid., 137.

13. Alma Luz Villanueva, *Weeping Woman: La Llorona and Other Stories* (Tempe, Ariz.: Bilingual Press/Editorial Bilingüe, 1994).

14. Alma Luz Villanueva, *Life Span* (Austin, Tex.: Place of Herons Press, 1985), 64.

15. Elizabeth Ordóñez, "Body, Spirit, and the Text: Alma Villanueva's *Life Span*," in *Criticism in the Borderlands: Studies in Chicano Literature, Culture, and Ideology,* ed. Héctor Calderón and José David Saldívar (Durham, N.C.: Duke University Press, 1991), 61–71.

16. Sánchez, "Birthing the Poetic 'I,'" 109.

17. Ibid., 111.

Chapter 7—Lorna Dee Cervantes

1. Marta Ester Sánchez, *Contemporary Chicana Poetry: A Critical Approach to an Emerging Literature* (Berkeley, Los Angeles, and London: University of California Press, 1985), 10.

2. Erika Krouse and Gregory Dobbin, "Calling Lorna Out: An Interview with Lorna Dee Cervantes," http://www.colorado.edu/creativewriting/lornaint.html.

3. Juan Bruce-Novoa, "Lorna Dee Cervantes," in *Heath Anthology of American Literature,* ed. Paul Lauter (Lexington, Mass. and Toronto: D. C. Heath and Co., 1990) 2: 2579.

4. Lorna Dee Cervantes, *Emplumada* (Pittsburgh and London: University of Pittsburgh Press, 1981), 45. Subsequent page references are given in the text.

5. Krouse and Dobbin, "Calling Lorna Out."

6. Ibid.

7. Tey Diana Rebolledo, *Women Singing in the Snow: A Cultural Analysis of Chicana Literature* (Tucson and London: University of Arizona Press, 1995), 96.

8. Krouse and Dobbin, "Calling Lorna Out."

9. Lynnette Seator, "*Emplumada:* Chicana Rites-of-Passage," *MELUS* 11 (Summer 1984): 23.

10. Sánchez, *Contemporary Chicana Poetry,* 103.

11. Seator, "*Emplumada,*" 37.

12. Lorna Dee Cervantes, *From the Cables of Genocide: Poems on Love and Hunger* (Houston: Arte Público, 1991), 57, l.15; Cervantes's emphasis. Subsequent page references are given in the text.

13. Juan Bruce-Novoa, *Revista Ibero-americana* 51 (1985): 565.

14. Ibid., 567.

15. Rebolledo, *Women Singing in the Snow,* 126.

16. Ada Savin, "Bilingualism and Dialogism: Another Reading of Lorna Dee Cervantes's Poetry," in An Other Tongue: Nation and Ethnicity in the Linguistic Borderlands, ed. Alfred Arteaga (Durham, N.C.: Duke University Press, 1994), 222.

17. Cordelia Candelaria, *Chicano Poetry* (Westport, Conn.: Greenwood Press, 1986), 225.

18. Seator, "*Emplumada,*" 34.

19. Elizabeth J. Ordóñez, "Webs and Interrogations: Postmodernism, Gender and Ethnicity in the Poetry of Cervantes and Cisneros," in *Chicana (W)rites on Word and Film,* ed. María Herrera-Sobek and Helena María Viramontes (Berkeley, Calif.: Third Woman Press, 1995), 176.

20. Krouse and Dobbin, "Calling Lorna Out."

21. Sánchez, *Contemporary Chicana Poetry,* 96.

22. Ibid., 21.

23. John F. Crawford, "Notes toward a New Multicultural Criticism: Three Works by Women of Color," in *A Gift of Tongues: Critical Challenges in Contemporary American Poetry,* ed. Marie Harris and Kathleen Aguero (Athens: University of Georgia Press, 1987).

24. Candelaria, *Chicano Poetry,* 157.

25. Krouse and Dobbin, "Calling Lorna Out."

26. Patricia Wallace, "Divided Loyalties: Literal and Literary in the Poetry of Lorna Dee Cervantes, Cathy Song, and Rita Dove," *MELUS* 18 (Fall 1993): 6.

27. Sánchez, *Contemporary Chicana Poetry,* 85.

BIBLIOGRAPHY

Author Bibliographies

Ana Castillo

Primary Bibliography

Castillo, Ana. "Extraordinarily Woman." In *Goddess of the Americas: Writings on the Virgin of Guadalupe,* edited by Ana Castillo, 72–78. New York: Riverhead Books, 1996.

———. *Loverboys: Stories.* New York and London: W. W. Norton, 1996.

———. *Massacre of the Dreamers: Essays on Xicanisma.* New York: Plume, 1995.

———. *The Mixquiahuala Letters.* New York: Anchor Books/Doubleday, 1986.

———. *My Father Was a Toltec and Selected Poems, 1973–1988.* New York and London: W. W. Norton, 1995.

———. "My Mother's Mexico." In *Latina: Women's Voices from the Borderlands,* edited by Lillian Castillo-Speed, 26–36. New York and London: Simon and Schuster, 1995.

———. *Peel My Love Like an Onion.* New York: Doubleday, 1999.

———. *Sapogonia (An Anti-Romance in 3/8 Meter).* Tempe, Ariz.: Bilingual Press/Editorial Bilingüe, 1990.

———. *So Far from God.* London: Women's Press, 1993.

———. "Yes, Dear Critic, There Really Is an Alicia." In *Máscaras,* edited by Lucha Corpi, 153–60. Berkeley, Calif.: Third Woman Press, 1997.

Secondary Bibliography

Alarcón, Norma. "The Sardonic Powers of the Erotic in the Work of Ana Castillo." In *Breaking Boundaries: Latina Writing and Critical Readings,* edited by Asunción Horn-Delgado, Eliana Ortega,

BIBLIOGRAPHY

Nina M. Scott, and Nancy Saporta Sternbach, 94–107. Amherst: University of Massachusetts Press, 1989.

Baker, Samuel. "Ana Castillo: The Protest Poet Goes Mainstream." *Publishers Weekly* 243 (12 August 1996): 417–18.

Bennett, Tanya Long. "No Country To Call Home: A Study of Castillo's Mixquiahuala Letters." *Style* 30 (Fall 1996): 462–78.

Bus, Heiner. "'I Too Was of the Small Corner of the World': The Cross-Cultural Experience in Ana Castillo's *The Mixquiahuala Letters.*" *Americas Review* 21 (Fall–Winter 1993): 128–38.

Castillo, Debra A. "Borderliners: Federico Campbell and Ana Castillo." In *Reconfigured Spheres: Feminist Explorations of Literary Space,* edited by Margaret R. Higonnet and Joan Templeton, 147–70. Amherst: University of Massachusetts Press, 1994.

Curiel, Barbara Brinson. "Heteroglossia in Ana Castillo's *The Mixquiahuala Letters.*" *Discurso: Revista de Estudios Iberoamericanos* 7. no. 1 (1990): 11–23.

Gomez Vega, Ibis. "Debunking Myths: The Hero's Role in Ana Castillo's *Sapogonia.*" *Americas Review* 22 (Spring–Summer1994): 244–58.

González, María. "Love and Conflict: Mexican American Women Writers as Daughters." In *Women of Color: Mother-Daughter Relationships in Twentieth-Century Literature,* edited by Elizabeth Brown Guillory, 153–71. Austin: University of Texas Press, 1996.

Gonzáles-Berry, Erlinda. "The (Subversive) *Mixquiahuala Letters:* An Antidote for Self-Hate." In *L'Ici et ailleurs: Multilinguisme et multiculturalisme en Amerique du Nord,* edited by Jean Beranger, Jean Cazemajou, Jean-Michel Lacroix, and Pierre Spriet, 227–40. Bordeaux, France: Presses de l'Université de Bordeaux; Centre de Recherches sur l'Amérique Anglophone, 1991.

McCracken, Ellen. "Rupture, Occlusion, and Repression: The Political Unconscious in the New Latina Narrative of Julia Alvarez and Ana Castillo." In *Confrontations et métissages,* edited by Benjamin Labarthe, Yves-Charles Grandjeat, and Christian Lerat, 319–28. Bordeaux, France: Maison des Pays Ibériques, 1995.

Pratt, Mary Louise. "'Yo Soy La Malinche': Chicana Writers and the Poetics of Ethnonationalism." *Callalloo* 16 (Fall 1993): 859–73.

Quintana, Alvina E. "Ana Castillo's *The Mixquiahuala Letters:* The Novelist as Ethnographer." In *Criticism in the Borderlands: Studies in Chicano Literature, Culture, and Ideology,* edited by Héctor Calderón and José David Saldívar, 72–83. Durham, N.C.: Duke University Press, 1991.

Saeta, Elsa. "Ana Castillo's *Sapogonia:* Narrative Point of View as a Study in Perception." *Confluencia: Revista Hispánica de Cultura y Literatura* 10 (Fall 1994): 67–72.

Sánchez, Rosaura. "Reconstructing Chicana Identity." *American Literary History* 9 (Summer 1997): 350–63.

Yarbro-Bejarano, Yvonne. "The Multiple Subject in the Writing of Ana Castillo." *Americas Review* 20 (Spring 1992): 65–72.

Lorna Dee Cervantes

Primary Bibliography

Cervantes, Lorna Dee. *Emplumada.* Pittsburgh and London: University of Pittsburgh Press, 1981.

———. *From the Cables of Genocide: Poems on Love and Hunger.* Houston: Arte Público, 1991.

Secondary Bibliography

Bruce-Novoa, Juan. "Lorna Dee Cervantes." In volume 2 of *Heath Anthology of American Literature,* 2579. Lexington, Mass., and Toronto: D. C. Heath and Co., 1990.

———. *Revista Ibero-americana* 51 (1985): 565–68.

Candelaria, Cordelia. *Chicano Poetry.* Westport, Conn.: Greenwood Press, 1986.

BIBLIOGRAPHY

Cota-Cárdenas, Margarita. "The Faith of Activists: Barrios, Cities, and the Chicana Feminist Response." *Frontiers* 14, no. 2 (1994): 51–80.

Crawford, John F. "Notes toward a New Multicultural Criticism: Three Works by Women of Color." In *A Gift of Tongues: Critical Challenges in Contemporary American Poetry,* edited by Marie Harris and Kathleen Aguero, 155–95. Athens: University of Georgia Press, 1987.

Krouse, Erika, and Gregory Dobbin. "Calling Lorna Out: An Interview with Lorna Dee Cervantes." http://www.colorado.edu/creativewriting/lornaint.html.

McKenna, Teresa. "'An Utterance More Pure than Word': Gender and the Corrido Tradition in Two Contemporary Chicano Poems." In *Feminist Measures: Soundings in Poetry and Theory,* edited by Lynn Keller and Cristanne Miller, 184–207. Ann Arbor: University of Michigan Press, 1994.

Monda, Bernadette, "Interview with Lorna Dee Cervantes." *Third Woman* 2, no. 1 (1984): 103–7.

Ordóñez, Elizabeth J. "Webs and Interrogations: Postmodernism, Gender, and Ethnicity in the Poetry of Cervantes and Cisneros." In *Chicana (W)rites on Word and Film,* edited by María Herrera-Sobek and Helena María Viramontes, 171–83. Berkeley, Calif.: Third Woman Press, 1995.

Rebolledo, Tey Diana. "Soothing Restless Serpents: The Dreaded Creation and Other Inspirations in Chicana Poetry." *Third Woman* 2, no. 1 (1984): 83–102.

———. "Tradition and Mythology: Signatures of Landscape in Chicana Literature." In *The Desert Is No Lady: Southwestern Landscapes in Women's Writing and Art,* edited by Vera Norwood and Janice Monk, 96–124. New Haven and London: Yale University Press, 1987.

———. *Women Singing in the Snow: A Cultural Analysis of Chicana Literature.* Tucson and London: University of Arizona Press, 1995.

Sánchez, Marta Ester. *Contemporary Chicana Poetry: A Critical Approach to an Emerging Literature.* Berkeley, Los Angeles, and London: University of California Press, 1985.

Savin, Ada. "Bilingualism and Dialogism: Another Reading of Lorna Dee Cervantes's Poetry." In *An Other Tongue: Nation and Ethnicity in the Linguistic Borderlands,* edited by Alfred Arteaga, 215–23. Durham, N.C.: Duke University Press, 1994.

———. "Lorna Dee Cervantes's Dialogic Imagination." *Annales du Centre de Recherches sur l'Amerique Anglophone* (Cedex, France [ACRAA]) 18 (1993): 269–77.

Seator, Lynette. "*Emplumada:* Chicana Rites-of-Passage." *MELUS* 11 (Summer 1984): 23–38.

Wallace, Patricia. "Divided Loyalties: Literal and Literary in the Poetry of Lorna Dee Cervantes, Cathy Song, and Rita Dove." *MELUS* 18 (Fall 1993): 3–19.

Yarbro-Bejarano, Yvonne. "Chicana Literature from a Chicana Feminist Perspective." In *Chicana Creativity and Criticism: Charting New Frontiers in American Literature,* edited by María Herrera-Sobek and Helena María Viramontes. Special issue, *Americas Review* 15, no. 3, 4 (Fall1–Winter 1987): 39–45.

Denise Chávez

Primary Bibliography

Chávez, Denise. "Artery of Land." In *Chicana Creativity and Criticism: Charting New Frontiers in American Literature,* edited by María Herrera-Sobek and Helena María Viramontes. Special issue, *Americas Review* 15, no. 3, 4 (Fall–Winter 1987): 70.

———. "Chekhov Green Love." In *Chicana Creativity and Criticism,* 79.

———. "Cuckoo Death Chime." In *Chicana Creativity and Criticism: Charting New Frontiers in American Literature,* edited by María Herrera-Sobek and Helena María Viramontes. Special issue, *Americas Review* 15, no. 3, 4 (Fall–Winter 1987): 76.

———. "Door." In *Chicana Creativity and Criticism: Charting New Frontiers in American Literature,* edited by María Herrera-Sobek and Helena María Viramontes. Special issue, *Americas Review* 15, no. 3, 4 (Fall–Winter 1987): 78.

———. *Face of an Angel.* New York: Warner Books, 1994.

———. "Grand Slam." In *Latina: Women's Voices from the Borderlands,* edited by Lillian Castillo-Speed, 135–40. New York and London: Simon and Schuster, 1995.

———. "Heat and Rain: Testimonio." In *Breaking Boundaries: Latina Writing and Critical Readings,* edited by Asunción Horno-Delgado, Eliana Ortega, Nina M. Scott, and Nancy Saporta Sternbach, 27–32. Amherst: University of Massachusetts Press, 1989.

———. "I Am Your Mary Magdalene." In *Chicana Creativity and Criticism: Charting New Frontiers in American Literature,* edited by María Herrera-Sobek and Helena María Viramontes. Special issue, *Americas Review* 15, no. 3, 4 (Fall–Winter 1987): 66.

———. *The Last of the Menu Girls.* Houston: Arte Público, 1986.

———. "Novena Narrativas y Ofrendas Nuevomexicanas." In *Chicana Creativity and Criticism: Charting New Frontiers in American Literature,* edited by María Herrera-Sobek and Helena María Viramontes. Special issue, *Americas Review* 15, no. 3, 4 (Fall–Winter 1987): 85–100. Reprinted in *Goddess of the Americas: Writings on the Virgin of Guadalupe,* edited by Ana Castillo, 153–69. New York: Riverhead Books, 1996.

———. "Silver Ingots of Desire." In *Chicana Creativity and Criticism: Charting New Frontiers in American Literature,* edited by

BIBLIOGRAPHY

María Herrera-Sobek and Helena María Viramontes. Special issue, *Americas Review* 15, no. 3, 4 (Fall–Winter 1987): 71.

———. "The State of My Inquietude." In *Chicana Creativity and Criticism: Charting New Frontiers in American Literature,* edited by María Herrera-Sobek and Helena María Viramontes. Special issue, *Americas Review* 15, no. 3, 4 (Fall–Winter 1987): 80.

———. "The Study." In *Chicana Creativity and Criticism: Charting New Frontiers in American Literature,* edited by María Herrera-Sobek and Helena María Viramontes. Special issue, *Americas Review* 15, no. 3, 4 (Fall–Winter 1987): 72.

———. "Tears." In *Chicana Creativity and Criticism: Charting New Frontiers in American Literature,* edited by María Herrera-Sobek and Helena María Viramontes. Special issue, *Americas Review* 15, no. 3, 4 (Fall–Winter 1987): 68.

———. "This River's Praying Place." In *Chicana Creativity and Criticism: Charting New Frontiers in American Literature,* edited by María Herrera-Sobek and Helena María Viramontes. Special issue, *Americas Review* 15, no. 3, 4 (Fall–Winter 1987): 67.

Secondary Bibliography

Adler, Jerry, and Tim Padgett. "Selena Country." *Newsweek,* 23 October 1995, pp. 76–77. Reprinted, http://www.latino.com/selena.html.

Anderson, Douglas. "Displaced Abjection and States of Grace: Denise Chávez's *The Last of the Menu Girls.*" In *American Women Short Story Writers: A Collection of Critical Essays,* edited by Julia Brown, 235–50. New York: Garland, 1995.

Bus, Heiner. "Gender Roles and the Emergence of a Writer in Denise Chávez's *The Last of the Menu Girls* (1986)." In *Gender, Self, and Society: Proceedings of IV International Conference on Hispanic Cultures of the United States,* edited by Renate von Bardelben, 277–86. Frankfurt, Germany: Peter Lang, 1993.

Candelaria, Cordelia. "The 'Wild Zone' Thesis as Gloss in Chicana

BIBLIOGRAPHY

Literary Study." In *Feminisms: An Anthology of Literary Theory and Criticism,* edited by Robyn R. Warhol and Diane Price Herndl, 248–56. New Brunswick, N.J.: Rutgers University Press, 1997.

Castillo, Debra A. "The Daily Shape of Horses: Denise Chávez and Maxine Hong Kingston." *Dispositio* 16, no. 41 (1991): 29–43.

Eysturoy, Annie O. *Daughters of Self-Creation: The Contemporary Chicana Novel.* Albuquerque: University of New Mexico Press, 1996.

———. "Denise Chávez." In *This Is about Vision: Interviews with Southwestern Writers,* edited by William Balassi, John F. Crawford, and Annie O. Eysturoy, 157–69. Albuquerque: University of New Mexico Press, 1990.

González, María. "Love and Conflict: Mexican American Women Writers as Daughters." In *Women of Color: Mother-Daughter Relationships in Twentieth-Century Literature,* edited by Elizabeth Brown Guillory, 153–71. Austin: University of Texas Press, 1996.

Gray, Lynn. "Interview with Denise Chávez." *Short Story Review* 5 (Fall 1988): 2–4.

Heard, Martha E. "The Theatre of Denise Chávez: Interior Landscapes with 'sabor nuevomexicano.'" *Americas Review* 16 (Summer 1988): 83–91.

Kelley, Margot. "A Minor Revolution: Chicano/a Composite Novels and the Limits of Genre." In *Ethnicity and the American Short Story,* edited by Julia Brown, 63–84. New York: Garland, 1997.

Rebolledo, Tey Diana. "Tradition and Mythology: Signatures of Landscape in Chicana Literature." In *The Desert Is No Lady: Southwestern Landscapes in Women's Writing and Art,* edited by Vera Norwood and Janice Monk, 96–124. New Haven and London: Yale University Press, 1987.

———. *Women Singing in the Snow: A Cultural Analysis of Chicana Literature.* Tucson and London: University of Arizona Press, 1995.

Rocard, Marcienne. "*The Last of the Menu Girls* by Denise Chávez: The Emergence of Self as Woman Writer." In *Gender, Self, and*

Society: Proceedings of IV International Conference on Hispanic Cultures of the United States, edited by Renate von Bardelben, 87–96. Frankfurt: Peter Lang, 1993.

Rosaldo, Renato. "Fables of the Fallen Guy." In *Criticism in the Borderlands: Studies in Chicano Literature, Culture, and Ideology,* edited by Héctor Calderón and José David Saldívar, 84–93. Durham, N.C.: Duke University Press, 1991.

Sandra Cisneros

Primary Bibliography

Cisneros, Sandra. *Bad Boys.* Chicano Chapbook No. 8. 1980.

———. "Cactus Flowers: In Search of Tejana Feminist Poetry." *Third Woman* 3, nos. 1 and 2 (1986): 73–80.

———. "Do You Know Me? I Wrote *The House on Mango Street.*" *Americas Review* 15 (Spring 1987): 77–79.

———. "From a Writer's Notebook. Ghosts and Voices: Writing from Obsession." *Americas Review* 15 (Spring 1987): 69–73.

———. "Ghosts and Voices: Writing from Obsession." *Americas Review* 15, no. 1 (1987): 69–72.

———. "Guadalupe the Sex Goddess." In *Goddess of the Americas: Writings on the Virgin of Guadalupe,* edited by Ana Castillo, 46–51. New York: Riverhead Books, 1996.

———. *The House on Mango Street.* 1984. 2d rev. ed. Houston: Arte Público, 1988.

———. "Living as a Writer: Choice and Circumstance." *Feminist Writers Guild* 10 (February 1987): 8–9.

———. *Loose Woman.* New York: Alfred Knopf, 1994.

———. *My Wicked, Wicked Ways.* Berkeley, Calif.: Third Woman Press, 1987.

———. "Notes to a Young(er) Writer." *Americas Review* 15 (Spring 1987): 74–76.

————. "Only Daughter." In *Máscaras,* edited by Lucha Corpi, 120–23. Berkeley, Calif.: Third Woman Press, 1997.

————. *Woman Hollering Creek and Other Stories.* New York: Vintage, 1991.

————. "A Writer's Voyages." *Texas Observer,* 25 September 1987, pp. 18–19.

Secondary Bibliography

Aranda, Pilar E. Rodríguez. "On the Solitary Fate on Being Mexican, Female, Wicked and Thirty-three: An Interview with Writer Sandra Cisneros." *Americas Review* 18 (Spring 1990): 64–80.

Badikian, Beatriz. "Writing out of Necessity: Interview with Sandra Cisneros." *Feminist Writers Guild* 10 (February 1987): 1, 6–8.

Binder, Wolfgang, ed. *Partial Autobiographies: Interviews with Twenty Chicano Poets.* Erlangen, Germany: Palm and Enke, 1985, pp. 54–74.

Bus, Heiner. "Chicano Literature of Memory: Sandra Cisneros, *The House on Mango Street* (1984) and Gary Soto, *Living up the Street* (1985)." In *Minority Literature in North America: Contemporary Perspective,* edited by Wolfgang Karrer and Hartmut Lutz, 159–72. International Symposium at the University of Osnabruck, 1988.

Busch, Juan Daniel. "Self-Baptizing the Wicked Esperanza: Chicana Feminism and Cultural Contact in *The House on Mango Street.*" *Mester* 22–23 (Fall–Spring 1993–1994): 123–34.

Candelaria, Cordelia. "The 'Wild Zone' Thesis as Gloss in Chicana Literary Study." In *Feminisms: An Anthology of Literary Theory and Criticism,* edited by Robyn R. Warhol and Diane Price Herndl, 248–56. New Brunswick, N.J. : Rutgers University Press, 1997.

Carabi, Angels. "Developing a Sense of Place: Sandra Cisneros in *The House on Mango Street.*" *Annari d'Angles* (Barcelona) 10 (1988):111–17.

BIBLIOGRAPHY

Carroll, Michael, and Susan Maher. "'A las Mujeres': Cultural Context and the Process of Maturity in Sandra Cisneros' *Woman Hollering Creek.*" *North Dakota Quarterly* 64 (Winter 1997): 70–80.

Carter, Nancy Corson. "Claiming the Bittersweet Matrix: Alice Walker, Sandra Cisneros, and Adrienne Rich." *Critique* 35 (Summer 1994): 195–204.

Doyle, Jacqueline. "Haunting the Borderlands: La Llorona in Sandra Cisneros's 'Woman Hollering Creek.'" *Frontiers* 16, no. 1 (1996): 53–70.

———. "More Room of Her Own: Sandra Cisneros's *The House on Mango Street.*" *MELUS* 19 (Winter 1994): 5–35.

Fiore, Teresa. "Crossing and Recrossing Woman Hollering Creek by Sandra Cisneros." *Prospero: Rivista di culture anglo-germaniche* 1 (1994): 61–75.

García, Alesia. "Politics and Indigenous Theory in Leslie Marmon Silko's 'Yellow Woman' and Sandra Cisneros' 'Woman Hollering Creek.'" In *Folklore, Literature, and Cultural Theory: Collected Essays,* edited by Cathy Lynn Preston, 3–21. New York: Garland, 1995.

González, María. "Love and Conflict: Mexican American Women Writers as Daughters." In *Women of Color: Mother-Daughter Relationships in Twentieth-Century Literature,* edited by Elizabeth Brown-Guillory, 153–71. Austin: University of Texas Press, 1996.

González-Berry, Erlinda, and Tey Diana Rebolledo. "Growing Up Chicano: Tomás Rivera and Sandra Cisneros." *Revista Chicano Requeña* 13, nos. 3–4 (1985): 109–19.

Griffin, Susan E. "Resistance and Reinvention in Sandra Cisneros' *Woman Hollering Creek.*" In *Ethnicity and the American Short Story,* edited by Julia Brown, 85–96. New York: Garland, 1997.

Grobman, Laurie. "The Cultural Past and Artistic Creation in Sandra Cisneros' *The House on Mango Street* and Judith Ortiz Cofer's *Silent Dancing.*" *Confluencia* 11 (Fall 1995): 42–49.

BIBLIOGRAPHY

Gutiérrez-Jones, Leslie S. "Different Voices: The Re-Bildung of the Barrio in Sandra Cisneros' *The House on Mango Street.*" In *Anxious Power: Reading, Writing, and Ambivalence in Narrative by Women,* edited by Carol J. Singley and Susan Elizabeth Sweeney, 295–312. Albany: State University of New York Press, 1993.

Gutiérrez-Revuelta, Pedro. "Género e ideología en el libro de Sandra Cisneros: *The House on Mango Street.*" *Crítica* 1, no. 3 (1986): 48–54.

Heredia, Juanita. "Down These City Streets: Exploring Urban Space in *El Bronx Remembered* and *The House on Mango Street.*" *Mester* 22–23 (Fall–Spring 1993–1994): 93–105.

Herrera, Andrea O'Reilly. "'Chambers of Consciousness': Sandra Cisneros and the Development of the Self in the BIG House on Mango Street." *Bucknell Review* 39, no. 1 (1995): 191–204.

Kanoza, Theresa. "Esperanza's Mango Street: Home for Keeps." Notes on *Contemporary Literature* 25 (May 1995): 9.

Kelley, Margot. "A Minor Revolution: Chicano/a Composite Novels and the Limits of Genre." In *Ethnicity and the American Short Story,* edited by Julia Brown, 63–84. New York: Garland, 1997.

Kessler, Elizabeth A. "A Sociolinguistic Study of Male-Female Interaction in Cisneros' *The House on Mango Street.*" *Conference of College Teachers of English Studies* 55 (1995): 10–17.

Klein, Dianne. "Coming of Age in Novels by Rudolfo Anaya and Sandra Cisneros." *English Journal* 81 (September 1992): 21–26.

Kolmar, Wendy. "Dialectics of Connectedness: Supernatural Elements in Novels by Bambara, Cisneros, Grahn, and Erdrich." In *Haunting the House of Fiction: Feminist Perspectives on Ghost Stories by American Women,* edited by Lynette Carpenter and Wendy Kolmar, 236–49. Knoxville: University of Tennessee Press, 1991.

Lee, A. Robert. "Chicanismo as Memory: The Fictions of Rudolfo Anaya, Nash Candelaria, Sandra Cisneros, and Ron Arias." In

BIBLIOGRAPHY

Memory and Cultural Politics: New Approaches to American Ethnic Literatures, edited by Amritjit Singh, Joseph T. Skerrett, Jr., and Robert E. Hogan, 320–39. Boston: Northeastern University Press, 1996.

Lewis, L. M. "Ethnic and Gender Identity: Parallel Growth in Sandra Cisneros' *Woman Hollering Creek.*" *Short Story* 2 (Fall 1994): 69–78.

Madsen, Deborah L. "(Dis)continuous Narrative: The Articulation of a Chicana Feminist Voice in Sandra Cisneros's *The House on Mango Street.*" In *Women on the Edge: Ethnicity and Gender in Short Stories by American Women,* edited by Corinne H. Dale and J. H. E. Paine, 3–18. New York and London: Garland Publishing, 1999.

Marek, Jayne E. "Difference, Identity, and Sandra Cisneros's *The House on Mango Street.*" *Hungarian Journal of English and American Studies* 1 (1996): 173–87.

Martín-Rodríguez, Manuel M. "The Book on Mango Street: Escritura y liberación en la obra de Sandra Cisneros." In *Mujer y literatura mexicana y chicana,* edited by Aralia López González, Amelia Malagamba, and Elena Urrutia, 249–54. Culturas en contacto 2. Mexico City and Tijuana: Colegio de México and Colegio de la Frontera Norte, 1990.

McCracken, Ellen. "Contemporary Chicano Narrative and Public Religious Display: Recuperating the Sacred in the Barrio Street and the Literary Text." In *Cultures de la rue: Les barrios d'Amerique du Nord,* edited by Geneviève Fabre and Catherine Lejeune, 163–77. Paris: L'Université de Paris, 1996.

———. "Sandra Cisneros's *The House on Mango Street*: Community Oriented Introspection and the Demystification of Patriarchal Violence." In *Breaking Boundaries: Latina Writings and Critical Readings,* edited by Asunción Horno-Delgado, Eliana Ortega, Nina M. Scott, and Nancy Saporta, 62–71. Amherst: University of Massachusetts Press, 1989.

BIBLIOGRAPHY

Morales, Alejandro. "The Deterritorialization of Esperanza Cordera: A Paraesthetic Inquiry." In *Gender, Self, and Society: Proceedings of IV International Conference on Hispanic Cultures of the United States,* edited by Renate von Bardelben, 227–35. Frankfurt: Peter Lang, 1993.

Mullen, Harryette. "'A Silence between Us Like a Language': The Untranslatability of Experience in Sandra Cisneros's *Woman Hollering Creek.*" *MELUS* 21 (Summer 1996): 3–20.

Norton, Jody. "History, Rememory, Transformation: Actualizing Literary Value." *Centennial Review* 38, no. 3 (1994): 589–602.

Olivares, Julián. "Entering The House on Mango Street (Sandra Cisneros)." In *Teaching American Ethnic Literatures: Nineteen Essays,* edited by John R. Maitino and David R. Peck, 209–35. Albuquerque: University of New Mexico Press, 1996.

————. "Sandra Cisneros's *The House on Mango Street* and the Poetics of Space." In *Chicana Creativity and Criticism: Charting New Frontiers in American Literature,* edited by María Herrera-Sobek and Helena María Viramontes. Special issue, *Americas Review* 15, no. 3, 4 (Fall–Winter 1987): 160–69.

Ordóñez, Elizabeth J. "Webs and Interrogations: Postmodernism, Gender, and Ethnicity in the Poetry of Cervantes and Cisneros." In *Chicana (W)rites on Word and Film,* edited by María Herrera-Sobek and Helena María Viramontes, 171–83. Berkeley, Calif.: Third Woman Press, 1995.

Restuccia, Frances L. "Literary Representations of Battered Women: Spectacular Domestic Punishment." In *Bodies of Writing, Bodies in Performance,* edited by Thomas Foster, Carol Siegel, and Ellen E. Berry, 42–71. New York: New York University Press, 1996.

Ricard, Serge. "La Desesperance d'Esperanza: Espace reve, espace vecu dans *The House on Mango Street* de Sandra Cisneros." In *L'Ici et l'ailleurs: Multilinguisme et multiculturalisme en*

BIBLIOGRAPHY

Amerique du Nord, edited by Jean Beranger, Jean Cazemajou, Jean-Michel Lacroix, and Pierre Spriet, 175–87. Annales du Centre de Recherche sur l'Amerique Anglophone 16. Bordeaux, France: Presses de l'Universite de Bordeaux, 1991.

Ríos, Katherine. "'And you know what I have to say isn't always pleasant': Translating the Unspoken Word in Cisneros' *Woman Hollering Creek.*" In *Chicana (W)rites on Word and Film,* edited by María Herrera-Sobek and Helena María Viramontes, 201–23. Berkeley, Calif.: Third Woman Press, 1995.

Rosaldo, Renato. "Fables of the Fallen Guy." In *Criticism in the Borderlands: Studies in Chicano Literature, Culture, and Ideology,* edited by Héctor Calderón and José David Saldívar, 84–93. Durham, N.C.: Duke University Press, 1991.

Sagel, Jim. "Sandra Cisneros." *Publishers Weekly,* 29 March 1992, pp. 74–75.

Sánchez, Reuben. "Remembering Always to Come Back: The Child's Wished-For Escape and the Adult's Self-Empowered Return in Sandra Cisneros's *House on Mango Street.*" *Children's Literature* 23 (1995): 221–41.

Satz, Martha. "Return to One's House." *Southwest Review* 82 (Spring 1997): 166–85.

Smith, Paula J. "Changing the Backdrop: Portraiture in Sandra Cisneros' 'Never Marry a Mexican.'" *Revista de Estudios Hispánicos, Río Piedras* 23 (1996): 249–62.

Spencer, Laura Gutiérrez. "Fairy Tales and Opera: The Fate of the Heroine in the Work of Sandra Cisneros." In *Speaking the Other Self: American Women Writers,* edited by Jeanne Campbell Reesman, 278–87. Athens: University of Georgia Press, 1997.

Thomson, Jeff. "'What Is Called Heaven': Identity in Sandra Cisneros's *Woman Hollering Creek.*" *Studies in Short Fiction* 31 (Summer 1994): 415–24.

BIBLIOGRAPHY

Valdés, María Elena de. "The Critical Reception of Sandra Cisneros's *The House on Mango Street.*" In *Gender, Self, and Society: Proceedings of IV International Conference on Hispanic Cultures of the United States,* edited by Renate von Bardelben, 287–300. Frankfurt: Peter Lang, 1993.

———. "In Search of Identity in Cisneros's *The House on Mango Street.*" *Canadian Review of American Studies* 23 (Fall 1992): 55–72.

Wyatt, Jean. "On Not Being La Malinche: Border Negotiations of Gender in Sandra Cisneros's 'Never Marry a Mexican' and 'Woman Hollering Creek.'" *Tulsa Studies in Women's Literature* 14 (Fall 1995): 243–71.

Yarbro-Bejarano, Yvonne. "Chicana Literature from a Chicana Feminist Perspective." *Americas Review* 15 (Fall–Winter 1987): 139–45.

Alma Luz Villanueva

Primary Bibliography

Villanueva, Alma Luz. *Bloodroot.* Austin, Tex.: Place of Herons Press, 1977.

———. *Desire.* Tempe, Ariz.: Bilingual Press/Editorial Bilingüe, 1998.

———. *La Chingada.* In *Five Poets of Aztlán,* edited by Santiago Daydí-Tolson. Tempe, Ariz.: Bilingual Press/Editorial Bilingüe, 1985.

———. *Weeping Woman: La Llorona and Other Stories.* Tempe, Ariz.: Bilingual Press/Editorial Bilingüe, 1994.

———. *Life Span.* Austin, Tex.: Place of Herons Press, 1985.

———. *Mother, May I?* Pittsburgh, Pa.: Motheroot Publications, 1978. Reprinted in *Planet with Mother, May I?* Tempe, Ariz.: Bilingual Press/Editorial Bilingüe, 1993.

————. *Naked Ladies.* Tempe, Ariz.: Bilingual Press/Editorial Bilingüe, 1994.

————. *Planet with Mother, May I?* Tempe, Ariz.: Bilingual Press/Editorial Bilingüe, 1993.

————. *Poems.* In *Third Chicano Literary Prize.* Irvine: University of California, 1976–1977.

————. *The Ultraviolet Sky.* Tempe, Ariz.: Bilingual Press/Editorial Bilingüe, 1988.

Secondary Bibliography

Fabre, Geneviève. "Leave-Taking and Retrieving in *The Road to Tamazunchale* and *Ultraviolet Sky.*" *Bilingual Review/Revista Bilingüe* 16 (1991): 171–83.

Herrera-Sobek, María. "The Nature of Chicana Literature: Feminist Ecological Literary Criticism and Chicana Writers." *Revista canaria de estudios ingleses* 37 (November 1998): 89–105.

Morales, Alejandro. "Terra Mater and the Emergence of Myth in *Poems* by Alma Villanueva." *Bilingual Review/Revista Bilingüe* 7, no. 2 (1980): 123–42.

Ordóñez, Elizabeth. "Alma Luz Villanueva." In *Chicano Literature: A Reference Guide,* edited by Julio A. Martínez and Francisco A. Lomelí, 415–19. Westport, Conn.: Greenwood Press, 1985.

————. "Body, Spirit, and the Text: Alma Villanueva's *Life Span.*" In *Criticism in the Borderlands: Studies in Chicano Literature, Culture, and Ideology,* edited by Héctor Calderón and José David Saldívar, 61–71. Durham, N.C.: Duke University Press, 1991.

Rebolledo, Tey Diana. *Women Singing in the Snow: A Cultural Analysis of Chicana Literature.* Tucson and London: University of Arizona Press, 1995.

Sánchez, Marta E. "The Birthing of the Poetic 'I' in Alma Villanueva's *Mother, May I?* The Search for a Feminine Identity." In *Beyond Stereotypes: The Critical Analysis of Chicana Literature,* edited by María Herrera-Sobek, 108–52. Binghamton, N.Y.: Bilingual Press/Editorial Bilingüe, 1985.

Sánchez, Marta Ester. *Contemporary Chicana Poetry: A Critical Approach to an Emerging Literature.* Berkeley, Los Angeles, and London: University of California Press, 1985.

Bernice Zamora

Primary Bibliography

Zamora, Bernice. "Archetypes in Chicana Poetry." *De Colores* 4, no. 3 (1978): 43–52.

———. "A Characteristic Fragility: The Native American in Chicano *Corridos.*" *Lore and Language* 12, nos. 1–2 (1994): 277–86.

———. "Notes from a Chicana Coed." In *Making Face, Making Soul: Haciendo Caras,* edited by Gloria Anzuldúa, 131–32. San Francisco: Aunt Lute Foundation, 1990.

———. "Piles of Sublime." In *In Other Words: Literature by Latinas of the United States,* edited by Roberta Fernández, 261. Houston: Arte Público, 1994.

———. *Releasing Serpents.* Tempe, Ariz.: Bilingual Press/Editorial Bilingüe, 1994.

———. *Restless Serpents.* Menlo Park, Calif.: Diseños Literarios, 1976. Reprinted in *Releasing Serpents,* 1994.

———. "Silence at Bay." In *Máscaras,* edited by Lucha Corpi, 21–34. Berkeley, Calif.: Third Woman Press, 1997.

———. "The Space Chicanos Inhabit in the *Corrido.*" *Nordic Yearbook of Folklore* 48 (1992): 153–63.

———. "Summer's Rage." In *In Other Words,* 260.

Secondary Bibliography

Bruce-Novoa, Juan. "Bernice Zamora." In *Chicano Authors: Inquiry by Interview,* edited by Juan Bruce-Novoa, 203–18. Austin: University of Texas Press, 1980.

———. *Chicano Poetry: A Response to Chaos.* Austin: University of Texas Press, 1982.

———. *RetroSpace: Collected Essays on Chicano Literature.* Houston: Arte Público, 1990.

Candelaria, Cordelia. "Bernice Zamora." In *Chicano Poetry: A Critical Introduction,* 146–56. Westport, Conn.: Greenwood Press, 1986.

Cota-Cárdenas, Margarita. "The Faith of Activists: Barrios, Cities, and the Chicana Feminist Response." *Frontiers* 14, no. 2 (1994): 51–80.

Desai, Parul. "Interview with Bernice Zamora, a Chicana Poet." *Imagine: International Chicano Poetry Journal* 2 (Summer 1985): 26–39.

Lawhn, Juanita Luna. "Bernice Zamora." In volume 2 of *Heath Anthology of American Literature,* edited by Paul Lauter, 2492. Lexington, Mass. and Toronto: D. C. Heath and Co., 1990.

Li, Gloria Elsa. "Bernice Zamora: Interview." In *Chicana (W)rites on Word and Film,* edited by María Herrera-Sobek and Helena María Viramontes, 283–303. Berkeley, Calif.: Third Woman Press, 1995.

Rebolledo, Tey Diana. "Soothing Restless Serpents: The Dreaded Creation and Other Inspirations in Chicana Poetry." *Third Woman* 2, no. 1 (1984): 83–102.

———. *Women Singing in the Snow: A Cultural Analysis of Chicana Literature.* Tucson and London: University of Arizona Press, 1995.

Saldívar, José David. "Towards a Chicano Poetics: The Making of the Chicano Subject, 1969–1982." *Confluencia* 1 (Spring 1986): 10–17.

Sánchez, Marta Ester. *Contemporary Chicana Poetry: A Critical Approach to an Emerging Literature.* Berkeley, Los Angeles, and London: University of California Press, 1985.

General Bibliography

Bibliographies

Campos Carr, Irene. "A Survey of Selected Literature on La Chicana." *National Women's Studies Association Journal* 1 (Winter 1988–1989): 253–73.

Castillo-Speed, Lillian. "Chicana Materials: A Selected List of Materials since 1980." *Frontiers* 11, no. 1 (1990): 66–84.

Eger, Ernestina. *A Bibliography of Criticism of Contemporary Chicano Literature.* Berkeley: University of California, Chicano Studies Library Publications, 1982.

Ordóñez, Elizabeth J. "Chicana Literature and Related Sources: A Selected and Annotated Bibliography." *Bilingual Review/Revista Bilingüe* 7 (May–August 1980): 143–64.

Chicana Lesbianism/Sexuality

de Alba, Alicia Gaspar. "Tortillerismo: Work by Chicana Lesbians." *Signs* 18 (Summer 1993): 956–63.

Moraga, Cherríe. *Loving in the War Years.* Boston: South End Press, 1983.
———. *Waiting in the Wings: Portrait of a Queer Motherhood.* Ithaca, N.Y.: Firebrand Books, 1997.

Pérez, Emma. "Irigaray's Female Symbolic in the Making of Chicana Lesbian *Sitios y Lenguas* (Sites and Discourses)." In *The Lesbian Postmodern,* edited by Laura Doan, 104–17. New York: Columbia University Press, 1994.

Rashkin, Elissa J. "Historic Image/Self Image: Re-Viewing Chicana Sexuality." In *Sex Positives? The Cultural Politics of Dissident Sexualities,* edited by Thomas Foster, Carol Siegel, and Ellen E. Berry, 97–119. New York: New York University Press, 1997.

Chicano/a Literature

Alarcón, Norma. "Making *Familia* from Scratch: Split Subjectivities in the Work of Helena María Viramontes and Cherríe Moraga." In *Chicana Creativity and Criticism: Charting New Frontiers in American Literature,* edited by María Herrera-Sobek and Helena María Viramontes. Special issue, *Americas Review* 15, no. 3, 4 (Fall–Winter 1987): 220–32.

Arteaga, Alfred. *Chicano Poetics: Heterotexts and Hybridities.* New York: Cambridge University Press, 1997.

Bruce-Novoa, Juan. *RetroSpace: Collected Essays on Chicano Literature.* Houston: Arte Público, 1990.

Calderón, Héctor, and José David Saldívar, eds. *Criticism in the Borderlands: Studies in Chicano Literature, Culture and Ideology.* Durham, N.C.: Duke University Press, 1991.

Cota-Cárdenas, Margarita. "The Chicana in the City as Seen in Her Literature." *Frontiers* 6 (Spring–Summer 1981): 13–18.

Fernández, Roberta. "*Abriendo caminos* in the Brotherland: Chicana Writers Respond to the Ideology of Literary Nationalism." *Frontiers* 14, no. 2 (1994): 23–50.

———, ed. *In Other Words: Literature by Latinas of the United States.* Houston: Arte Público, 1994.

Feyder, Linda, ed. *Shattering the Myth: Plays by Hispanic Women.* Houston: Arte Público, 1992.

Herrera-Sobek, María, ed. *Beyond Stereotypes: The Critical Analysis of Chicana Literature.* Binghamton, N.Y.: Bilingual Press/Editorial Bilingüe, 1985.

Herrera-Sobek, María, and Helena María Viramontes, eds. *Chicana Creativity and Criticism: Charting New Frontiers in American Literature.* Special issue, *Americas Review* 15, no. 3, 4 (Fall–Winter 1987). Reprinted, Albuquerque: University of New Mexico Press, 1996.

Herrera-Sobek, María, and Helena María Viramontes, eds. *Chicana (W)rites on Word and Film.* Berkeley, Calif.: Third Woman Press, 1995.

Huerta, Jorge, and Carlos Morton. "Chicano Theatre in the Mainstream: Milwaukee Rep's Production of a Chicana Play." *Gestos* 8
(November 1993): 149–59.

Jiménez, Francisco, ed. *The Identification and Analysis of Chicano
Literature.* New York: Bilingual Press/Editorial Bilingüe, 1979.

Lucero-Trujillo, Marcela Christine. "The Dilemma of the Modern
Chicana Artist and Critic." In *The Third Woman: Minority Women
Writers of the United States,* edited by Dexter Fisher. Boston:
Houghton Mifflin Co., 1980.

Martínez, Julio A., and Francisco A. Lomelí, eds. *Chicano Literature:
A Reference Guide.* Westport, Conn.: Greenwood Press, 1985.

McCracken, Ellen. "Latina Narrative and the Politics of Signification:
Articulation, Antagonism and Populist Rupture." *Crítica* 2 (Fall
1990): 202–7.

Quintana, Alvina E. *Home Girls: Chicana Literary Voices.* Philadelphia: Temple University Press, 1996.

Rebolledo, Tey Diana. "Abuelitas: Mythology and Integration in Chicana Literature." *Revista Chicano Requeña* 11 (Fall–Winter 1983):
148–58.

———. "The Chicana Guerillera Literary Critic." In *Speaking the
Other Self: American Women Writers,* edited by Jeanne-Campbell
Reesman, 79–89. Athens: University of Georgia Press, 1997.

———. "The Politics of Poetics: Or, What Am I, a Critic, Doing in
This Text Anyhow?" In *Chicana Creativity and Criticism: New
Frontiers in American Literature,* edited by María Herrera-Sobek
and Helena María Viramontes, 129–38. Albuquerque: University
of New Mexico Press, 1996.

———. "Tradition and Mythology: Signatures of Landscape in Chicana Literature." In *The Desert Is No Lady: Southwestern Landscapes in Women's Writing and Art,* edited by Vera Norwood and
Janice Monk, 96–124. New Haven: Yale University Press, 1987.

BIBLIOGRAPHY

———. "Walking the Thin Line: Humor in Chicana Literature." In *Beyond Stereotypes: The Critical Analysis of Chicana Literature,* edited by María Herrera-Sobek, 91–107. Binghamton, N.Y.: Bilingual Press/Editorial Bilingüe, 1985.

———. "Witches, Bitches and Midwives: The Shaping of Poetic Consciousness in Chicana Literature." In *The Chicano Struggle: Analyses of Past and Present Efforts,* edited by John A. García, Theresa Córdova, and Juan R. García, 166–77. Binghamton, N.Y.: Bilingual Press/Editorial Bilingüe, 1984.

———. *Women Singing in the Snow: A Cultural Analysis of Chicana Literature.* Tucson and London: University of Arizona Press, 1995.

Rivero, Eliana S. "The 'Other's Others': Chicana Identity and Its Textual Expressions." In *Encountering the Other(s): Studies in Literature, History, and Culture,* edited by Gisela Brinkler-Gabler, 239–60. Albany: State University of New York Press, 1995.

Rocard, Marcienne. "The Chicana: A Marginal Woman." In *European Perspectives on Hispanic Literature of the United States,* edited by Geneviève Fabre, 130–39. Houston: Arte Público, 1988.

———. "The House Theme in Chicana Literature: A New Sense of Place." *Hispanorama. Chicanoliteratur* 106–7 (February 1990): 146–47.

———. "The Remembering Voice in Chicana Literature." *Americas Review* 14 (1986): 150–59.

Rosaldo, Renato. "Fables of the Fallen Guy." In *Criticism in the Borderlands: Studies in Chicano Literature, Culture and Ideology,* edited by Héctor Calderón and José David Saldívar, 84–93. Durham, N.C.: Duke University Press, 1991.

Salazar-Parr, Carmen. "La Chicana in Literature." In *Chicano Studies: A Multidisciplinary Approach,* edited by Eugene E. García, Francisco A. Lomelí, and Isidro D. Ortiz, 120–34. New York: Teachers College. Press, 1984.

BIBLIOGRAPHY

Salazar Parr, Carmen, and Genevieve M. Ramirez. "The Female Hero in Chicano Literature." In *Beyond Stereotypes: The Critical Analysis of Chicana Literature,* edited by María Herrera-Sobek, 47–60. Binghamton, N.Y.: Bilingual Review Press, 1985.

Saldívar, José David. *The Dialectics of Our America: Genealogy, Cultural Critique, and Literary History.* Durham, N.C.: Duke University Press, 1991.

Saldívar, Ramón. *Chicano Narrative: The Dialectics of Difference.* Madison: University of Wisconsin Press, 1990.

Saldívar Hull, Sonia. "Political Identities in Contemporary Chicana Literature: Helena María Viramontes's Visions of the U.S. Third World." In *'Writing' Nation and 'Writing' Region in America,* edited by Theo d'haen and Hans Bertens, 156–65. Amsterdam: VU University Press, 1996.

Sánchez, Rosaura. "Deconstructions and Renarrativizations: Trends in Chicana Literature." *Bilingual Review Revista Bilingüe* 21 (January–April 1996): 52–58.

———. "Reconstructing Chicana Identity." *American Literary History* 9 (Summer 1997): 350–63.

Sommers, Joseph, and Tomás Ybarra-Frausto, eds. *Modern Chicano Writers.* Englewood Cliffs, N.J.: Prentice Hall Inc., 1979.

Stockton, Sharon. "Rereading the Maternal Body: Viramontes' *The Moths* and the Construction of the New Chicana." *Americas Review* 22 (Spring–Summer 1994): 212–29.

Tatum, Charles M., ed. *New Chicana/Chicano Writing,* vol. 2. Tucson: University of Arizona Press, 1992.

———. *New Chicano/Chicana Writing.* Tucson: University of Arizona Press, 1993.

Thurston, Kay. "Barriers to the Self-Definition of the Chicana: Gina Valdés and *There Are No Madmen Here.*" *MELUS* 19 (Winter 1994): 61–73.

BIBLIOGRAPHY

Velásquez-Treviño, Gloria. "Cultural Ambivalence in Early Chicana Literature." In *European Perspectives on Hispanic Literature of the United States,* edited by Geneviève Fabre, 140–46. Houston: Arte Público, 1988.

Vigil-Piñón, Evangelina, ed. *Woman of Her Word: Hispanic Women Write.* 2d ed. Houston: Arte Público, 1987.

Viramontes, Helena María. *The Moths and Other Stories.* Houston: Arte Público, 1995.

———. *Under the Feet of Jesus.* New York: Penguin/Dutton, 1995.

Ybarra-Frausto, Tomás. "I Can Still Hear the Applause: La Farándula Chicana: Carpas y Tandas de Variedad." In *Hispanic Theatre in the United States,* edited by Nicolas Kanellos, 45–61. Houston: Arte Público, 1984.

Comparative Studies

Bak, Hans, ed. *Multiculturalism and the Canon of American Culture.* Amsterdam: University of Amsterdam Press, 1992.

Baker, Houston A., Jr. ed. *Three American Literatures: Essays in Chicano, Native American, and Asian-American Literature for Teachers of American Literature.* New York: Modern Language Association, 1982.

Bardelben, Renate von, Dietrich Briesemeister, and Juan Bruce-Novoa, eds. *Missions in Conflict: Essays on U.S.-Mexican Relations and Chicano Culture.* Tübingen, Germany: Gunter Narr Verlag, 1986.

Fabre, Geneviève, ed. *European Perspectives on Hispanic Literature of the United States.* Houston: Arte Público, 1988.

Jennings, James, ed. *Blacks, Latinos and Asians in Urban America: Status and Prospects for Politics and Activism.* New York: Praeger Publishers, 1994.

Karrer, Wolfgang, and Hartmut Lutz, eds. *Minority Literature in*

North America: Contemporary Perspective. International Symposium at the University of Osnabruck, 1988.

Keating, Analouise. *Women Reading Women Writing: Self-Invention in Paula Gunn Allen, Gloria Anzuldúa, and Audre Lorde.* Philadelphia: Temple University Press, 1996.

Lawhn, Juanita. "Victorian Attitudes Affecting the Mexican Women Writing in *La Prensa* during the Early 1900s and the Chicana of the 1980s." In *Missions in Conflict: Essays on U.S.-Mexican Relations and Chicano Culture,* edited by Renate von Bardelben, Dietrich Briesemeister, and Juan Bruce-Novoa, 65–71. Tübingen, Germany: Narr, 1986.

Lee, A. Robert. "Ethnic America: The Non-European Voice." *British American* 3 (June 1991): 9–10.

———, ed. *A Permanent Etcetera: Cross-Cultural Perspectives on Post-War America.* London: Pluto Press, 1993.

Norwood, Vera, and Janice Monk, eds. *The Desert Is No Lady: Southwestern Landscapes in Women's Writing and Art.* New Haven and London: Yale University Press, 1987.

Ruoff, A. LaVonne Brown, and Jerry W. Ward eds., *Redefining American Literary History.* New York: Modern Language Association, 1990.

The Yearbook of English Studies 24 (1994), special issue, "Ethnicity and Representation in American Literature."

Culture

Anaya, Rudolfo, and Francisco Lomelí, eds. *Aztlán: Essays on the Chicano Homeland.* Albuquerque: University of New Mexico Press, 1989.

Morales, Sylvia. "Filming a Chicana Documentary (1979)." In *Chicanos and Film: Representation and Resistance,* edited by Chon A. Noriega, 308–11. Minneapolis: University of Minnesota Press, 1992.

BIBLIOGRAPHY

Ruiz, Vicki, L. "'Star Struck': Acculturation, Adolescence, and the Mexican-American Woman, 1920–1950." In *Between Two Words: Mexican Immigrants in the United States,* edited by David G. Gutiérrez, 125–47. Wilmington, Del.: Scholarly Resources, 1996.

Wertheimer, Eric. *Imagined Empires: Incas, Aztecs and the New World of American Literature, 1771–1876.* New York: Cambridge University Press, 1999.

Feminism

Alarcón, Norma. "Cognitive Desires: An Allegory of/for Chicana Critics." In *Listening to Silences: New Essays in Feminist Criticism,* edited by Elaine Hedges and Shelley Fisher Fishkin, 260–73. New York: Oxford University Press, 1994.

Anzaldúa, Gloria. *Borderlands/La Frontera: The New Mestiza.* San Francisco: Aunt Lute, 1987.

———, ed. *Making Face, Making Soul: Haciendo Caras.* San Francisco: Aunt Lute Foundation, 1990.

Bardelben, Renate von, ed. *Gender, Self, and Society: Proceedings of IV International Conference on Hispanic Cultures of the United States.* Frankfurt: Peter Lang, 1993.

Billings, Linda M., and Alurista. "In Verbal Murals: A Study of Chicana Herstory and Poetry." *Confluencia* 2 (Fall 1986): 60–68.

Candelaria, Cordelia. "The 'Wild Zone' Thesis as Gloss in Chicana Literary Study." In *Feminisms: An Anthology of Literary Theory and Criticism,* edited by Robyn R. Warhol and Diane Price Herndl, 248–56. New Brunswick, N.J.: Rutgers University Press, 1997.

Castillo-Speed, Lillian, ed. *Latina: Women's Voices from the Borderlands.* New York and London: Simon and Schuster, 1995.

Cota-Cárdenas, Margarita. "The Faith of Activists: Barrios, Cities, and the Chicana Feminist Response." *Frontiers* 14, no. 2 (1994): 51–80.

BIBLIOGRAPHY

Fisher, Dexter, ed. *The Third Woman: Minority Women Writers of the United States.* Boston: Houghton Mifflin Co., 1980.

Fregoso, Rosa Linda. "Chicana Film Practices: Confronting the 'Many-Headed Demon of Oppression.'" In *Chicanos and Film: Representation and Resistance,* edited by Chon A. Noriega, 168–82. Minneapolis: University of Minnesota Press, 1992.

Herrera-Sobek, María. "Social Protest, Folklore, and Feminist Ideology in Chicana Prose and Poetry." In *Folklore, Literature, and Cultural Theory: Collected Essays,* edited by Cathy Lynn Preston, 102–16. New York: Garland, 1995.

Horno-Delgado, Asunción, Eliana Ortega, Nina M. Scott, and Nancy Saporta Strenbach, eds. *Breaking Boundaries: Latina Writings and Critical Readings.* Amherst: University of Massachusetts Press, 1989.

Huaco-Nuzum, Carmen. "(Re)Constructing Chicana, Mestiza Representation: Frances Salome España's *Spitfire.*" In *The Ethnic Eye: Latino Media Arts,* edited by Chon A. Noriega and Ana M. López, 260–74. Minneapolis: University of Minnesota Press, 1996.

Lucero, Marcela C. "Resources for the Chicana Feminist Scholar." In *For Alma Mater: Theory and Practice in Feminist Scholarship,* edited by Paula A. Treichler, Cheris Kramarae, and Beth Stafford, 393–401. Urbana: University of Illinois Press, 1985.

Melville, Margarita B. *Twice a Minority: Mexican American Women.* Saint Louis: C. V. Mosby Co., 1980.

Moraga, Cherríe, and Gloria Anzuldúa, eds. *This Bridge Called My Back: Writings by Radical Women of Color.* Watertown, Mass.: Persephone Press, 1981. Reprinted, New York: Kitchen Table, Women of Color Press, 1983.

Sternbach, Nancy Saporta. "'A Deep Racial Memory of Love': The Chicana Feminism of Cherríe Moraga." In *Breaking Boundaries: Latina Writing and Critical Readings,* edited by Asunción Horno-Delgado, Eliana Ortega, Nina M. Scott, and Nancy Saporta Sternbach, 48–61. Amherst: University of Massachusetts Press, 1989.

BIBLIOGRAPHY

Yarbro-Bejarano, Yvonne. "Chicana Literature from a Chicana Feminist Perspective." In María Herrera-Sobek and Helena María Viramontes, *Chicana Creativity and Criticism: Charting New Frontiers in American Literature,* edited by María Herrera-Sobek and Helena María Viramontes. Special issue, *Americas Review* 15, no. 3, 4 (Fall–Winter 1987): 139–45.

Fiction

Eysturoy, Annie O. *Daughters of Self-Creation: The Contemporary Chicana Novel.* Albuquerque: University of New Mexico Press, 1996.

Herrera-Sobek, María. "The Politics of Rape: Sexual Transgression in Chicana Fiction." In *Chicana Creativity and Criticism: Charting New Frontiers in American Literature,* edited by María Herrera-Sobek and Helena María Viramontes. Special issue, *Americas Review* 15, no. 3, 4 (Fall–Winter 1987): 171–81.

Lomelí, Francisco A. "Chicana Novelists in the Process of Creating Fictive Voices." In *Beyond Stereotypes: The Critical Analysis of Chicana Literature,* edited by María Herrera-Sobek, 29–46. Binghamton, N.Y.: Bilingual Press/Editorial Bilingüe, 1985.

Martínez, Eliud. "Personal Vision in the Short Stories of Estela Portillo Trambley." In *Beyond Stereotypes: The Critical Analysis of Chicana Literature,* edited by María Herrera-Sobek, 71–90. Binghamton, N.Y.: Bilingual Press/Editorial Bilingüe, 1985.

Sánchez, Rosaura. "Chicana Prose Writers: The Case of Gina Valdés and Sylvia Lizarraga." In *Beyond Stereotypes: The Critical Analysis of Chicana Literature,* edited by María Herrera-Sobek, 61–70. Binghamton, N.Y.: Bilingual Review Press, 1985.

History

Broyles-Gonzáles, Yolanda. "The Living Legacy of Chicana Performers: Preserving History through Oral Testimony." *Frontiers* 11, no. 1 (1990): 46–52.

BIBLIOGRAPHY

Castillo, Ana, ed. *Goddess of the Americas: Writings on the Virgin of Guadalupe.* New York: Riverhead Books, 1996.

García, Richard A. *The Chicanos in America, 1540–1974.* Dobbs Ferry, N.Y.: Oceana Publications, 1977.

Gutiérrez, Ramón, and Genaro Padilla, eds. *Recovering the US Hispanic Literary Heritage.* Houston: Arte Público, 1993.

Herrera-Sobek, María, ed. *Reconstructing a Chicano/a Literary Heritage: Hispanic Literature of the Southwest.* Tucson: University of Arizona Press, 1993.

Zamora, Lois Parkinson. *The Usable Past: The Imagination of History in Recent Fiction of the Americas.* New York: Cambridge University Press, 1998.

Interviews and Author Testimonials

Agosin, Marjorie. "A Dream of Shadows: Writing, Speaking, Becoming." Translated by Monica Bruno. In *Máscaras,* edited by Lucha Corpi, 99–108. Berkeley, Calif.: Third Woman Press, 1997.

Alvarez, Julia. "An Unlikely Beginning for a Writer." In *Máscaras,* edited by Lucha Corpi, 189–99. Berkeley, Calif.: Third Woman Press, 1997.

Binder, Wolfgang, ed. *Partial Autobiographies. Interviews with Twenty Chicano Poets.* Erlangen, Germany: Palm and Enke, 1985.

Bruce-Novoa, Juan. *Chicano Authors: Inquiry by Interview.* Austin: University of Texas Press, 1980.

Castillo, Ana. "Yes, Dear Critic, There Really Is an Alicia." In *Máscaras,* edited by Lucha Corpi, 153–60. Berkeley, Calif.: Third Woman Press, 1997.

Cisneros, Sandra. "Only Daughter." In *Máscaras,* edited by Lucha Corpi, 120–23. Berkeley, Calif.: Third Woman Press, 1997.

Cofer, Judith Ortiz. "And Are You a Latina Writer?" In *Máscaras,* edited by Lucha Corpi, 11–19. Berkeley, Calif.: Third Woman Press, 1997.

BIBLIOGRAPHY

Corpi, Lucha, ed. *Máscaras.* Berkeley, Calif.: Third Woman Press, 1997.

Fernández, Roberta. "Depicting Women's Culture in Intaglio: A Novel in Six Stories." In *Máscaras,* edited by Lucha Corpi, 73–96. Berkeley, Calif.: Third Woman Press, 1997.

Hoyas, Angela de. "The Natural Imperfections of the Cloth." In *Máscaras,* edited by Lucha Corpi, 163–67. Berkeley, Calif.: Third Woman Press, 1997.

Moraga, Cherríe. "En busca de la fuerza femenina." In *Máscaras,* edited by Lucha Corpi, 179–87. Berkeley, Calif.: Third Woman Press, 1997.

Pineda, Cecile. "Deracinated: The Writer Re-Invents Her Sources." In *Máscaras,* edited by Lucha Corpi, 57–70. Berkeley, Calif.: Third Woman Press, 1997.

Ponce, Mary Helen. "On Language." In *Máscaras,* edited by Lucha Corpi, 111–17. Berkeley, Calif.: Third Woman Press, 1997.

Quiñónez, Naomi. "*Molcajete* Mamas and the Feathered Pens." In *Máscaras,* edited by Lucha Corpi, 169–76. Berkeley, Calif.: Third Woman Press, 1997.

Vando, Gloria. "A Stain upon Silence." In *Máscaras,* edited by Lucha Corpi, 133–50. Berkeley, Calif.: Third Woman Press, 1997.

Villanueva, Alma Luz. "Abundance." In *Máscaras,* edited by Lucha Corpi, 37–55. Berkeley, Calif.: Third Woman Press, 1997.

Viramontes, Helena María. "The Writer's Ofrenda." In *Máscaras,* edited by Lucha Corpi, 125–31. Berkeley, Calif.: Third Woman Press, 1997.

Zamora, Bernice. "Silence at Bay." In *Máscaras,* edited by Lucha Corpi, 21–34. Berkeley, Calif.: Third Woman Press, 1997.

Poetry

Bornstein, Miriam. "The Voice of the Chicana in Poetry." *Denver Quarterly* 16 (Fall 1981): 28–47.

Bruce-Novoa, Juan. *Chicano Poetry: A Response to Chaos.* Austin: University of Texas Press, 1982.

BIBLIOGRAPHY

Candelaria, Cordelia. *Chicano Poetry.* Westport, Conn.: Greenwood Press, 1986.

Del Río, Carmen M. "Chicana Poets: Re-Visions from the Margin." *Revista Canadiense de Estudios Hispánicos* 14 (Spring 1990): 431–45.

Gutiérrez Spencer, Laura. "Mirrors and Masks: Female Subjectivity in Chicana Poetry." *Frontiers* 15, no. 2 (1994): 69–86.

Herrera-Sobek, María. "The Acculturation Process of the Chicana in the *Corrido.*" *Proceedings of the Pacific Coast Council on Latin American Studies* 9 (1982): 23–34.

Ordóñez, Elizabeth. "Sexual Politics and the Theme of Sexuality in Chicana Poetry." In *Women in Hispanic Literature: Icons and Fallen Idols,* edited by Beth Miller, 316–39. Berkeley, Calif.: University of California Press, 1983.

Ordóñez, Elizabeth J. "The Concept of Cultural Identity in Chicana Poetry." *Third Woman* 2, no. 1 (1984): 75–82.

Pérez-Torres, Rafael. *Movements in Chicano Poetry: Against Myths, against Margins.* New York: Cambridge University Press, 1995.

Pratt, Mary Louise. "'Yo soy la Malinche': Chicana Writers and the Poetics of Ethnonationalism." In *Twentieth Century Poetry: From Text to Context,* edited by Peter Verdonk, 171–87. London: Routledge, 1993.

Rebolledo, Tey Diana. "Game Theory in Chicana Poetry." *Revista Chicano Requeña* 11 (Fall–Winter 1983): 159–68.

———. "The Maturing of Chicana Poetry: The Quiet Revolution of the 1980s." In *For Alma Mater: Theory and Practice in Feminist Scholarship,* edited by Paula A. Treichler, Cheris Kramarae, and Beth Stafford, 143–58. Urbana: University of Illinois Press, 1985.

Sánchez, Marta Ester. *Contemporary Chicana Poetry: A Critical Approach to an Emerging Literature.* Berkeley, Los Angeles, and London: University of California Press, 1985.

INDEX

INDEX

Bergholz Literary Services for permission to quote from works appearing in *Resiembra,* ed. Jim Sagel (University of New Mexico, © 1982 by Denise Chávez); *Chicana Creativity and Criticism: Charting New Frontiers in American Literature* (special issue, *Americas Review* 15, no. 3, 4, © 1987 by Denise Chávez; reprinted by University of New Mexico Press, 1996); and *The Journal of Ethnic Studies* Spring 1987 (© 1987 by Denise Chávez).

Grateful acknowledgment is made to the following for permission to quote from the works of Sandra Cisneros: to Susan Bergholz Literary Services for permission to quote from *The House on Mango Street* (Vintage Books, a division of Random House, Inc., © 1984 by Sandra Cisneros; in hardcover by Alfred A. Knopf, 1994); *My Wicked, Wicked Ways* (Third Woman Press, © 1987 by Sandra Cisneros; in hardcover by Alfred A. Knopf); *Woman Hollering Creek and Other Stories* (Vintage Books, a division of Random House, Inc., © 1991 by Sandra Cisneros; first published in hardcover by Random House, Inc.); and works appearing in *Goddess of the Americas: Writings on the Virgin of Guadalupe,* ed. Ana Castillo (Riverhead Books, © 1996 by Ana Castillo).

Grateful acknowledgment is made to the following for permission to quote from the works of Alma Luz Villanueva: to Alma Luz Villanueva and Place of Herons Press for permission to quote from *Bloodroot* (© 1977 by Alma Luz Villanueva); to Bilingual Press/Editorial Bilingüe for permission to quote from *Desire* (1998); *Naked Ladies* (1994); *Planet with Mother, May I?* (1993); *The Ultraviolet Sky* (1998); and *Weeping Woman: La Llorona and Other Stories* (1994).

Grateful acknowledgment is made to the following for permission to quote from the works of Bernice Zamora: to Arte Público Press for permission to quote from works appearing in *In Other Words: Literature by Latinas of the United States,* ed. Roberta Fernández (1994).

Grateful acknowledgment is also made to Arte Público Press for permission to quote from works by Angela de Hoyos and Naomi Quiñónez appearing in *In Other Words: Literature by Latinas of the United States,* ed. Roberta Fernández (1994).